Evict Evil

A Paranormal Memoir

Timothy L Drobnick Sr

Contents

1. Chapter 1   1

2. Chapter 2   10

3. Chapter 3   16

4. Chapter 4   22

5. Chapter 5   30

6. Chapter 6   35

7. Chapter 7   41

8. Chapter 8   47

9. Chapter 9   53

10. Chapter 10   59

11. Chapter 11   64

12. Chapter 12   70

13. Chapter 13   76

14. Chapter 14   81

15. Chapter 15   87

16. Chapter 16   92

17. Chapter 17   98

18. Chapter 18   104

19. Chapter 19   110

20. Chapter 20   117

21. Chapter 21   123

22. Chapter 22   129

23. Chapter 23   136

24. Chapter 24   142

25. Chapter 25   148

26. Chapter 26   154

27. Chapter 27   160

28. Chapter 28   166

29. Chapter 29   172

30. Chapter 30   178

31. Chapter 31   183

32. Chapter 32   190

33. Chapter 33   197

34. Chapter 34   203

35. Chapter 35   209

36. Chapter 36   215

37. Chapter 37   221

38. Chapter 38   227

39. Chapter 39   232

40. Chapter 40   238

41. Chapter 41   244

42. Chapter 42   250

43. Chapter 43   256

44. Chapter 44   262

45. Chapter 45   268

Disclosure   275

About the Author   276

Free Audiobook   278

Please Leave Review   279

Other Books   280

Chapter 1

T HE WHITEHALL OFFICE HAD a soul. I entered her with respect. The phone rang as I opened the door.

"Do you really offer free coffee?" The man on the phone asked. "I saw your help wanted ad for telemarketing, you said that coffee's on you."

"That's right," I said. "Coffee's free. We pay cash daily. Are you a telemarketer?"

"I have been. Right now, I'm living under a bridge. My name's Michael."

"Wow, how long have you been under that bridge?"

"A month now. My clothes are shit, I can't shave and it's hard to get a job." I heard him sigh. A sigh of a beaten man. "I hate begging for money. Makes me feel like pond scum."

"Well, come on in. I'll give you a chance. Have you eaten today?"

"No."

"Okay, I have sandwiches here."

"Oh, thank you." I heard a bit of hope in his voice. I gave him instructions to find our office. The newspaper advertisement generated thirty phone calls that morning. Columbus was proving to be ripe for harvesting salespeople.

The front doorbell rang as a man in rumpled clothing entered. His patchy, curly beard had a three-day growth which left his cheeks bare. His face barely contained his smile as he walked to me, extending his hand.

"Hi, I'm Kwame. I'm here for a telemarketing job. I spoke to you on the phone earlier."

"Kwame, it's great to meet you! Have you done sales before?"

"I've worked for years at telemarketing. I own a business, but right now, I need cash." He scratched his head and wrinkled his brow. "I have bigger plans than being a telemarketer. But this'll do for now."

"Yeah, I know the recession is hitting people hard. We pay cash daily, twenty percent straight commission; there's no guarantee."

"That's fine with me, I don't like guarantees because I can get a higher commission if I'm not compensating for the non-producers." He frowned and shook his head at the idea of free loaders.

"That's always been my answer. That's one way I know that you actually know how to sell. Fill out this application. We can't start selling yet. We're waiting on a license from the state. Hopefully, it'll be this week."

"Can I have some of that coffee you advertised?"

"Of course, Kwame, it's over there. There's sugar and cream if you want it. Sandwiches are in the fridge."

Another man on crutches arrived. Kwame saw him and ran to open the door.

"I can get my own damn door, thank you," the man growled. He had one pant leg tied over his amputated leg.

"Sorry," Kwame said. "I don't want any problems." The man scowled at Kwame and hobbled toward me.

"I'm here for the job," he said.

"I'm Tim. Have you done telemarketing before?"

"I was doing telemarketing before your mama was in diapers."

"On a crank phone and party lines?"

He looked at me and raised his right eyebrow. "What are we selling?"

"Light bulbs."

"Yeah, I've sold those for other people. How long have you guys been in business?"

"We're not actually in business yet. We're still waiting for the license, but we've come here from Colorado. We were running telemarketing rooms in Denver. I was the top salesperson."

"So, you think you're a hotshot?"

"I'm great at sales. Nobody ever beat me."

"Nothing wrong with a cocky salesman if he's good." He showed his yellow teeth.

"Here's an application. What's your name?"

"Don."

"Nice to meet you, Don. Have a table if you like. There's coffee, cream and sugar in the back."

"That's great." He took the application and grabbed his crutches and swung over to the coffee machine. He filled his cup after pouring the cream. Then he asked, "Hey can you set my coffee on the table?"

"Sure, not a problem." I grabbed his coffee. He sat, resting his crutches against the table. He took a sip and began filling out the application.

A couple strode up to my desk. He had a ten-day beard and a ten-day smell. The lady behind him had matted hair and watched the floor as she followed him. Her hair may have been dirty blonde. Or maybe just dirty.

"Hey, I'm Kenny, and this is Cheryl," he said.

"Pleased to meet you," I said. "Are you here for the job?"

"Yeah, we saw your sign in the window. It says cash paid daily, is that right?"

"Yes, that's right as soon as we open. We're waiting on our license from the state."

"Oh, so no cash today?" Kenny looked at Cheryl. She stepped closer to him.

"I'm sorry, not today. It's going to be fantastic when we open. Everybody will make good money. There's coffee and sandwiches, in the meantime," I pointed to the back.

"Okay, thanks," Kenny said. He walked toward the coffee. Cheryl followed, keeping a close eye on her feet.

The bus slowed with a hiss of air brakes and squeaks of metal on metal in front of our office. It stopped with a last burst of air. A man hopped off and trotted over.

"Hi, I'm Michael. We talked on the phone," he said.

"Oh, Michael from under the bridge?"

"Yeah, that's me." He smiled. He looked the part of a bridge dweller, yet he smelled better than Kenny.

"Coffee's over there and sandwiches are in the fridge. When you're ready, I'll give you an application to fill out."

"Thanks a lot, man, you don't know how much I appreciate that." He went to the refrigerator and grabbed a sandwich, unwrapped it, and shoved it into his mouth like a starved beast. He closed his eyes and hummed as he chewed. Then he poured hot coffee, grabbed another sandwich, and sat at a table.

The beige phone rang again and I picked up the handset. It was Candy. "Hi Candy, what's up?"

"What time do you need me to pick you up today?"

"Well, from what I understand, we're supposed to be here till nine PM. Why don't you and Colin come by this afternoon? We can have lunch together and talk."

"We're going to the store to get Colin new clothes. We can come over after that."

"Alright, Candy, see you then." I hung up and sat in my chair. It had been a busy day. The economy was poor. The deluge of calls from job seekers surprised me. Even though we offered a straight commission. No guaranteed income. *What if Dagger can't get licensed?* I thought. *What would I tell these people? Their eyes searched me +for salvation from their poverty.*

A snazzy man came in the front door. He wore a silk, three-piece suit, his shoes shined like a mirror, and he had groomed his hair with a glowing substance. He walked up to my desk.

"I'm Vernon," he said. "I called about the ad earlier."

"Yes, Vernon. Thanks for coming in. Have you done telemarketing before?"

"I do it often, when I don't have enough money to pay all the bills." He said to me quietly, "My parishioners don't always tithe."

"Oh, so you're a minister?"

"Yes, I am."

"Where's your church at?"

"Wherever we can meet. Usually, it's in the homes of my members. But we're looking to get our own building soon."

"Well, good luck with that. Here's an application for you. If you'd like coffee, it's over there." I pointed.

Vernon scanned the room. "You have quite a diverse crowd here."

"Yes, this recession is creating desperate people of all types."

"Tell me about it," he said.

I handed him an application. "Sit anywhere, pens are on the tables."

"Timmy." Dagger and Harley walked in the back door from the alley. The alley stretched along the back of our shopping center. More of a strip mall. Delivery drivers used it to avoid congestion in customer parking. This center included a trophy shop, pizza to go, and Shorin-Ryu Karate operated by Master Moore, triple black belt. At least, that's what his sign in the window said.

"It's Tim, sir."

"How's the recruiting going?"

"I've got nine people, sir." Dagger stared at me. My heart beat increased. He had an enormous presence. His thick neck muscles magnified his stare. He shook his head, glared at Harley, then wandered the room. He chatted with the new recruits, each time, spreading his legs and standing with crossed arms, chin up, shoulders back, stomach in. It appeared he was leading his own military. His stomach was larger than military regulation, but not by much. He established himself to be the alpha male of anyone he encountered. He spoke at a volume that drowned out other conversations. He wore a US Marines ball cap with the bill bent to form an upside-down U shape. He concentrated his glare at whoever he spoke with. When he smiled, it was sideways. Like he was half happy to see you. Half pissed. Harley shook my hand.

"When will we have the license, Harley?"

"We should have it this week. Things are looking really good."

"I sure hope so. These people need money."

"It'll happen soon, Tim. Real soon." Harley patted me on the back.

Dagger walked back toward me. He stopped, took his cap off, and slapped it against his leg. He put it back on, using both hands while glaring at me. "Timmy, keep on top of this. Fill this room up, you hear me?"

"Yes sir. My name is Tim, not Timmy."

He turned to Harley. "Why did you put an inexperienced man in charge of our flagship office?"

"I have faith in him," Harley said. Harley's cadence deferred to his brother. His little brother. Dagger's demeanor wasn't that of a little brother. He was commander of all he surveyed.

"He's a married man. Married men can't make it in this business," Dagger growled.

Dagger walked away toward the alley. Harley patted me on the back again, smiled, then followed Dagger. I could hear

Dagger screaming at Harley in the alley. This was the Dagger I had observed in Denver. Total asshole. Harley promised I'd never see or talk to Dagger. He busted that promise. Maybe Dagger wouldn't return. I hoped.

"Hey buddy," Michael said. He walked over with his coffee and sandwich. "One thing I learned from living under a bridge is you can't let scary people control your life."

"Thanks," I said. "He scares the shit out of me." His formidable appearance must have been boot camp training. Scary training 101. How to intimidate anyone and anything 102. The front doorbell rang again. I turned to see a man with scruffy hair, goatee and mustache walking in. He wore a McDonald's uniform.

"Welcome, are you here for the job?" I asked.

"Yeah, I saw the cash paid daily ad in the newspaper and I called you a while ago. I'm Gary." Gary looked around the room, then back at me.

"Oh yeah, Gary, I remember you. I see you're working at McDonald's?"

"Yeah, I'm working full time there but I'm looking for something better."

"Have you done any sales before?"

"No, never."

"I can teach you. It takes most people three to seven days to learn. We work on a straight commission, but experienced salespeople make fifty to one hundred dollars per day."

"That's more than I'm making at McDonald's. I'd love that."

"Alright, just remember, there's no guarantee, but I'll do my best to train you. Don't count on much income in the first week. Fill out this application. There's coffee in the back here."

"I've had McDonald's coffee all day, no thank you." Gary sat at a table next to Bernie to fill out the application.

Three more applicants came in. I invited everyone to hang out and have free coffee and sandwiches. By nine o'clock, it was time to close the shop, and Candy arrived with Colin.

"Hi Candy, nice to see you." Colin jumped into my arms.

"Okay, everybody, I'm closing, but you're welcome to come back tomorrow. I'll keep the coffee hot and sandwiches in the fridge. Hopefully, we'll get the license this week." Everyone sauntered out, mumbling, "See you later," and "Talk to you later."

I walked to the back to turn off the lights. I flicked the switch and stood facing toward the front door, where Candy and Colin waited for me. I remembered a week earlier, when I first entered it. Someone had ripped tile from the front area, leaving bare glue in square shapes on the concrete floor. The windows and walls were dusty. Rite Rug had delivered a roll of carpet before my arrival. I rolled it out in the front area and pulled it tight to the corners. Then, I spent the day washing the windows, walls, bathroom, and the tile floor in the back area as the technicians from Ohio Bell installed fifteen telephone lines in the carpeted room.

My first entrance to the office showed it to be lifeless. Dead. Void of energy. But as I cleaned, organized, and filled the room with furniture, a ten-gallon coffee pot, and my faith in the future, life formed in that workspace where we launched our hopes and dreams.

The office gained a soul. I don't know where it came from, but I suspect it was from my energy and from the souls of my salespeople as they joined our company and our dream. I took a long look, then walked toward Candy and Colin.

"Candy, thank you for coming to pick me up." We went out to the car and I got behind the driver's wheel. Candy got in the Phoenix Oldsmobile after strapping Colin in the car seat.

"Candy, would you like to go to Denny's for dinner? I'm starving."

"Yes, that'd be great, thank you. How'd it go today?"

"It's working. I've got a sales crew. We can make money when we get the license. The inventory hasn't arrived yet, though, and Dagger's been scaring me. Harley promised I'd never have to deal with him. I don't know if I can work for him." I started the car and backed out of the parking spot, then turned left onto Main Street toward Denny's.

"What would you do if you quit?" Candy looked at me with her eyebrows pinched. I could see she was worried.

"I can sell for another company, or I can stay until I get enough to start my cleaning company."

"I worry about you starting a cleaning company. What if it doesn't work again?"

"Candy, I've explained this to you so many times. It'll work great. When I was at ServiceMaster, I turned that job into a gold mine. I could turn my company into a gold mine."

"Well, okay," Candy said. She looked out the window. I wished Candy would have faith in me. It was hard to keep motivated some days without her support. We remained quiet as I stopped at three red lights, got lucky on two green lights, and made a yellow light. Almost. We pulled into Denny's. The row of booths next to the window was half full. Some were eating, some were talking. We had our dinner with little talking.

Chapter 2

A T NINE, THE NEXT morning, Candy dropped me off at the office. I gave her a kiss and handed her thirty dollars so she and Colin could have fun.

"Please come by and visit me this afternoon if you get a chance, okay, honey? I miss you guys."

"Okay, Tim." Candy turned to look behind her as she backed out. I doubted she would visit me that afternoon. She hadn't before.

At two o'clock, a rusty, beat-up sedan pulled into the parking lot. Five people piled out. I recognized them from our office in Colorado. Brett staggered toward the door.

Brett's eyes were half open and he had Einstein's hair. His clothing, as always, looked like rejects from a thrift store. I wondered if he dug through the rubbish cans that held the discards from charity boxes. He wobbled through the door and stopped to absorb his new environment. He took one step and tripped but grabbed a chair to steady himself.

"What are you guys doing here?" I asked.

"Don't you want us?" Brett asked. He sat on the chair. His eyes and head wobbled. The other four Denver refugees entered.

"Of course, I just wasn't expecting you. Everyone, there's coffee and sandwiches. Welcome to Ohio."

"This place better be worth it. You guys burnt the shit out of Colorado. Nobody wants to buy anything," Rod said. Rod stretched his arms and yawned.

"That wasn't me, that was Harley and Dagger."

Brett weaved back toward the bathroom. The other guys grabbed a coffee. "Can we work?" Rod asked. Rod had a three-day beard. I'd always seen him clean shaven. They must have driven non-stop from Denver.

"No, we're still waiting on the license. Hopefully, it'll be here this week," I said. "In the meantime, I've been filling up the room."

Rod looked at the crowded room. "Will there be phones for us?"

Rod looked at me for an answer. "I'll work it out the best I can. Nobody told me you were coming. Dagger's been screaming at me to pack the phones."

"How many phones have you got here?"

"Fifteen. With morning and night shifts, we can handle thirty people. And you know half will quit."

"Alright." Rod sauntered over to the table with his coffee.

"Hey Tim." Harley walked in from the back door. I walked back to him.

"Harley, you said I wouldn't have to deal with Dagger. He's frying my nerves."

"I think he'll be okay once we get started, he's worried we won't have a business."

"I don't want to deal with him. You promised me I wouldn't have to."

"I know. Give me a chance to get it worked out. Do you have a driver yet?"

"No, I don't have an ad for drivers, just for telemarketers."

"Well, we need to get one. Somebody has to deliver these products." Harley walked into the main room, "Hey everybody." Everyone turned to look. "We need a driver for when we open up. Does anyone have a friend or a relative that needs a delivery job?"

"I've got one. I bet he'd like this job," Vernon said.

"Get him in here," Harley said.

"Yes sir," Vernon said. Vernon picked up the phone and made a call. Within an hour, Vernon's friend arrived. Vernon stood and gave him a hug, then brought him over to me.

"This is my cousin Marcus; he'd love to do deliveries for us." Marcus was thin and neat. Drivers needed to look professional for our customers. I wouldn't be able to send most of our salespeople in their current fashion.

"Alright, Marcus, that'd be great. We're not open for business yet, but as soon as we get our license, I'll put you to work."

"That sounds good to me," Marcus said. He smiled, which showed a gold tooth. One of his two middle teeth. "What's the pay?"

"Two dollars for every box you deliver. Most orders are only one box but sometimes two or three boxes."

"I'm great at delivering. I can handle it," Marcus said. Vernon patted Marcus on the back. Marcus gave Vernon a golden smile.

"Thanks, Marcus. Hang out with us if you want to."

"I can't, but I'll come back when you open."

"I need you to fill out an application and give me your phone number." Vernon sat with him as he filled it out.

The coffee and water I drank demanded an exit strategy, so I walked to the bathroom. When I shut the door, I could hear Dagger chewing out Harley in the alley.

"This isn't the man we want running an office," Dagger said. "I offered him an advance on his pay until we get started. He said he didn't need it. He doesn't need our money; we can't control him. I advanced all our Colorado salesmen money so they could have a hotel and food. That gives us control. We can't trust a man that doesn't owe us money. And we sure as hell can't control him."

I finished my business and went back to the front. Ten minutes later, Dagger and Harley walked in. Dagger looked at the twenty recruits.

"Timmy, we've only got fifteen phones. Why do you have twenty people?"

"Dagger, you told me to fill up the phones. That's what I was doing. I wasn't expecting a crew from Colorado."

"You better figure it out. I don't want one phone being manned by someone who can't sell."

"Should I stop hiring? People are calling from the ad."

"You think you're a manager. You figure it out." Dagger stomped away. Harley followed him.

For the next five days, we heard nothing from Dagger. I kept recruiting because I knew only half the people would stay. On the sixth day, Dagger arrived waving a paper. Harley was right behind him.

"We got our license, let's go to work!" Dagger said.

I had prepared the numbers to dial and the scripts to use during our waiting period. I told everyone to get on the phone and start calling.

The room was abuzz. All fifteen phones were in use. Five more people were waiting for the chance to make phone calls. Harley and I roamed the room to encourage the salespeople for thirty minutes. What if we couldn't make sales in Ohio like we did in Colorado? Pain stabbed at my temples.

This brought back the fear I had when I hired my very first telemarketer. That was before Columbus, before Denver, before Harley. It was in Sheridan. I sat at my desk, listening to my one and only telemarketer calling to offer free estimates for my carpet cleaning company. It had been my last hope. My last fifty dollars. If it had failed, I'd have nothing. The wait was excruciating.

It brought back the fear I had selling alarm systems in Denver. After many weeks, I made no sales but I had figured out the problem was the product. I didn't believe in it. But I believed in our light bulbs. Maybe, our salespeople didn't believe in the light bulbs. They couldn't sell them if they didn't believe it to be an excellent product.

Another thirty minutes passed and still, no sales. It was very odd. In Colorado, we would make sales every five minutes. We should've had twelve sales. Maybe all of this was for nothing. Maybe I'd have to go find another sales job.

And then, Vernon raised his hand. We walked over and he was closing a sale. We patted him on the back as he filled out the ticket. Immediately, everybody started making sales. We had pierced the veil.

Harley showed me how to pin the tickets on a wall map to dispatch the orders. We had one driver, Vernon's cousin. We loaded him up with products and gave him tickets. Sixty minutes later, he called into the office.

"Hey, this is Marcus, my car broke down." My throat fell into my stomach. What would we do if we can't deliver the sales?

"Does anybody know anyone that wants to do deliveries?" I asked the room. Several called friends and within an hour, we had two more drivers, Ralph and Jacob.

Ralph, who looked like a janitor with a baseball sized clump of keys hanging from his baggy pants, jumped in his car and took off. He wasn't dressed to impress, but I was desperate. Within an hour, he called.

"I need more tickets," Ralph said.

"Did you get the others delivered?" I asked.

"Yes, all of them were delivered. I need more." My spirits rose. I read seven more tickets to him. The other driver called in and he had delivered his. I gave him two more tickets. We had a business going full blast.

"Hey Tim," I turned, and Vernon was standing there with a ticket.

"Yes, Vernon."

"This lady wants to know if we can deliver tomorrow afternoon instead of tonight?" His voice expressed a tone of impatience. I understood why. He had a sale, almost, if only we could deliver it. At any minute, his customer may change her mind and hang up the phone. A thin phone connection tied the salespeople to the customers. It could be cut easily by an impatient prospect.

Before I could answer, Brett jumped in. "Hey golden boy."

"Yes Brett," I said. I turned away from Vernon. I could see from the corner of my eye that Vernon became agitated that I hadn't solved his problem.

"This lady wants a delivery after nine o'clock tonight, but I told her we're only going up till nine. What should I do?"

"Hold on a second, Brett, I need to help Vernon," I said.

"But I might lose the sale if I don't answer her now," Brett said.

"I might lose mine, also," Vernon said. "I was here first."

"Okay, guys, hold on," I said. But before I could answer either of them, Kwame chimed in.

"Tim," Kwame said, "this lady isn't in this area we're calling. She wants to know if she can get it delivered to her sister across town."

"Kwame, hold on, I'm helping Brett," I said.

"You were helping me first," Vernon said. He stepped in front of Brett to get my attention.

"I'm going to lose this sale if I don't get a fast answer," Kwame said.

I started getting dizzy, trying to answer everyone at the same time. When I built my cleaning company in Sheridan, I had eighteen employees. It was easy for me to manage them. But they didn't need help at the same time. My brain went into overload. The effect was that I could help no one. I couldn't even speak. Then, three other salespeople wanted my attention. I was frozen in place.

Chapter 3

H ARLEY HAD BEEN WATCHING my meltdown. He took over. "Hold on, everybody, let's give Tim a chance here." He looked at me. "So, Tim, pick one person, take care of them and then move onto the next. Everybody can wait."

I inhaled slowly, then took Vernon's ticket. "Vernon, we can deliver tomorrow between two and four or between five and nine." Vernon smiled and went back to his phone. I answered each person one at a time. I relaxed.

"Thank you, Harley, for helping me. My brain was frying."

"Yes, Tim, I know, but you'll figure it out," Harley said. He patted my shoulder and walked out front to light his cigarette. Harley must have learned hard lessons from having his brother for a boss. I was thankful he helped me cope with that situation.

After the morning shift, everybody left for lunch. The afternoon gave me a break to catch up and breathe. I wondered if I'd be able to handle this new job. It was more complicated than I expected. But at least in the afternoon, I could relax and prepare myself for the evening shift. The phone rang, I picked it up, and I answered, "New Day Marketing."

"Who's this?" A gruff voice demanded.

"This is Tim Drobnick, I'm the manager."

"Do you know who this is?"

"No sir, no idea."

"This is Murphy. What are you doing out there?"

"I'm working for New Day Marketing."

"You're not allowed to work in Ohio. What's your name again?"

"Tim Drobnick."

"I remember you. You're my top salesman in Colorado. Why are you in Ohio?"

"Harley invited me to come out."

"Harley ain't shit. Is he with that piece of garbage brother of his?"

"Yes, Dagger's the owner. Harley's running the company for him."

"Dagger is not the owner. I never gave him permission to leave my company."

"Do you want me to leave them a message, sir?"

"Yeah, tell them this. Tom Murphy is putting out a contract on their heads. I'm putting one on yours too." He hung up the phone. *Oh crap, what now*? I thought.

I called Harley. He answered the phone. "Harley, a guy named Murphy just called here. He says he didn't give you permission to open a business in Ohio. He said he's putting a contract on you, me, and Dagger."

"Oh, don't worry about that, Tim," Harley said. "We'll take care of it." Harley hung up immediately.

Thirty minutes later, Dagger's Bronco pulled up in front of the office. Dagger and Harley both jumped out and came inside. Dagger had a swagger and targeted me with his eyes.

"What's this call you got from Murphy?"

"He said he didn't give you permission to come to Ohio. He's putting a contract on our heads, including mine."

"Yeah, he's full of shit. He's just pissed that he lost his best crew."

Dagger picked up a corner phone in the empty room and made a call. He talked in low tones. Harley walked over to listen. I stayed at my desk. Dagger hung up and turned to me.

"Not to worry, we put a contract on Murphy. If he kills us, he'll be a dead man," Dagger said.

This brought flashbacks of my accidental dealings with the mafia in Denver. Oh my God, did I just go into business with the mafia? Who were these guys? Why did they know a hitman? Why would somebody be placing a contract on us? My breathing and pulse increased. I needed to calm the panic before depression attacked me, but I started to hyper-ventilate. I sat after Dagger and Harley left and meditated on a geranium on my desk. After twenty minutes, I gained my wits back.

After the evening shift, Candy came to pick me up. Colin came running into the office to meet me. I picked him up and swung him around as he laughed with a snort. I finished paying everybody thirty minutes later, got in the car, and drove home with Candy and Colin.

"Candy, something weird happened today. A man named Tom Murphy put a contract on our heads."

"Whose heads?"

"Harley, Dagger, and mine. He said he didn't give us permission to come out here."

"Who's Murphy?"

"I guess he's who we worked for in Colorado. I never met him."

"What are we going to do now?" Candy asked.

"I'm not sure. Something else strange happened. Dagger came into the office this afternoon and made a phone call. After he finished, he told me he had a contract on Murphy. If anything happened to us, a hitman would kill Murphy."

"That seems kind of crooked, don't you think?" Candy asked.

"Yeah, no kidding." We made it home. I relaxed at the dining room table and Candy brought me dinner.

"Can you sit down and talk with me?" I asked. Candy pulled out a chair and looked at me.

"Honey, we're going to need a doctor soon for prenatal care."

"Yes, I know, Candy. I can afford a doctor after I get paid, this Saturday."

"Okay, and I still need more maternity clothing."

"Let's visit the mall on Sunday. I'll walk with Colin while you shop for clothing. Then we could have lunch."

"That'd be great," Candy said.

On Friday morning, a five-foot-tall man in a baseball cap scurried in. He peered up at me, scrunched his face and grunted, "Who are you?" He reminded me of an animated gargoyle. Or an imp. His presence was unsettling. I wasn't sure why, but I could feel it in my gut. His expression showed hate. A burning, soul consuming hate.

"Tim Drobnick." My voice squeaked. Then I said it more clearly, "I'm Tim Drobnick."

"Are you the manager?" He cleared his throat of what sounded like gravel and mucus. He squinted at the salespeople, growled, then looked back at me.

"Yes, I am. Why?"

"Who put you in charge here?"

"Harley did."

"Harley is a pissant. He's not in charge of anything, where's Dagger?"

"I assume he's at his house."

"Get him on the phone for me." He pointed at the phone with his tiny finger and frowned.

"Excuse me sir, who are you?"

"I'm Dale Lewis. I'm supposed to be in charge here. I just got into town. You're not supposed to be running this office. I am." He clenched his jaw and deepened his facial gargoyle features.

"Okay, Dale, hold on." I took one step from him and grabbed the phone. Dale stood with his arms dangling like rubber bands and his face crinkled like old newspaper. I called Harley. "Hey Harley, Dale Lewis is here."

"Put him on," Harley said.

Dale expelled a full body spasm as he took the phone, as if a demon had violently evacuated or entered his body. Not that I believed in demons but Dale could be a good argument for their existence. I took three steps back.

"This is Dale. I need to talk to Dagger." He cleared his throat again and put his hand on his hip. "What do you mean, you're in charge? This is total bullshit. I thought I was managing this place." Dale listened for twenty seconds, shaking his head, then slammed the phone. He fisted his hands, growled at me and the other salespeople, then left. I shuddered. He looked to be a compact lump of evil as he marched to his car, leaning forward with his fists clenched.

"What the hell was that?" Don asked. Rod stood to watch Dale get into his car.

"I don't know. Armageddon on legs?" I asked.

When Saturday afternoon arrived, it was time to get paid. It was my first week, and we had $8000 in sales. For my first week, I didn't think that was too bad.

Harley arrived at five after one. The salespeople, having finished a long week, were visiting with each other. They were waiting for me to pay them. They had to wait until after the drivers returned and I checked them in.

Harley was carrying a case of Bud Light. "Hey everyone, you did a great job this week. Beers are on me!" He sat the case on the table next to the front window, then stood back and laughed. In Denver, I watched Harley do this for his crew. He loved to make them happy.

"Thanks a lot, Harley," Rod said. He patted Harley on his back, then grabbed a cold can. Since Rod worked with us in Denver, he knew Harley was a jovial man and bought drinks for the crew.

"Wow, I've never worked in a phone room where the boss bought us beer," Don said. "Thanks, Harley."

"Yeah, thanks Harley," Larry said. Others joined in. Harley stood with his hands on his hips, an enormous smile on his face, watching the crew grab a beer. Then he grabbed a Bud for himself and walked over to me.

"Harley, thanks for bringing the beer. Hey, we broke $8,000 this week," I said.

"Good job, Tim. I knew you could do this. As soon as the drivers get back, we'll count your inventory and close you out for the week.

"Sure thing," I said. I put my pen down and walked over to grab a beer and talk with my crew. Harley followed.

Ralph backed his car to the front door. His muffler was hanging by wire and rattling against the underside. He turned the engine off, which gave three loud pops, then halted.

Chapter 4

"HEY, GUYS, DOES ANYBODY want to help Ralph get his inventory in here? The faster we get him checked out, the faster I can pay you," I said.

"Sure," Rod and Larry said. They walked out to help Ralph. The other driver pulled up next to Ralph's car and two other salespeople went to help him.

After the drivers were checked in and the salespeople were paid, Harley counted my inventory, then he sat with me to review my paperwork for the week.

"You did $8,233 in sales this week," Harley said. "I think that's good for your first week."

"Thank you, Harley, I'll get better, I promise. Sometimes I get overwhelmed, but I'll get used to it."

"I'm confident you will, Tim. You should have $756 in cash left over in your payroll bag."

"Yes, the bag is in my drawer," I said. I counted the money in front of Harley, which came to $556. I scratched my head. "I've been careful with the payroll, Harley. I don't get how it could be short."

"Well, it's exactly $200 short, so it looks like it was a mistake you made. That comes out of your pay for the week. You get ten percent, so your pay is $823, minus the 200 bucks." Harley counted out $623 for me. I put it in a separate bag.

"Thank you, Harley. I'm sure I'll get it straight next week."

"I'm sure you will, Tim." Harley picked up the closeout paperwork, put it in his briefcase and left. I looked out the window until Candy pulled up in the Phoenix. I locked up the office and took the driver's seat. Candy walked to the passenger side. We drove toward Kroger to get groceries.

"Candy, I got paid $623. I actually made $823. There's $200 missing. I don't know how it could've happened. I never let the money bag out of my sight. And I brought it home every night."

"Does that mean I can't have money this week?" Candy pushed her bottom lip out, her pout. Didn't she care that I lost $200?

"I'll give you $300 for clothing and groceries. I'll make better money next week and I'll watch it like a hawk."

"Okay, honey." Candy smiled and clasped her hands on her lap. We were quiet until we arrived at Kroger.

"Why is this place packed?" Candy asked. Nine people were pushing carts into the automatic sliding doors of the store, dressed in vacation clothing. Denim, shorts, straw hats, ball caps, loose-fitting shirts. Three had small children in tow. One mother had one child in tow, while placating the baby in the child seat of the cart.

"Independence Day is next week. I assume people are getting ready to barbeque and have parties. Geez, no parking spaces are open." I stretched my neck looking for an empty space.

"There's one," Candy pointed at two people entering their vehicle. I approached and waited for the car to back out. Their brake lights came on. After ten seconds, their backup lights lit for twenty seconds.

"What the hell? Are they leaving or not?" I asked.

"Tim, Colin can understand you," Candy said.

"Sorry." We waited another half a minute and the car backed out. I claimed my prize.

"You got lucky," Candy said.

"Candy, look, my ghosts made it to Columbus."

"What, where?"

"Candy, see the people coming to the car next to us?"

"Yeah, okay?" Candy frowned.

"Now on the other side," I said.

"Okay, I remember you said this is how your ghosts prove they're with you. I don't get it."

"It's odds and probability. When you–"

"No, stop. That hurts my head," Candy said.

"Look, now the car in front of us, their owner's coming to it. Three sides. This is amazing."

"I'm glad your ghosts made it to Columbus," Candy said. She crawled out of the car and grabbed a shopping cart in the corral of silver pipes. A sign asked us to return the carts to the corral for the promise of lower prices. Candy's walk had become a waddle as her baby bump grew. I thought she was cute, but she didn't agree. I plucked Colin from the car and put him in the cart's child seat. I pushed the cart, letting Candy lead us at her own pace.

As we walked into the store, the blast of cool air hit us. It was even cooler because our sweat from the scorching sun magnified the chill. But it felt good. The entrance led us directly into the produce, where the sweet aroma of fresh, unhusked corn greeted us. Five people were bagging them as if they were disappearing, they probably were. People loved to grill corn on Independence Day. They'd cook whatever wouldn't slip through the grate of their stainless-steel propane grills on their brick or stone patios. Candy pulled a plastic bag from the roll, opened it, and shoved ears of corn into it. I didn't understand how anyone could open those plastic bags so fast. I could rub and pick for twenty minutes, looking like a fool. Finally, I'd decide I didn't need vegetables.

Colin ran to grab an orange squash shaped like a club. He swung it, pretending to be some supernatural creature, I assumed. I pulled him back near me to avoid wounding frenzied shoppers.

As I followed Candy, she threw groceries into the cart, and I placed the items Colin picked and tossed in the cart back on the shelf. Soon, the cart was full, and we checked out. Candy loved shopping. I would have rather stayed home and entertained Colin, but I wanted family time.

When we made it home, Colin jumped into my lap as I leaned back in the easy chair. It was nice that Colin was tired and snuggled with me. I closed my eyes.

"Tim, I have lunch for you." Candy set a heavy ceramic plate on the table. Candy had found an entire dinner set at Target for the incredibly low price of fifty dollars. She loved the blue flower design.

"Thank you, honey." I picked up Colin and set him on a chair next to me at the table. He helped me eat my BLT on toast. Mostly the bacon.

The next morning on Sunday, Candy let me sleep in till ten. I needed the rest after that stressful week. The fear of Dagger, Murphy, and Dale Lewis was like residing in a popcorn popper. You never knew when they would explode.

We arrived at the mall holding the hand of a bouncing Superball that we called Colin. Candy shopped for maternity clothes. I intercepted five clothing racks that tipped too far after Colin pulled on the shirts hanging from it.

"Oh, honey, how about this one?" she asked. She pulled a dress up over her maternity bump.

"That will look beautiful on you."

"Well, I'm four months along now. I don't think I'm going to be beautiful."

"Yes, you are Candy. You're gorgeous. What do you think?" I asked Colin. "Do you think mommy is pretty?"

Colin paused, put his finger in his mouth, and looked at Candy.

"Well, you see that, he's speechless; he must think you're beautiful."

Candy laughed.

We waited on Candy while she paid for three dresses, then we went to Calle's restaurant on the second floor of the mall. Calle's entrance had stained glass windows framed in cherry wood. Maybe just cherry wood color. The carpet was burgundy and plush. They kept the lights low for ambiance. The seating was at wooden booths or tables with varnished tops. With Colin, we couldn't visit a cafe with tablecloths as he would yank it off. And he was a disaster with crayons. I didn't understand why a tablecloth restaurant would supply crayons.

"Colin, are you hungry yet?" I asked.

"Yes!" he yelled. Everyone turned to look at him.

"Sorry, everyone, he gets excited," I said. I held up the kiddie menu with pictures of food. "Colin, point at what you want." He pointed at every picture on the menu. "Candy, I think that means he's getting our choice." We both laughed.

"Tim, did you learn more about that..." Candy lowered her head to the table, "...contract on your head?" Candy sat back and unrolled her napkin as she frowned at me.

"Nothing new." I scanned the menu.

"How can Dagger put out a contract?" Candy asked.

"I don't know, I've been wondering about that myself. I sure hope I haven't joined the mafia. I have a propensity for that."

"I've always wondered about their names," Candy said. "It seems odd for parents to name their kids Dagger and Harley. Do you think that's their real name?"

"Harley said it's their legal names, the ones their parents gave them. You're right, it is weird somebody would name their kids that." I leaned back in my chair and put my hands on the table. "Candy, I don't understand how I lost $200 this week. I was so careful. Our funds are getting low. After giving you $300 this week, we had enough to pay our bills, but nothing left for savings."

"If you're making money with these boys, you'll keep working for them, right?"

"Candy, I don't know. Dagger keeps telling Harley he doesn't want me running that office. And that other guy, Dale Lewis, he's trying to snatch the office away from me. I don't know how long I'll be working for these guys but I'll do my best to stay." We finished our day at the mall and returned home.

Monday morning, we had an additional help wanted ad in the paper for drivers. The phone rang at nine o'clock.

"Hello, this is New Day Marketing," I said.

"Hey, this is Kermit Cook. I'm calling about your driver's ad. Is the job still open?"

"Hi, Kermit, this is Tim. Yeah, I still have driver positions open. Come in and check it out."

"Sure will, buddy. Give me your address and I'll be there."

"We're at 3872 East Main St. in Whitehall."

"Okay, I'll be there in about fifteen minutes."

Sure enough, fifteen minutes later, a man with wire-rimmed glasses, perfectly feathered hair parted in the middle, and chewing gum walked in. He walked up to me, stuck his hand out with a jerk, turned his head slightly sideways.

"I'm Kermit Cook, I'm here about the delivery job."

"Howdy, Kermit. I'm Tim. Thanks for coming in. You know, Kermit was my nickname in college."

"Really? Why'd they call you Kermit?"

In a high-pitched voice I said, "This is Kermit T. Frog, coming to you live from Sesame Street."

"Wow, you really sound like Kermit," he said.

"And apparently, I looked like him too."

"So, tell me about this driver's job," Kermit asked.

"We're paying two dollars per box you deliver. Most deliveries are one box, but I run bonuses for doubles or triples."

"How do you map out your deliveries?" He asked.

"Come back here. I'll show you the tickets pinned on the map. When the drivers are calling on the phone, I read the ones that are close together."

Kermit put his hands on his hips and snapped his gum, studying the board. "So, if I called in right now, how would you dispatch me?"

"Well, first I'd ask where you were at."

"Right here," Kermit pointed at an intersection.

"Then, I'll give you these four tickets right here."

Kermit stood back and snapped his gum again. "Okay, buddy. I can do this job. The way you dispatch, I could do fifty deliveries a day."

"Seriously? That's how much I'm producing, but that'll increase. I'm training and hiring new salespeople."

"Yeah, make me your only driver. I'll take care of you."

"You can be one of my two primary drivers. I need backup drivers in case somebody breaks down. I learned that the hard way. Besides, I'm sure I'll get you all the deliveries you can handle."

"Okay, buddy." Kermit turned to me, stuck out his hand and nodded with a jerk. "I'm your man."

"Great Kermit, I can give you tickets to deliver now, if you like?"

"Sure, I'm ready to go full time."

"Okay, I have to get information from you. Fill out this application, plus I need your mother's phone number and address."

"Seriously? Why?"

"I had a driver, Jacob, disappear with inventory. I found him at his mother's house. If I can't find you, I know your mother can."

Kermit laughed and sat to fill out the application.

Next, I filled out an inventory form for Kermit. He nodded his head and snapped his gum as I explained his responsibility and accounting for the light bulbs.

Then, he loaded his car with the boxes. He had a four-door Bonneville and a spacious back seat for cargo. The sun had bleached the paint on the hood.

"I'm going to get this painted soon." Kermit explained, patting the hood. "It'll look like new."

"As long as it gets the job done," I said. Kermit crawled behind the wheel and drove away.

I returned to my desk, then Dagger stomped in.

Chapter 5

ELECTRICITY SHOT THROUGH MY brain. I held my breath, and my legs went weak. He stood staring at me, just inside the door, like Clint Eastwood in a spaghetti western. His formidable body blocked the sun, leaving a glowing edge on his shape's perimeter. *Christ, why is he staring at me?* I thought.

He held a lone sheet of paper in his hand and lifted it to show me and clenched his other fist. Then he walked toward me, his steps were deliberate and slow. As he got closer, I could see he was holding a copy of my close-out summary Harley helped me fill out two days earlier. Harley, jovial, bringing beer, patting my back, said I did good for my first week. Dagger shook the paper in my face.

"What's this?" he asked, more of a growl.

"That's my sales summary from last week," I said.

"Do you consider this acceptable?"

"For my first week, yes."

"Bullshit. I told Harley you shouldn't be running this office. This office should do $15,000 per week." He slammed the paper onto my desk with his open palm.

"I'm training salespeople and I'm hiring more of them. I'll keep the phones busy all day." My shivering legs couldn't keep me vertical much longer. I needed to sit, but I dared not look disrespectful.

"Next week better be stellar." He picked up my coffee mug, threw it across the room, and shattered it on the wall. He marched across the room and kicked the door open with his foot.

After he left, I sat and shivered uncontrollably. Thirty minutes later, Dale Lewis walked in the front door. He clutched his tiny little paws, and he had a tiny little grimace on his tiny little face.

"Dagger told me about your shitty week. $8000? I should be the one running this office. I could do $8000 in my sleep. Harley's insane for putting you in charge. You're a newbie. You don't know what the hell you're doing. I'll make sure Dagger fires you if it's the last thing I do." Dale kicked my trash can, turned around, and stomped his tiny little feet out the door.

I was still shaking from Dagger. Dale turned me into an earthquake. I doubted Dale had enough influence to hurt me, but I wasn't sure. I had just started a new job, and I already had two enemies. My friend Harley didn't have control, as he promised.

I continued to train and hire more salespeople during the week. Kermit and Ralph were excellent drivers, plus I had two part-time drivers for back-up. It was hard to enjoy success because my fear of Dagger and Dale poisoned my days. Something about them scared me to the core. They attacked at random, like the villains of a horror movie.

Finally, it was Saturday night, time for closeout. Harley came in to count my inventory.

"Well, you did $10,252 this week. That's an improvement over last week," Harley said.

"Yeah, Dagger and Dale were telling me they could do $15,000."

"Don't listen to them," Harley said. He stuffed the closeout paperwork into the folder inside his brown leather briefcase.

"But they keep popping in like jack-in-the-boxes and screaming at me. How can I ignore that? It makes it hard for me to do my job and to keep my mind positive." I dropped my pen onto my desk and leaned back in my chair. *I should just quit now,* I thought.

"I'll talk to them, Tim; you're doing a good job. Keep up what you're doing. Now, according to our summary, you should have $1,497 for payroll after you paid everyone."

I laid it out on the desk as I counted $1,197. Three hundred missing. Exactly. Again.

"Dang it," I said. "I didn't let that bag of money out of my sight all week. I don't understand how I lost it." I searched my mind for any mistake I had made. I didn't remember letting the payroll out of my sight unless it was in my desk drawer. Even then, I kept an eye out for anyone moving near my desk.

"Well, it's even money again. Seems someone is grabbing twenties. Your ten percent this week is $1,252, minus the $300 leaves you $952."

"Alright, thank you, Harley. It really hurts losing that much money."

"Close up and head home. You deserve a day off." Harley patted my back. "You'll do better next week."

"Thank you, Harley." Harley left and I locked up the office. Candy arrived. I walked out to the car and entered the passenger side. I didn't feel like driving.

"Hi, honey," I said.

"Hi Tim, did you make a lot of money this week?" Candy looked at me. I sighed. It would be nice if she greeted me another way. Sometimes I wondered if she didn't care about me, only how much money I made. On the way out from Denver, she was excited about coming here to get rich. She got really excited and made love to me every night. I wondered if it was just because the idea of money excited her, I hoped not.

"I made $1,252, but $300 of it was missing. I can't figure out where it's going. The money doesn't leave my sight."

"Can I still get $300 this week?" Candy asked, showing no concern for the lost money.

"Yes, of course, honey. After taxes, we only have enough to pay this week's bills. At this rate, I'll never save enough for a carpet cleaning company."

"We'll be okay as long as you keep working for Harley, right?"

"I don't know, Candy. I don't know." I sat quietly for twenty seconds. "I feel like eating at a Mexican restaurant. Do you?"

"Yes, that sounds great. How about you, Colin? Want to go to a Mexican restaurant?"

"Yes," Colin said. Colin would go anywhere if there were crayons and chocolate milk.

After the host seated us at the restaurant, I looked out the window. I thought about my lost money. It never left my hand, or desk, or vision unless I was in bed. This made me wonder if perhaps Candy was taking it. I hated to think that, but unless I was crazy, it wasn't happening while I was at work. I decided I'd count the money before I went to sleep and then count it again in the morning. We tucked Colin in, then Candy and I went to bed.

"Candy? Honey?"

"Yes Tim?"

"Could we make love? It's been a couple weeks since we have." I sat on the bed hopeful. Candy was wearing a loose-fitting pajama top that easily draped over her baby belly. It must have been new. I didn't recognize it. She sure looked good in them.

"I'm pretty tired tonight, maybe tomorrow night." Candy lifted the covers, sat on the bed, put her feet under the blanket, and pulled them over her. She lay on her side, facing away from me.

"Okay, honey. Good night, I love you." I longed for her. Her hair spread beautifully on her pillow. Every time I asked, she said maybe tomorrow. That tomorrow had never arrived.

"Good night, Tim, I love you too."

The next morning when I woke up, I opened my money bag and counted. One-hundred dollars was missing. Did I count it wrong the night before? I didn't think I did.

Candy dropped me off at eight on Monday morning. I got the office ready to open. At nine o'clock, Dagger pulled up, squealing his tires in front of the office. He jumped out, slammed his car door, and yanked the office door open. He marched in with a red face and gritting his teeth. His clenched right fist held a baton, which he snapped open.

Chapter 6

H E WALKED UP TO my desk, slammed it with the baton, and screamed, "$10,000? All you gave me was $10,000? I told you this office must do $15,000."

I was panting before he walked in the door. When he slammed the baton on my desk, I quivered. I didn't know if he would hit me.

"Sir," I said. I paused. "I did $2,000 better this week than the previous week. Each week will get better, I promise. I'm still hiring salespeople and training them, and I've got an excellent set of drivers."

"Not good enough, Timmy, not good enough." He stressed the word, Timmy.

"I'm sorry sir, I'm doing my best."

"Your best isn't good enough." He hit the desk again with his baton, then hit the wall. He put his hands on his hips and stood glaring at me for thirty seconds. I squirmed, unsure of what to do. Finally, he turned and left. I sat down in my chair, breathing hard and fighting panic.

An hour later, Dale Lewis came in, walked up to me with his mouth clinched, his baseball cap covering his head and looked up at me.

"I don't understand why they let you in here. I could do $20,000 and all you did was 10,000? You took my job. This is my office. There's no way you're going to stay here. I'll see to it with my last dying breath if I have to."

He turned around and tramped away. Although his stomps were smaller, his evil overshadowed Dagger's. Maybe, angry garden gnomes spawned him.

Thirty minutes later, a man walked into my office. He wore a neatly pressed white business shirt, rolled up at the sleeves, and a loosened collar. He had brown shoes and khaki pants. He carried a black sales case in one hand and a tan briefcase in the other. He set them on my desk.

"Good afternoon, sir, my name is Roger."

"Hi Roger, I'm Tim. What can I do for you?"

"I have office supplies for you." He started taking out staplers, pens, and rubber bands. I was miffed that he didn't ask permission to commandeer my desk.

"Does that briefcase lock?" I asked.

"Oh yes." He opened the briefcase. "You can change the combination inside to anything you want. If you lock the case and forget it, you're out of luck. So be careful."

"That's perfect. How much do you want for that?" I spun the lock. It seemed cheap. The inside was a fake plastic leather. The outside looked like a higher quality faux leather.

"Fifty dollars."

"That's crazy."

"Alright, thirty dollars."

"I'll take it, nothing else though." I handed him cash. He slipped the money into a brown envelope with a clasp inside his sales case.

"Alright, buddy, I'm going to be back in this area next week. Talk to you later." He put the goodies back in his bag.

"Roger, Roger," I said.

That night, before I retired to bed, I counted the money. I wrapped it up in rubber bands and included a note with the amount. Then, I locked it in my briefcase and slid it under my side of the bed. Candy didn't know the combination. Perhaps this would solve the mystery.

The next morning, I awoke looking at the ceiling. I patted Candy's side of the bed. Empty. I looked at my alarm clock. 6:58. Damn. I had two more minutes to sleep. Why did I wake up early? I sat up and pushed the alarm off. Then, I remembered the briefcase. I stood, kneeled and pulled it out from under the bed. I had left the combination on 427 in case Candy tried to unlock it. I doubted she would notice. After attempting to hack the lock, it would change the setting. It was still on 427. I dialed in the combination and opened the case. I had left the payroll in a business size white envelope in the middle pocket facing away. Just in case she broke in, she may not remember to place it back in the middle pocket. The envelope was still in the middle pocket, facing away. It looked untouched.

I counted the money. It was a hundred dollars short. Dammit. There's no way Candy could break into this case. She didn't know the combination. I looked at the hinges. The faux leather when the case was closed hid them. They looked unharmed. Maybe I miscounted. Maybe I'm going crazy. I showered, dressed, and went to help Candy with breakfast.

Maybe her face would give her away. I watched her as we ate our eggs. I saw nothing unusual. After breakfast, I went to work.

That evening, at eight PM, salespeople filled my phones. There were three standing against the wall, waiting for one to open. The sun was low and reflected through the window. I saw Dale Lewis walking across the parking lot toward me. I held my breath, anticipating another assault.

He walked in the room, stopped, looked around, lifted his hat, which revealed a pure white bald dome with a startling tan line. Sunlight hadn't peeked under his cap since the garden gnomes spawned him. He scratched his head, snorted, slapped his hat back on, turned around and trudged over to the Brass Rail Bar.

I gave Candy a call. "Candy, Dale's at the Brass Rail. I'm going to talk to him after work and try to reason with him. Don't come pick me up, I'll grab a taxi to come home, okay?"

"Okay, Tim. I hope you fix things."

"Thanks, Candy. I love you, honey."

"I love you too, Tim," Candy said.

After I closed the office, I saw Dale's car still in the parking lot. I walked over to the Brass Rail Pub. When I opened the door, the air greeted me with the aroma of stale beer. The lounge was empty save Dale and a woman at the bar. They had wrapped around each other like octopi; she was bending her neck down to kiss him, while Dale looked up. There was massive suction and slurping between their mouths. I sat four bar stools over to wait for a chance to get his attention. For ten minutes, they devoured each other. Weren't they embarrassed doing that in public? He had his hat off, which showed his white dome.

Dale opened one eye and saw me sitting at the bar. He pushed the girl back and grunted and put his hat back on.

"What do you want?" he said.

The lady stood up, excused herself, and headed toward the bathroom.

"Dale, I want to talk to you. I want you to know I'm not your enemy."

"Oh, yes you are," Dale said.

"Dale, are you angry with me because I have this office?"

"I'm angry with you because you're a pissant. And yes, Dagger gave me this office. Somehow, you snuck in here and took it away. I hate devious people."

"Dale, back in Colorado, Harley asked me to open the first office here. I didn't even know you existed, or that Dagger promised this office to you."

"Harley is not supposed to be in charge out here." Dale lifted his hat and scratched. White flakes fell to his shoulders.

"Dale, I just want to get along with you. I don't want to be your enemy."

"Fine, then give me back my office."

"Harley promised me this office before I left Denver. I brought my family. I'm depending on the income."

"Yeah, Dagger told me you're a family man. You're doomed. Family men die in our world."

"Okay, Dale. I tried." I slid off the stool.

"I'll haunt you. You'll never have peace. I'll make sure you are gone." Dale stood.

"What do you mean, gone?" I asked. I stopped and faced him.

"You'll find out." He clenched his tiny hands. His lady came out of the restroom and Dale walked over to her. They moved to the other end of the bar. I assumed Dale wanted to watch the door. I returned to my office, unlocked the door, and called a cab to take me home.

After dinner with Colin and Candy, I went upstairs to the bathroom. I locked the door and started the shower. Then I slid a screwdriver from my pocket, took off the light switch cover, counted my money, and rolled it up with rubber bands. I slipped it inside the crevice next to the switch. I then replaced the cover, took my shower, and went to bed. I wrote what the count was on a piece of paper and put it inside my locked briefcase.

The next morning, I went to the bathroom, locked the door, took the money out, counted it and it was short one-hundred dollars. Dammit, how can this possibly be happening? I'm counting it several times. I know I can't be wrong. Candy had to have taken it. But how'd she find the money in the wall?

The next night, I removed the cover and then pulled out the switch. I put the money roll inside of plastic and used black electricians' tape to wrap it up next to the black wire. It was far enough down the wire you couldn't get to it or see it unless you removed the light switch. I put the slots on the four screws pointing at noon, three o'clock, six o'clock, and nine o'clock. I went to bed, confident that the money was secure.

Chapter 7

I N THE MORNING, I entered the bathroom and started the water in the sink. I removed the cover. The screws were at the positions I expected. But, when I removed the switch, retrieved the payroll, and counted the money, a hundred dollars was missing. Again.

It seemed impossible, but Candy must be the thief. I didn't think we had poltergeists in our building. It wasn't old enough. It was the only logical conclusion. The idea that Candy was stealing from me hurt. Another pain tacked onto the painful memory of when she cheated on me. I wondered what it would be like if I just took Colin and left her. It might be good for me, but not for Colin. I couldn't break up the family. I'd have to live with Candy and hope our marriage would improve.

That night, I found a hiding spot for my money in the office, counted it and wrapped it up. The next morning, Saturday, I counted the money, and it was all there. The money had only disappeared when it was at my house. It had to be Candy.

Damn, that woman had skills. Maybe, she should have been a detective, or psychic.

It was time for the Saturday night close out, and I was short 300 bucks. At least I knew what was happening and I could control the losses.

"You did $12,358 this week," Harley said.

"Thanks Harley, but your brother says anything under 15,000 is not acceptable. He's coming here every week intimidating and scaring the hell out of me because I'm not performing well."

"Just ignore him."

"I can't ignore him. Did you know he slammed his baton on my desk and threatened me this week? If I was working anywhere else, I could sue him for harassment."

"Yeah, don't do that, that would make it worse." Harley shook his head.

"Harley, when will you control this business? You said I'd never have to deal with Dagger and you never mentioned Dale Lewis."

"Oh, you mean Oompa Loompa?" Harley laughed.

"What's Oompa Loompa?"

"Remember Willy Wonka, the little orange guys? Just put green hair on Dale."

I looked up and thought about that. "Yeah, that's funny." I laughed.

"He's always pissed off. Don't worry about him."

"I haven't learned how to not worry. Both guys scare me. It's hard to keep my mind right and keep motivating my crew to make sales."

"Hang in there, Tim," Harley said. He gave me his signature pat on the back.

After we closed, Candy pulled up in the car to take me home. Candy opened the door and walked to the passenger side. I guess she wanted me to drive. I got in the driver's seat. Colin was in the back seat, fastened into his safety chair.

"Hi daddy!" Colin said. I reached back and tickled his tummy.

Candy buckled up. "Do you think you're going to get your own car soon?" Candy asked.

"I could've by now if I hadn't lost $1,500," I said. Candy didn't reply. "Let's go get Mexican food, okay? I love Chi-Chi's."

"Okay, that sounds good. Do I still get $300 this week?" Candy asked.

"Candy, didn't you already get $300 this week?" I looked at her and squinted.

"What are you talking about?" Candy's mouth opened like she had no clue.

"You stole one-hundred dollars out of my payroll three nights this week."

"No, I didn't, I don't know what you're talking about." She crossed her arms and pouted.

"Well, it doesn't matter. I solved the problem. Yes, I'll give you another $300. I just wish you'd be honest with me. You know I need to collect $50,000 to start a cleaning company, right? Then I'll have all the money you'll ever want, but I can't do it if you keep stealing from payroll."

"I worry about that cleaning company."

"I know, I know, I know, I know." We said nothing else as we drove to the restaurant.

On Monday mornings, I expected a visit from the evil duo. Not to disappoint, Dagger busted in the door and screamed. Everybody had to hang up their phones.

"If you don't give me $15,000 this week, I'll bury you. I don't care what Harley says, this is just bullshit." Dagger grabbed the cactus on my desk and smashed it on the tile floor. The ceramic pot blew apart and flew past me, one coming dangerously close to my eye. Three shards flew on the telemarketer's table next to the show window. The soil sprayed over the tile and the poor cactus split into five pieces.

Dagger walked to me and pressed his index finger on my forehead, raised his thumb and made an action like shooting a gun. "I'm dead serious," he said. He said the word, dead, slowly. Then he turned and walked out.

That incident reminded me of the time in Colorado when I saw him smash Harley's mug on the wall. Poor Harley tried to recompose himself, and after he did, he walked around the room to encourage the salespeople. I followed his lead. Soon, everybody was back to normal, and we had sales going again. How-the-hell could Dagger expect us to increase sales with his tantrums?

The goblin didn't show this time. That was a positive thing. Except it wasn't. His evil wormed its way into my skull. I thought maybe it was my imagination. But I couldn't shake it.

That night, after our family dinner, Candy put Colin to bed. Thirty minutes later, we went to bed.

"Candy?"

"Yes, Tim?"

"Could we make love tonight? We haven't since we got into this townhouse."

"Not tonight, maybe tomorrow night."

"I really miss being with you and touching you."

"I know, Tim."

I lay, trying to sleep, but I couldn't. I felt someone in the room. I bolted out of bed, but I saw nothing. I lay down again. Just as I transitioned into a light sleep, I felt Dale's evil energy around me. I woke up and stood. Again, I saw nothing, but I could feel the air as thick as black syrup surrounding me. Somehow, this was Dale.

"Dear God, Sheena, ghosts, please help me." I lay down and closed my eyes. After thirty minutes, I fell asleep.

That Saturday at the end of my fourth week, I had $13,000 in sales. It wasn't 15,000, but I was getting there. An excellent performance, considering I had hired and trained a crew of salespeople from scratch, except for the five from Colorado.

When Harley walked into the office, Dagger and a stranger followed him. Dagger was whistling as he walked past me. He stood and spread his feet, shoulders back, chin up, paunchy stomach in, and smiled. He seemed wickedly happy.

The stranger had a black wool topcoat with the collar turned up. A fedora sat on his blonde head. He stood next to Dagger and put a cigarette into his mouth with two fingers. He puffed and squinted as the smoke rolled under the brim of his hat. I put his age at about thirty. He had a gold and diamond ring on his left pinky finger. It winked in the light as he lifted his cigarette. He kept a poker face as he stared at me. Dagger continued to grin.

"I'm here for your close out," Harley said.

"Hi Harley, I'm ready for you." I looked to Harley and ignored Dagger and his costumed pet.

Harley moved the inventory away from the wall. He hadn't moved them on previous close outs, but I knew it was to check for holes. He grabbed the pen tucked behind his ear and used it to point as he counted, then he wrote the count on the inventory form on his clipboard. He turned and gave me a big smile. Harley was always good for smiles. I believed he wanted everyone to be happy.

Harley sat at my desk and subtracted the inventory count from the week's beginning inventory, then used the calculator to multiply the difference times the retail price of each box. He took the paper off the clipboard, lifted it up, and leaned back in his chair. He held it up and observed it for five seconds, then, he looked at me.

"You had a great week, Tim," Harley said. "You did $13,473." He gave me his big smile. In the corner of my eye, I saw the pet smirk. Dagger shook his head and pivoted on his heel. He snatched the Marine's ball cap from his head and slapped it on his leg.

Harley noticed their response and frowned at them. He looked back at me. "It's time to count payroll. You should have $1,332."

I counted out the payroll, $1,332. No money missing. "It's all here," I said. Candy couldn't take her bonus money.

"Ok, give it to me so I can recount it," Harley said. He hadn't counted the money on previous close outs. I handed it to him. Harley laid out the cash on the desk, separating it by denomination. He then picked up each pile, counted it, then wrote it on the clipboard. He used the calculator to add all the pile numbers. Then he gave me my commission, $1,347.

"Thank you, Tim," Harley said. "We're replacing you. This is your last week."

Chapter 8

H ARLEY PLACED THE BUNDLE of money into his briefcase, closed it, then stood.

"Harley, at the rate I'm going, I'll do $15,000 next week." I looked at him, hoping his smile would keep me employed.

"It's not my choice." He patted me on the shoulder. He had a sympathetic look, and I knew it was genuine. Dagger's face stretched over his smile. I knew that was genuine as well.

Dagger stuck his hand out to me. "Give me the keys." I handed them to him, and he held them above the outstretched gloved hand of the stranger. He let them drop, and his fingers snapped closed, snatching the keys.

Dagger looked at me, put his hands on his hips. "This is Tony, one of my best friends from New Jersey. He knows how to run a phone room. He's going to kick ass and show you how it's really done."

"But I can be a telemarketer, right?" I asked.

"No. I don't want you near my business." Dagger's smile became a sneer. *If I can't be here, how will he show me?* I thought.

I looked at Harley. Harley looked at the floor as his younger brother yanked his puppet strings. I had trusted Harley's promise that I wouldn't have contact with Dagger. I trusted the wrong man. Candy pulled up in the Phoenix. I grabbed the picture of my family from my desk, picked up my briefcase, and left, saying nothing more.

"How was your day?" Candy asked, as I crawled into the passenger seat.

"I don't want to talk about it now, let's go home." I looked out the window so my face wouldn't reveal my anger and hurt. Candy backed out and turned left on Main Street.

I needed a plan to support my family. Should I do it by finding another sales job and risk working for another idiot? Or should I start a cleaning company? Candy stopped at a red light at Hamilton Road. I looked at the people standing by the bus stop. I didn't want to be one of them. I needed a plan.

The challenge in starting a disaster restoration business was that I didn't have $50,000 to buy the equipment and rent a warehouse, but I knew a man that might solve my problem, Buster McCade. He was the insurance agent in Denver that worked with ServiceMaster. Perhaps, he'd recommend me to the same insurance company in Columbus and maybe they'd finance me with his recommendation.

Candy pulled into the front of our townhouse. I had said nothing to her on the ride home. I opened the back door and picked Colin out of his seat.

"Tim, what's wrong?" Candy asked, as she unlocked the door.

"I'll tell you inside. I need to mix a drink first."

"Okay." Candy looked at me, her eyebrows furrowed into a worried look.

Colin ran toward the trucks he had waiting on the living room floor. I walked into the kitchen. I opened the top cupboard and grabbed the Absolute, vermouth, and stainless-steel martini shaker.

"Candy, would you like a virgin drink?" I asked.

"Orange juice would be good." Candy was sitting at the table in the dining room. It flowed into the living room with no divider.

I pushed the icemaker with the martini shaker and filled it half with ice. I grabbed orange juice from the fridge, poured twelve ounces, covered the top and shook it. I poured it into a tall glass decorated with blue flowers. It was from another collection Candy found at Target. I handed it to Candy and walked back to start my martini.

"So, Candy," I said as I returned to the kitchen. "Dagger fired me today." I could see Candy through the opening above the kitchen counter.

"What? On no! Why?"

"Because he's an asshole, that's why. He replaced me with some mafia-looking smartass. Said he'll show me how to do it right."

"Can you be a salesman?"

"No. Dagger said he doesn't want me near his business."

"How's he going to show you how to do it right then?" Candy asked. That surprised me. Candy rarely noticed contradictions. She produced them.

"That's an excellent question, Candy. Very smart."

Candy looked at the ceiling, then took a drink. "What'll you do now?"

"I'll see if I can get a cleaning company started on the bit of money we have. If not, I'll get a sales job somewhere else."

"Oh." Candy sipped her orange juice.

"Candy, can you see why it's important to start a business? We don't want to depend on someone else for a job."

"Yes. I can see that." She sipped again and sat quietly for thirty seconds. "But that cleaning business really worries me."

"I know, Candy. I know." I sat next to her to enjoy my martini. Shaken, dry, a bit dirty, and three olives.

On Monday, I called Buster, and he answered the phone. "Hello, Buster, this is Tim Drobnick. I used to work with you at ServiceMaster. You said I could call you?"

"Oh yes, thank God." He said it *Gawad*. "Are you ready to do disaster restoration?"

"Well, I have bad news. I was working for a telemarketing company that could've helped me save the $50,000 for start-up capital, but they moved to Ohio, so, I moved with them. I was wondering if you'd recommend me to your insurance company in Columbus. I'm sorry I'm not there to help you out."

"Oh man, I'm disappointed." He sighed. "I understand you have to go where the money is." He paused for five seconds. "Yeah, I'd be happy to give you a recommendation. None of the agents in Columbus know me, but maybe it'd help."

"Thank you, Buster. Another question. Do you think the insurance company would loan me $50,000? I could be exclusive to them for disaster restoration."

"I doubt it, but you can ask. I'll give you the number of the main office."

"Alright, Buster, thank you. So, it's okay if I give them your name when I call?"

"Yes, they can call me. I'll give them an excellent report." Buster paused for twenty seconds. "Okay, man, here's the number 614-555-9232. Man, I wish you were in Denver."

"I'm sorry, Buster, you were a great agent to work with."

"Tim, thank you. Good luck to you." I sat the phone receiver on the cradle and held my breath for ten seconds, then exhaled.

I called the number Buster gave me. No luck. They said they needed no more contractors. So much for that idea.

Maybe, I thought, *I could buy an owner-financed carpet cleaning company. That would give me most of what I needed to add disaster restoration to my services.*

I got phone numbers for Columbus cleaning companies from the Yellow Pages at the library. This was telemarketing, one of my skills. I only needed one sale. I went home and got on the telephone and started calling.

"ABC carpet cleaning, how may I help you?"

"This is Tim Drobnick. I assume you're the owner?

"Oh no, Josh Jacobs is the owner. How can I help you?"

"I need to speak with Mr. Jacobs. Is he available?"

"He's in his office. I'll send you back to him." She put me on hold. I was entertained by Rod Stewart's "Lay Down Sally" for thirty seconds until Mr. Jacobs answered the phone. "Hello, this is Josh Jacobs."

"Hello, Mr. Jacobs. This is Tim Drobnick. You don't know me from Adam, but you've got a wonderful company there, and I'd like to buy it."

"Well, it's my lucky day," Josh laughed. "But, unless you're offering five million cash up front, it's not for sale."

"I see. When do you think you might retire from the business?"

"I'm only fifty years old. I have a long way to go. So, unless you got five million to help me retire early, no dice." He was very polite, considering I had interrupted his valuable time.

"Well, I'm sure your company is worth it, but I don't have that much cash. I appreciate you taking the time to talk to me."

"You're welcome. Good luck to you, son." Josh hung up the phone.

Candy had come home and was listening to my calls. She looked worried but said nothing. I knew she wasn't happy with me owning a cleaning company. I think she was going to get her wish.

I spent seven days calling one-hundred companies. No one would sell. That was seven days without income. I needed to get a job. I had the choice of working for a cleaning company, or a sales company. The odds of me finding another disaster restoration company that'd pay me fifty percent were slim. Competition in Columbus was stiffer than it had been in Denver. Sales was my better option.

I spent the next week Monday through Friday, going to interviews for sales companies, and trying to decide who I wanted to work for. I couldn't find a match.

That Saturday I slept in. I had a late breakfast with my family. The phone rang, and I picked it up. It was Harley.

"Hi, Tim, this is Harley." There was no party in the background. I heard a muffler challenged vehicle driving by.

"Yeah, I recognize your voice. What's up?"

"My car is in the shop. I need to get to Newark. Would you give me a ride?"

It was odd getting this call. In my mind I had already cut off Harley, Dagger, the beast and telemarketing from my world. A call from Mars wouldn't have surprised me more.

Chapter 9

"HARLEY, YOU HAVE AT least a dozen people that could give you a ride. Why are you calling me?"

"I need somebody who won't spill the beans that I'm headed there." A passing siren interrupted Harley.

I weighed the pros and cons in my mind in the seconds the emergency vehicle was screaming by. I couldn't think of any. Harley had always been in my corner, defending me from Dagger. He sucked at it. But he tried. Harley had faith in me to give me that first office. That was worth a lot to me.

"Alright, Harley, I'm not doing anything else today, anyway. I'll come pick you up. Where're you at?"

"I'm at the Bob Evans on Main Street in Reynoldsburg."

"I'll be there shortly."

"I'll be waiting outside for you."

I hung up the phone. "Candy, I'm giving Harley a ride out to Newark."

"Why's he calling you? Didn't he fire you?"

"Harley didn't want to fire me, Dagger did. He says he wants me to drive him out there so nobody else figures out he's on the way. I don't know. I'll take him out. I know he did his best to protect me even though he didn't live up to his word."

"Okay, honey." Candy frowned.

"I'll be back later." I leaned in to kiss her, and she let me. I grabbed my keys and left. I found Harley on a wooden rocking chair outside the Bob Evans restaurant. He stood and waved at me and got in the car.

"Hey Tim, how are you doing?" he asked.

"I've been better."

"I'll buy you lunch for this, okay? Pull through Wendy's." Harley pointed at the entrance.

"Sure, Harley, thank you. Why do you need a ride to Newark?"

"Well, we put Brett in charge of the office. He's been drunk, sales are in the toilet, and he's threatening to burn the place down."

"Burn the place down, seriously?"

He looked at me, "Yep."

"He's the most negative man I've ever met. Well, no, I take that back. There's Dale Lewis and your brother. What possessed you to put Brett in charge?"

"It was Dagger's idea. Order me Dave's Triple Combo," Harley said. I had just pulled up to the Wendy's order board. I gave our orders, got the food, and headed out to Newark.

"So, Dagger's in charge, isn't he?" I asked.

"Yes. He promised I'd be in charge, and he'd be a silent owner. I suspect he lied to me, so I'd agree to come with him."

"And this is your little brother, right?"

"Yes."

"I don't understand the dynamics of your family. Do you mind if I ask you a personal question?" I exited I-270 onto Rt 16 toward Newark, Ohio.

"Sure, go-ahead Tim."

"How did your parents pick your names? I mean, Harley is pretty cool, you know, Harley motorcycle and all that. But Dagger?"

"Yeah, there's a story to that. My dad loves Harleys. I was the first born, and he named me after the bike."

"And Dagger?"

"Yeah, that's another story. Can't tell you about that one."

"Oh." I paused for a second. "Why are you and Dagger so different? You're kind and he seems, well, evil." I slowed at a yellow light that became red. I stopped. I reached into the Wendy's bag to grab two fries.

"He wasn't always like that." Harley sipped on his coke. "Something bad happened, and he changed. I like to believe he'll change back some day. I know there are good parts inside of him, he just doesn't let anyone see them."

"Said like a big brother," I said. The light turned green and I waited for the four cars in front of me to move. "I'm a big brother. I can understand your point of view. Then, another personal one, which I probably shouldn't even ask."

"Okay, what is it?"

"How do you, Dagger, and Murphy know a hitman?"

Harley was chewing a bite of his Dave's Triple Combo. He watched the blonde lady in the red Corvette next to us. After he finished, he said, "We best not go there, Tim."

"Okay, Harley."

I held my Dave's Single, with enough unwrapped to bite it, in my right hand and gripped the steering wheel with my left. The drive to Newark was country, or mostly. There were houses and businesses along the way with stretches of soybean and corn. Barns stood like mile markers and silos like watchmen. A few painted barns told me to chew Mail Pouch Tobacco.

Harley, having finished his meal, sat quietly, staring out the window, sipping his Coke from the plastic straw.

We arrived in Newark. Harley directed me to the office and I pulled up behind it. A man stood in the stairwell that led to the basement office. We got out of the car and I followed Harley to the stairwell.

"How's it going, Steve?" Harley asked the man.

"Glad you guys are here. Brett's hysterical." Steve said. He pointed at the office with his thumb and rested his other arm on the cinderblock wall. Harley walked inside.

As I came near the office, I felt it had a broken soul. It lived, but not well. I could sense a strained desire for success hampered with negativity. A soul had been born to that office, but it hadn't been allowed to thrive.

I stopped to shake Steve's hand. "Hi, I'm Tim."

"Are you the new manager here?"

"No, Harley asked me for a ride. They fired me a couple weeks ago."

"Why'd they fire you?"

"Dagger said I had to do $15,000 per week. I only had $13,000 in my fourth week."

"Oh, you're the guy from Whitehall?"

"Yeah, I was."

"They put that new guy in charge, Tony. He's a real ass. He hasn't broken $4,000 since you left."

"Really? Dagger said he'd show me how to run a room. Which made little sense since he banned me from his business."

Steve rolled his eyeballs and went back to his smoke while leaning on the cinder blocks. We were at eye level to the parking lot, where we could see underneath the cars. The sun glistened off the chrome and windshields. Crickets were calling, announcing a hot day.

I liked Steve right away. He had a sympathetic spirit about him, although he tried to appear cynical. He was a big man; I'd guess 500 pounds and six feet tall.

"Hey, why is there a bomb on your gas tank?" Steve asked, as calm as if noticing a penny in the driveway.

I looked. "What are you talking about?"

He pointed. "Look at the gas tank. There's a tiny box with an antenna coming off it."

"Oh, my God." I squinted and saw it. I walked to the car and lay on the gravel for a closer look. It was something foreign. The gravel stung my hands as I pushed myself back to my knees. I stood and stepped back as if the car may explode any minute. I brushed the sand from my hands and knees.

"Oh, my God, Steve, I think you're right." Steve didn't move. He kept smoking and watching the bomb. I walked into the office to grab Harley. He was talking to Brett, who was melting down.

"You guys gave me the worst area there is. Nobody will buy anything out here. And you know I make sales." Brett said. His eyes were rolling from intoxication.

"Yes Brett, you were always good for $1,200 a week," Harley said.

"Not out here. This area is crap. Nobody out here wants to buy anything." Brett tipped back on his chair and fell onto the floor. Harley tried to catch him but missed. Brett hit his head on the tile, and he went limp.

"Hey, Harley, sorry to interrupt. There's a bomb on my gas tank."

"What?" Harley's eyes widened. "Damn, I got Brett and a bomb to deal with." Harley looked at Brett, then went outside. He stood next to Steve.

"Yeah, Steve saw it. I crawled under the car. It sure looks like one." Steve pointed it out. Harley squinted.

"I think we should call the cops," I said.

"We may need an ambulance," Harley said. "For Brett." I followed Harley back into the office and Brett was sitting up again, whining about how Dagger cheated him into that shitty office.

"Brett, are you okay?" Harley asked. Brett got on his hands and knees to stand. We could see blood matted in his hair. "I guess he'll be okay if we keep him awake."

I called 911 for the bomb. Within ten minutes, seven police cars pulled into our parking lot and in front of the building.

"Who found the bomb?" One officer asked. Steve and I pointed at the car. I was in the stairwell next to Steve, prepared to dive at any second.

"It's on the gas tank, sir," I said.

Two of them looked underneath the car. One officer pinched the microphone on his shoulder. "We need to clear a six-hundred-foot area. Call the Dayton bomb squad." He turned to us. "You need to move across the street." He walked inside the office and told everyone to exit and cross the street.

Chapter 10

BRETT STUMBLED OUT. TWO of the salespeople were steadying him, holding his arms. "I told you, this place is terrible. They're trying to bomb us," Brett said.

"Ok, Brett," Harley said. The two salespeople helped him across the street and positioned him next to a light pole. Brett held onto it.

"I told you, I told you. This place is a shit hole." Brett still couldn't focus his eyes. They rolled this way and that as two lost marbles.

As we stood, watching the bomb show, I met the other salespeople. There was Crystal, Steve's wife. There was Barry, Julie, and Butch.

"So, how are sales out here?" I asked them.

"Brett's right, nobody wants to buy out here. It's a terrible place to make sales," Barry said. He pulled a pack of Marlboro's from his front pocket.

One of the police officers came toward us. As he walked across the street, Brett, hanging on that pole, reflected in his aviator sunglasses. He stopped in front of us. "Whose car is this?"

"It's mine," I said.

"Why would anybody put a bomb in your car?"

"I don't know. I love everybody and everybody loves me." I smiled. His face was stoic and eyes hidden by the shades. He didn't see the humor.

"The Dayton bomb squad is en route. It'll take them an hour and a half to arrive. We've got a six-hundred-foot area blocked off. Stay here, I may have questions." The officer turned and strode back toward the group of police cruisers.

A white van with a gigantic telescoping satellite antenna on top pulled up in front of us. The side panel announced that Channel 6 News had the latest and most accurate news. A man jumped out from the driver's seat, dressed in khakis and a tan jacket covered with pockets. A female reporter exited from the passenger side. She was dressed for business, hair perfect, and was holding a wireless microphone.

The officer walked over to them. The lady asked him something, to which, the officer shook his head. Another khaki-clad man pushed out the back van doors with a shoulder camera. He walked in front of the officer and the lady pointed the microphone at the officer's mouth. The officer shook his head again and walked back to the bomb scene.

A thought came to my mind. It made my stomach roll and blood drain from my head. What if this was a hit? I remembered the hushed call Dagger made, then announcing he had put a contract out on Murphy. Maybe I was one of the intended targets, as Murphy promised.

"Harley," I asked, "do you think Murphy put that bomb there?"

Harley took a drag on his cigarette, then let the smoke escape his nostrils. He said nothing.

"And, Harley, if he did, how did he find my car? He doesn't know where I live, does he?"

Harley bent his head toward his left shoulder. His neck cracked. He still said nothing. We stood quiet for five minutes.

"Harley, what'll you do with this office?" I asked. He cleared his throat and looked at me.

"We're going to shut it down. It's a poor area, we can't make sales here."

"Oh, come on, Harley, you know that's not true. How long is your lease for?"

"We've got four more months."

"How about you let me take it over for four months? In the worst-case scenario, I can make $3,000 a week alone. How much has it been doing?"

"Brett hasn't brought in more than $1,000 for us in a week. That's with four salespeople."

"Harley, you know Brett. That man is negative. He should've been able to sell $1,200 per week working alone."

I looked at Brett. He had slid down to sit on the grass, leaning against the light pole. He was mumbling. "I told you. I told you. This place is shit. They're going to bomb us to hell."

Harley sucked his cigarette, looked at Brett, then gazed at the clouds. "You could be right, Tim."

"What'll it hurt? You already have to pay for the office for four months. I'll see what I can do with it, okay?" I waited in silence for a minute, looking at Harley for an answer.

"Okay, Tim. I'm game."

"Thanks, Harley. What'll Dagger say about you hiring me again?"

"I'm sure he'll have plenty to say."

"Harley, what about Murphy? Is he going to kill me?"

Harley looked at me. He shook his head. "This will never happen again."

"How do you know that?"

"Trust me on this one, Tim." Harley threw his cig butt on the ground and stepped on it.

Trust him? Like, I trusted him to keep Dagger away from me? I thought. Maybe I should have got out then. Walked away from

Dagger and his cruel dictatorship. Something inside was gnawing at me, telling me I wasn't finished with this telemarketing company yet. Mostly, my instincts had taken care of me in the past. I trusted them again. I wasn't sure if this was my instincts or Sheena prompting me.

We waited around for an hour and the bomb squad from Dayton showed up. We, plus a growing crowd of people, and the news cameras watched as the technicians in bomb suits examined the object under my car. They transferred it to a metal box and sealed the lid. Then, they took it to the field next to our office and exploded the box.

The evening news had it on television that night and I recorded it on VHS.

On Monday, I went out to open the Newark office. I had Candy drop me off since I still only had the one car.

"Tim, it takes thirty minutes to drive here. Do I have to get you tonight?" Candy asked. She frowned as I leaned into the driver's side window to kiss her goodbye.

"Well, what do you expect?" I stood away and frowned back at her.

"It's a long drive." She expelled air to show her disapproval.

"Fine," I lifted my hands above my head, "I'll just sleep in the office, come back and get me on Saturday night."

"Okay, Tim." She backed away and left without hesitation. I didn't expect that response. I was being sarcastic. Shit, now what would I do?

I opened the office at eight AM, made some coffee, cleaned up the mess Brett left, and waited for the salespeople to arrive. The first was Barry.

"Barry, we're closing this office. This is poor sales territory. You'll need to find another job," I said.

"What, are you sure?" He asked.

"Yes, I'm sure. How were your weekly sales?

"The best I did was $300."

"So, you earned sixty dollars, which isn't worth your time. I'm sorry, you'll have to find another job."

"Okay," he said. He walked out with his hands in his pockets. I could see I disappointed him. Next, Julie and Butch came in. I explained the situation and they left, also disappointed.

Last to appear were Crystal and Steve. I gave them the same story.

"If you're shutting it down, why are you out here?" Steve asked.

I looked at Steve. "Alright, Steve, I know Brett's negative attitude infected everybody who was working here. I can sell $3,000 by myself. I'll hire more salespeople, but ones that weren't poisoned by Brett."

"We're not poisoned. We knew Brett was a negative man."

"What were you doing, before here?"

"I was a delivery driver. Crystal was a salesperson."

I looked at Crystal. "What's the best week of sales you've had?"

"Probably $300," she said.

"I'm going to expect at least $1,500 per week from any salesperson." Steve took a long drag on his cigarette and looked at Crystal. Crystal sat down and covered her eyes. Tears fell from her hands.

"I'm sorry, Crystal, I didn't mean to make you cry."

"I really need this job. I'd love to do $1,500 in sales. If you show me how to make it, I promise I'll work on it."

I took a deep breath and looked at Steve. He raised his eyebrows as he held onto his cigarette.

"Crystal, you were making sixty dollars commission for a week. That's not much to lose. You can make more at McDonald's."

"I don't want to work at McDonald's. I want to be a salesperson, that's why I'm here," Crystal said. "If you'll show me how to sell 1,500 per week, I promise you, I'll do it."

Chapter 11

I LOOKED AGAIN AT Steve. He folded his arms, spread his legs, and looked up at the ceiling.

"Well, Crystal, I'll tell you what. It's just you and me in here. I think we can keep the room positive."

"I promise you; I'll be positive."

"I really do like you and Steve. You seem like talented people," I said. I pulled out a chart from my briefcase. "I'm going to show you a system I've been using for years. If you follow it, I guarantee you'll get at least $1,500 per week in sales, okay?"

"Yes, I promise. I promise. I'll do it." Crystal's eyes lit up and she sat forward with her shoulders back, looking right at me. I looked at Steve. He crossed his arms and had a big smile on his face.

"So, Steve, do you still want to be our driver?"

"Of course."

"I'll be writing at least 2,500 a week. Crystal will write 1,500. That's over twenty deliveries a day. Can you handle that?" I asked. Steve inhaled a slow drag from his cigarette, let the smoke puff into the air, and stared at me. "I'll take that as a yes," I said. Steve smiled and nodded.

"Crystal, this is my strategy. When we call people, we're not speculating about sales, we're connecting with them and making them feel good about what we're doing. We count our presentations, not our sales."

"I don't understand. Why don't we count sales?" Crystal looked at me with one eyebrow up. The morning sun was peeking through the front window, creating an angelic glow on Crystal's face. Dusty spider webs covered the outside of the glass, which sat right at ground level.

"Because, if you count presentations, you no longer worry about getting sales. Get it?"

"I get it," she said. She looked up and wrinkled her nose and pressed her lips with her index finger.

She doesn't get it; I thought.

"For me, I make a sale for every four presentations. Since you've had less practice, we're going to assume that you need ten presentations to make a sale, okay?"

"Okay. What's a presentation?"

"A presentation is when you read the entire script and your prospect tells you either yes or no."

"So, if they don't buy, it counts?" Crystal frowned.

"Yes, that's correct. Can you do that?"

"That seems easy to me."

"Let's get started, Crystal. Here's your numbers and here's a chart to keep track of your presentations." I handed the papers to her. "Make a call. I want you to read this script."

She put on her glasses and read it. "This script isn't what Brett gave us." She sat the paper down on the table and shook her head.

"This one will work, I promise you."

Crystal looked at me, then picked up the phone. After five calls, somebody answered. She read the entire script, and the prospect turned her down.

"Thank you," Crystal said. She hung up the phone. "I didn't get a sale." Crystal stuck out her lower lip.

"It doesn't matter, Crystal. Add a hash mark for one presentation. Here's a tip. You need to sound optimistic when you call, even if you're not. Okay?"

"Okay, Tim." Crystal made another call and presentation. She was cheerier but didn't get the sale.

"That person still said no." Crystal's eyebrows tipped inward. She was worried.

"It's okay, Crystal, you've got seven more rejections and then you'll have a sale. Okay?"

"Okay," Crystal said. She made four more calls and then got a sale. She wrote out the ticket and jumped to hand it to Steve. She squealed and gave him a hug, then hugged me. Steve picked up a light bulb box and walked out. Crystal pinched his butt as he lumbered up the stairs and squealed again. She danced back to me like a first day schoolgirl.

"Now, Crystal, we're talking about averages. My guess is that your average is one sale for every ten presentations. That means you'll need fourteen more presentations to get another sale, okay? I could be wrong. Maybe your ratio is better, but we won't know that until you've made lots of calls."

Light filled Crystal's eyes and she sat in her chair with her shoulders straight and smiled at me. "Yes, I get it."

Now, I thought, *she gets it.*

As Crystal made calls, I coached her how to use inflection and how to listen. Twenty minutes later, Steve showed up with a check for the first ticket he delivered.

"Thanks Steve! See Crystal? You got this."

"Eeee!" Crystal waved her hands, jumped up, and hugged Steve.

"Crystal, I'm going to teach you a powerful sales technique that a dear friend of mine taught me." I wanted to tell her that Sheena was my teacher. I worried that explaining about Sheena would cause a deluge of help requests like in Denver. I kept her a secret.

"When you're talking to people, I want you to concentrate on them. Forget everything around you. Listen to your prospect. Sometimes you'll notice something in the background. Perhaps it's a mom taking care of kids. You can make a comment about kids. Or maybe they sound like they're not paying attention. If so, just stop talking. Most of the time, they'll ask if you're still there. Then, you say, 'yes, I'm here, I'm sorry,' and then continue. But don't wait too long; sometimes they'll just hang up."

"And then, this part is crucial. Listening will help you imagine that you're there with them. Imagine you're in the room speaking with them. Imagine you're becoming their friend and that they like you. What you're doing is connecting with them spiritually, which I know sounds like mumbo-jumbo, but it's one reason I've always been a top salesperson."

"Okay, Tim. I believe you," Crystal said. She smiled. By the end of the day, Crystal had sold $200, and I had $400. When nine PM came, I checked Crystal and Steve out, paid them, and they left. I turned to look at the room. Where was I going to sleep? I didn't even have a blanket. Then someone knocked on the door. It was Steve.

"Tim, Crystal and I would like to take you to Tee Jay's for dinner," Steve said.

"You know, that'd be nice. I'm not going home tonight so I have nothing else to do."

I got in their car and Steve drove us to the restaurant. His side of the car rode lower than the passenger's side. We arrived and found a table. Steve couldn't fit in a booth.

"You two did a great job today. I'm very proud of you."

Steve looked sideways at me and nodded. Crystal giggled, "Thank you. I'm overjoyed that you're teaching me how to sell." She patted Steve's thick hand. I could tell they loved each other. I tried not to think about it, but I wondered how the hell skinny

Crystal and 500-pound Steve got along in bed. I brushed the thought away with a mental broom.

"How long will you be our manager?" Steve asked.

"I don't know. Probably until Dale or Dagger gets in a tizzy and fires me."

"Who's Dale?"

"A troll. An evil troll. He's jealous of me and wants me gone. Actually, I think he wants me dead."

"I heard Dagger fired you for being an incompetent manager in Whitehall, but the salespeople know the difference. Word is out that they made more money when you were running it. Tony is a total ass. No one wants to work for him," Steve said.

"Well, that's good to know. A bit of revenge for me," I laughed.

"Yeah, I have a couple of friends working there. Tony hasn't broken $4,000 in a week since you left."

"Crap. We'll do more than that on four phones. I'm sure Dagger will torment and scare me no matter how many sales we make." I picked up the menu.

"I've had bosses on a power trip. I don't allow them to do that to me." Steve sipped his coffee and put his arm around Crystal.

"I get the impression you don't take shit from anyone," I said.

"Nope! But I can see you're competent and fair. We'll enjoy working for you."

"Thank you, Steve."

"You said you're not going home tonight," Crystal said. She reached over for the sugar and poured enough in her coffee to turn it into syrup.

"No, I only have one car and I let my wife keep it. She doesn't want to drive out twice a day. I'll sleep in the office this week and buy a car next weekend after I get paid."

"Well, that sucks. Come stay with us," Steve said.

"I hate to be an imposition."

"Fiddle farts. You won't be an imposition."

"Maybe later this week, I'll see how camping out goes."

"Okay, my friend. You're making things hard on yourself." Steve folded his hands and rested them on his belly. The chair groaned as Steven leaned back.

"I appreciate your offer, Steve, I really do."

Chapter 12

S TEVE AND CRYSTAL DROVE me back to the office after
we finished eating. As I approached the door, I felt its soul.
It had more life than that day I drove Harley to replace Brett.
Like Elvis, the negativity had left the building. Crystal, Steve,
and I had provided nourishment for it. It was growing in love,
hope, and faith.

I entered and lay down on the hard floor. Sleeping wouldn't be
easy. The tile was cold against my head. I grabbed a coffee can
for a pillow. I lay on the floor and put my neck over it. That
wouldn't work. I got back up again. Maybe the table wouldn't
hurt my back. I crawled up and stretched out. My legs hung over
the end, which stressed my lower back. I put my feet up on the
table, which was also uncomfortable. I slid off the table and
looked out the window. There was a restaurant across the street.
It was closed right now. I was thinking that the next day, I'd
have lunch there.

Then, I got an idea. I took off my shoes and put my head on
the toes of them. It worked better than the coffee can. I rolled
back-and-forth trying to keep my body from getting too cold on
the tile. But I couldn't sleep. I got back up again.

If I had a car, I could sleep in it. Well, if I had a car, I could
drive home and sleep in my bed, even better. Although, my bed
had been cold too. I stood and looked out the window and

pondered that Candy hadn't made love to me since we got into the townhouse two days after arriving in Columbus. On our vacation trip from Denver, she became loving, and I thought our marriage was on the way to being fixed.

Our marriage. It almost wasn't. If she hadn't tricked me into getting her pregnant, I'd never have taken her back after she ran home to mother. But there was no way I'd abandon my children. And then, we had a second one, without my vote. I wanted my children to have a solid home. I didn't want their parents to be divorced. I'd do whatever I could to keep our marriage working, and hopefully, loving. Then when they grew up, if our marriage still wasn't fixed, I'd leave Candy.

At that moment, the memory of catching Candy cheating cut into my consciousness. It still hurt. I didn't think the hurt would ever go away. And trust. I lost trust with her. I wondered, sometimes, what she did when I was at work, but I couldn't worry about that, or I'd go insane. That cheating was another event that would have broken us up. I'd have walked out instantly. I didn't deserve to be treated like that, but we had children. The children needed a stable home.

Being alone in that office at night brought up too many bad memories. I needed to keep my mind busy. But I also needed to get some sleep. I went to my desk, sat down in my chair, folded my arms and rested my head on them.

The phone rang at eight AM. I woke up and answered.

"New Day Marketing," I said.

"Is this Timmy?" I recognized Dagger's sharp voice.

"Yes, sir."

"Do you know why I'm calling?" He asked.

"I have no idea, sir."

"Harley put you in charge without consulting me. Yesterday, you turned in a lousy six-hundred dollars. Why are you wasting my phones and office?" His voice thundered. I expected lightning to come through the phone line.

"We'll do more. This was my first day out here," I said.

"You always have excuses. I need five thousand from you this week or your ass is grass, do you understand?"

"Yes sir." With that, he hung up. It set me in a panicked state. My breathing rate increased. I could feel my heart pumping. I made some coffee and closed my eyes. At nine, Crystal and Steve arrived.

"You're looking like shit, my friend," Steve said. He closed the door behind Crystal. Steve treated Crystal like a lady. I liked that.

"He's looking sweet," Crystal said. She smiled at me.

"Sweet or shit, same thing," Steve said. He folded his arms. I looked at Steve's feet. He had untied tennis shoes. Either they wouldn't close all the way, or he couldn't reach them.

"Thanks guys. I had a drive-by call from Dagger this morning. I'm calming down. I don't know how he expects salespeople to get motivated by demeaning and yelling at them."

"Don't put up with his shit," Steve said.

"He scares me," I said.

"You can't let scary people rule your life." He sucked on his cigarette and stared at me. Steve tried to look scary. It didn't work. His eyes showed a kind heart.

"I've heard that before. Thanks. Let's get to work. I brewed coffee for you."

After our morning shift, Crystal and Steve left and I walked to the restaurant across the street. They built it in the 60s, but it was still warm and inviting. It had an old greasy aroma, but it appeared to be clean. Mostly. I sat down in the booth. Oh, my gosh, I could've laid in that booth and taken a nap.

The server came over. "What can I get for you, hon?" Her hair was pulled into a ponytail by a pink scarf. She had six homemade bracelets on her right hand. Ceramic beads and charms on a macrame cord. Her left wrist had a lone copper bracelet. She had a brown plastic name tag pinned to her blouse.

There was masking tape over the previous owner's name. Bridget was inked on the tape.

"I'd like a BLT sandwich and some fries, please, and some water."

"Okay, dear, I'll bring it out for you soon." She walked away, her bracelets jingling. I looked out the window. It was a splendid view of the cars driving by on the Main Street intersection. Where were they going? Didn't they have jobs? I watched a utility truck drive by with six aluminum ladders attached to the top. He was followed by a Ford F-150 truck filled with new cut lumber. They must be together.

Watching the traffic was hypnotic. I nodded off and was awakened when Bridget returned to my table.

"Here you go, darling," she set the plate in front of me.

"Thank you, that looks delicious." I rubbed my eyes and yawned.

"Holler if you need me." She gave me a concerned look, then walked away.

I nibbled my lunch slowly and relaxed for an hour. Then, I paid my bill and walked to the office. I could hear the phone ringing before I opened the door.

I picked up the phone, "Hello, this is New Day Marketing."

"Do you know how many times this phone rang?" I recognized Dagger's voice.

"No, I just walked into the office."

"Where were you? Why weren't you answering the phone? Do you realize how many times the phone rang before you picked it up?" The gravel in his voice sounded like coal mining scrapers on a service road.

"I don't know how many times the phone rang. I was having lunch at the cafe across the street."

"I'm confining you to that office. What if a job applicant arrived?" I could hear telemarketers in the background. Some poor souls had likely been demotivated with a Dagger attack.

"I could see the office. If someone came in, I'd wave them over to the restaurant."

"What if the job applicant called the office?"

"We don't have an ad in the paper, sir. Do you want me to stay here for twelve hours? I can't even take a break?"

"It doesn't matter. This is your last week, anyway. There's no way in hell you're making $5000 this week." Dagger hung up. At five o'clock, Crystal and Steve returned.

"Hey Steve, could you pick up something for me at RadioShack?"

"Sure, what do you need?"

"I need a wireless phone that will reach across the street."

"What'll you do with that?"

"I'm going to have lunch. Alright guys let's get to work."

Our first week, with only Crystal and I, we turned in $3,500 in sales. Steve delivered them superbly. On Saturday, Harley arrived to close me out.

"Good job, Tim," Harley said. He put rubber bands around the closeout papers and placed them in his briefcase on the floor between his feet. Harley wore his standard Hawaiian shirt, this one in blue. He had sandals, no socks. He sat on the edge of his chair with his legs spread.

"It wasn't just me; Steve and Crystal were great." I nodded at Steve, then Crystal.

"But we made more money with you than we did with Brett," Crystal said.

"Also, Tim didn't get drunk on the job." Steve added.

I sighed. "It doesn't matter. Dagger said my ass was grass if I didn't pull in 5,000 this week. I guess that means you'll be closing the office."

"Hell no," Harley said. "I'll take care of Dagger."

You haven't so far, I thought.

"Okay, Harley, I'll plan on opening up on Monday." Steve nodded at Crystal. Her face exploded into an enormous smile.

Candy had showed up for the closeout. She and Colin waited in the office with me while we finished counting. Harley paid me $353.

"You earned more in Whitehall," Candy said. She stretched her neck to look at the money Harley handed me.

"Honey, I made $460 from my personal sales. I couldn't do that in Whitehall. So combined, that's almost eight hundred. Pretty good, considering I didn't lose any of the money." I raised one eyebrow and looked at Candy. She frowned and looked away.

"Okay, everyone, I'll see you next week. Good luck to you," Harley said. I picked up Colin, locked the door, and went to our car. Steve and Crystal said goodbye as they walked to their car.

"That Crystal is pretty hot, don't you think?" Candy asked. She looked over her shoulder at Crystal walking away in her tight jeans and halter top.

"What? I don't think about that. No one is as beautiful as you, honey." Candy didn't look convinced. We drove home in silence. It still pissed me off. I had to sleep on the tile floor all week. Candy didn't seem to care. But I'm sure if I'd stayed with Steve and Crystal, Candy would have wigged out now that she's seen her. Candy's right, Crystal was hot.

Chapter 13

T HE NEXT DAY, SUNDAY, I found a used Volkswagen Rabbit, for $400 in an expensive neighborhood. Their son used it for college and now they wanted to get rid of it. Buying used cars from rich people was an excellent strategy.

I paid for the car, gave three hundred to Candy, which left almost nothing for the next week. I knew, however, that I would make more money. A lot more. I gave the Phoenix to Candy, as it was the better car. I worried about her breaking down while pregnant and with our tiny child.

The most Brett's regime had done in a week was $1,000. Yet, Dagger promised to fire me if I did less than $5,000. I waited for Monday morning to see what would happen.

On Monday, Barry showed up. He dipped his head below the top of the doorway. With his hands on his hips, he frowned and surveyed the room.

"Hey, I thought you guys closed this office?"

"Hi Barry. I thought it best to start with a brand-new crew."

"Then why is Crystal here?"

"It was just me and Crystal. I can convert one negative person at a time. No more. Last week, she wrote $1,200 in sales by following my coaching. I did $2,300."

"Twelve hundred? That's fantastic. Would you give me a chance?"

"Barry, I expect at least $1,500 per week out of every salesperson. I'm sure Crystal is going to hit that this week. If you follow my system, I'll let you have a chance. But I need you to understand this is not a poor territory. Brett infected all of you with a negative attitude."

"I'm sure I can do it, just show me what you do," Barry said.

"Sure, welcome to the team." I walked over to shake his hand, looking up at his face.

"Barry, here's the numbers, and here's how we do it." I explained my system. Barry focused on me and my instructions and then got on the phone. Barry had experience; I could tell. He had mastered his vocal inflection.

I waited for Dagger to call or show up to fire me. He never did on Monday. Or Tuesday. By Wednesday, I assumed I still had my job.

At the end of that week, Barry had written $2,000 in sales. He was a natural. Crystal did her $1,500 and was jumping so much I thought she'd blast off to the moon. I did my $2,500. So, the office in total turned in $6,000 in sales. Steve delivered all the sales by himself, always within thirty minutes. He'd even help resell on very rare occasions a client was having second thoughts. I was forming the perfect crew.

The next week, Julie appeared. "I saw cars here. I thought you closed this office."

"Yes, Julie, I lied to you. Everybody was so negative after Brett, I knew there was no point in trying to convince you otherwise."

"Then why are Barry and Crystal here?"

"I gave Crystal a chance. She brought in $1,500 last week. Then I gave Barry a chance and he wrote $2,000 last week. I couldn't bring back an infected crew simultaneously. I can only cure one attitude at a time. Do you want a shot at this?"

"Yes," Julie said. I went through the same process with her, and Julie wrote $1,500 her first week with us. That week, we brought in $7,500.

That week, I set aside $500 toward my cleaning business after taxes, personal bills, and giving Candy $300. Maybe, I could save $50,000 before Dagger fired me.

I drove my Rabbit out to Newark the next Monday morning to open the office. I started the coffee, which filled the room with its aroma, then organized the numbers for my crew for the week. The phone rang.

"New Day Marketing, this is Tim," I answered. The coffee was brewing, dripping into the pot. Within ten minutes, my crew would arrive to start the day. The coffee had a good aroma to energize them.

"How is it you keep snagging all the best territory?" I recognized Dale's congested, raggedy voice.

"Are you referring to the Newark territory?"

"Yes. You keep convincing Harley to give you the good stuff. It's not fair."

"What are you talking about? Brett convinced everybody this place was rotten. Dagger was going to close it."

"I knew Newark could make sales," Dale said.

"Well, why didn't you take it, then?"

"Because I'm stuck in the Dayton office. It's not fair that Harley's giving you favorable treatment. I keep getting stuck in these dumps. Dayton sucks." Dale cleared his throat. I imagined his face turning red, emphasizing that bald, white dome of his.

"Dale, I'm busy, I'm hanging up now, bye." I hung up. The phone rang immediately and I picked it up. Before I could say anything, Dale blasted me.

"Don't ever hang up the phone on me, you insolent little twerp. You won't keep taking advantage of me. You're going to get yours. You'll disappear." Then he hung up.

I felt a presence in the room. My heart stopped, and I turned my head slowly to look behind me. The room was empty, but something brushed the hairs on my arm. It made my stomach turn and my skin sweat. I stood and walked to the corner to escape it, but it followed me. It invaded my breath, making me gasp for air. I closed my eyes, breathed slowly in and slowly out, and slipped to the floor, leaning against the wall. "Sheena, ghosts, God, please help me. Push this evil away from me," I asked.

I remember Sheena telling me that there would be hard lessons for me to learn in Ohio. This must be one of them. But what was I supposed to learn? How does being attacked by evil people teach me anything?

The door opened and Steve and Crystal entered. Steve looked at me.

"What are you doing in the corner on the floor?" Steve asked.

"Drive-by calling." I put my hand on my heart and inhaled a raspy sound. Steve walked over and held out his hand. I took it and he helped me stand.

"Thank you, Steve," I said. I felt the evil presence melt away.

Despite the rough start, we had a good morning of sales and when lunch break came; I took my portable phone across the street in case Dagger called. Except for Dagger and Steve, nobody ever called. Well, there was the troll.

I was biting into my BLT when the phone rang. I answered, "New Day Marketing, this is Tim."

"Honey?" I heard Candy's voice, much frailer than normal.

"What is it, Candy?"

"The Phoenix broke down. A lady stopped and gave us a ride. I'm at the Bob Evans in Reynoldsburg." I could hear Candy was upset.

"Are you hurt? Is everybody okay?"

"Yes, Colin and I are fine. Steam spurted from the hood, so I drove faster to get home. Then the engine stopped."

Many times, I explained to Candy that steam means pull over immediately. She must have forgotten. I didn't remind her. It would only make her feel worse.

"Okay, honey, I'll be there. It'll take me about thirty minutes."
I put ten dollars on the table, walked across the street and got
into my Rabbit. It took half an hour to reach the Bob Evans
restaurant. She was at a booth inside.

"Hi Candy, hi Colin, are you guys, okay?" I asked.

"Yes, we're okay. We've been staying cool here and having
lunch," Candy said. The server lifted a tray of steaming steaks
above my head as she walked past. I moved out of her way and
sat in the booth.

"That's good. Ride with me to the office and then I'll let you
take the rabbit home."

"Do I have to come pick you up tonight?"

"No, I won't make you do that. I'll sleep in the office again
and buy another car this weekend."

"What'll you do with the Phoenix?"

"I'll have it towed to a mechanic."

"Okay," Candy said. She looked out the window. The server
delivering the steaks whizzed by our booth toward the kitchen.

"Daddy, draw a picture for me," Colin asked. I took the paper
and drew a tree with the crayons. After they finished eating,
Candy rode with me to Newark. I kissed her and Colin and let
her take the Rabbit. I'd been away for three hours. Hopefully,
Dagger hadn't called while I was helping Candy.

Chapter 14

THE CREW CAME IN at five o'clock. Steve walked through the door, sucking on a cigarette, letting the smoke out slowly, gathering against the low ceiling. "Where's your car?" He asked.

"Candy blew the heads. I picked her up and gave her my car."

"Does that mean you'll be sleeping in the office this week again?" Steve asked.

"I guess so."

"Well, that's just ridiculous. Come stay with Crystal and me." Steve looked sideways at me and crossed his arms.

"I think I'll accept your offer this time. Sleeping in this office stinks big time. I'll buy you guys' dinner at Tee Jay's after work for your kindness."

"I never turn down a free meal," Steve said. He walked back outside. Everybody started making calls. The phone room felt alive with a pure, productive energy. We transferred that energy to our prospects, which yielded many sales.

After work I went to dinner with Crystal and Steve at Tee Jay's, and they gave me a ride back to their house. It was small, but cozy, filled with blanket-covered chairs and couches. The kitchen sink was piled with rinsed dishes. The counters were wiped clean, and a folded towel hung from the cupboard door.

"Crystal and I sleep in separate bedrooms because I snore. You can share her bed tonight if you like," Steve said

"Oh, I don't think that's a good idea. My wife would have a cat fit."

"Well, why does she have to know?"

"I always assume she'll find out, it's easier to live my life that way. That woman has supernatural senses."

"Well, you can sleep on the couch then," Crystal said. "I'll bring blankets and a pillow. But my bed is a lot more comfortable. And we could cuddle." She smiled at me.

"No, really, that's too complicated. I wouldn't want Steve to get jealous."

"We don't get jealous," Crystal said, "we're swingers." Crystal opened a closet in her bedroom and grabbed a handful of blankets.

I looked at Steve. He raised his eyebrows.

"Oy vey," I said. "I respect that, but I'll stay on the couch, okay? Thank you very much for your hospitality." I thought about what would happen if Candy knew I was staying overnight at a swinger's house. She had told me *it was just sex* when I caught her fucking that man in Denver. But I bet she wouldn't see it that way if I cheated. I decided that was the last night I'd sleep over. Crystal and Steve were polite and kind to me. In the morning, we returned to the office.

"Hey, Crystal, I'll sleep in the office tonight. I'm sure if my wife finds out I'm staying at your house, she'll freak out. But I'd love to borrow a blanket and pillow."

"I understand. And yes. We also have a rolled-up foam mattress. You can borrow that," Crystal said.

"That would be fantastic. Dinner will be on me again tonight," I said.

For the next six weeks, we broke records. One week, we hit $8,000 in sales. Fortunately, I hadn't heard from Dagger, but

Dale still harassed me. When he did, I hung up the phone. That morning, I got a call, it was Dagger.

"Timmy," he said.

"Yes, sir. It's Tim." I held the phone out from my ear, expecting the rage of his wrath to blow, but it didn't happen.

"I'm calling to give you kudos. Your office is beating the other ten offices. Our top office this week made $7,000 and they have fifteen phones."

"Well, thank you sir, I appreciate that." I wondered what the hell he was up to. Why would he admit to me that sales were low in other offices?

"Anyway, good job Timmy," Dagger said.

"Thank you, sir," I said. Dagger hung up. I bet Dagger was goading the other managers that the tiny Newark office was beating them. I'm sure he teased Dale, which would throw gasoline on Dale's glowing embers of hate and jealousy for me.

It was time to switch the calling area. Since I started managing Newark, we'd been using clean, unmarked paper sheets of phone numbers, but we were running out of territory. We could only call prospects once every six months. I started the rotation in August when I first came to Newark. Brett had already called through the Buckeye Lake territory. I wondered if I should call them early. I gave Harley a call.

"Hey, Harley, this is Tim. I'm glad I caught you at home."

"Hi Tim, how are you?"

"Doing good. Your brother even called and congratulated me. That was a shock."

"Will wonders ever cease?" Harley said. I laughed.

"We're near the end of finishing our territories until January. What do we do now?"

"We'll have to shut down the office until January." I could hear glasses clinking. Harley must have been having a party.

"That's going to hurt my people. They depend on this income. There must be something we can do."

"Not that I can think of. If you get an idea, let me know and call me back," Harley said.

"May we call the unfinished Buckeye Lake numbers? That's the area Brett managed. We could call those who hadn't answered the phone."

"Yeah, that seems okay, do that."

"Thanks, Harley."

I slid the side drawer open from my gun metal gray desk and lifted the Buckeye Lake numbers. There were less than ten sales on them, but over 500 rejections. I could see why Bret was threatening to burn down the office. But this was the only work left.

I prepared a pot of gourmet coffee to cheer up my workers. The blank basement walls did little to inspire my crew. Aroma treats and contests would perk them up. After they sat; I handed out the strips of numbers. Crystal picked it up and peered at it with her mouth hanging open.

"We can't call these," Barry said. He squinted his eyes. He leaned back in his chair and stretched his long legs across the tile floor.

"Why not?" I asked.

"This is the worst area ever. We couldn't make any sales there." Barry laid the paper on the desk and folded his arms.

"Yeah," Steve said, "when they got the rare sale, half the time nobody answered the door." Steve shook his head and lifted his eyes at the ceiling as if reliving the pain of failed deliveries.

"Come on, guys, we've been kicking butt out here. Before I arrived, you thought Newark and Heath were terrible. We proved that wrong. We'll make lots of sales in Buckeye Lake," I said. Julie pushed back from the desk. Crystal folded her arms.

"Okay, everybody, let's get to work," I said. Everyone groaned and leaned forward. They picked up the telephone and started calling. After I made seven presentations, I made a sale.

"See, guys? You can make sales here." I raised my ticket to show them.

"They won't answer the door when Steve tries to deliver," Barry said.

"Barry, I'm sure that you sounded depressed to the customers back then. That's probably why they didn't answer the door. They weren't excited about the purchase. You know my magic technique now. Come on, let's make sales."

After seven more presentations, I produced another sale. The rest of the team had zilch. Six o'clock rolled around and their eyes were hollow, as if they were rotting inside. Crystal propped her head with her elbow on the desk. Julie cradled the phone on her shoulder and shielded her eyes with her hands. Barry stretched his legs as far as he could without sliding off the chair. He hung his head back like a ragdoll. I knew they believed they couldn't sell and therefore, they were not.

"Okay, everybody off the phone," I said. Everybody hung up their phones and looked at me. "Do you remember how I taught you to imagine yourself in the living room talking with your prospects?"

"Yes," Crystal said.

"Well, are you doing that?" I asked. No one responded. Barry looked at his shoes. "I promise this is an excellent area. The only reason you're not making sales is because you are associating these number sheets with a negative experience. I'm sorry we had to use the same marked papers. I bet if I had given you new ones, you'd make your usual sales." Julie covered her eyes with her hands, as if the light were painful. Crystal slumped down in her chair. "Will you concentrate on your prospects? Imagine you're there talking with them?" I asked.

"I'll try," Julie said.

"Me too, I'll try," Crystal said.

"You can do this. Remember everything you've learned. Let's get back to work."

They continued to work, but the room resonated like a funeral. My salespeople were mourning their dead abilities. A body in a casket would have improved the mood. It couldn't be worse. Eight o'clock rolled around and my crew had no sales.

Chapter 15

"OKAY, EVERYBODY, HANG UP the phone again, please," I said. The crew laid their phones down and slumped onto the desks.

"You guys, normally you fill this room with positive energy, but tonight it's like you're auditioning for a zombie movie. Come on guys, you can do it. Just get your mind right."

They nodded and picked up the phones, but by 8:20, nothing had happened. I knew tonight would poison my crew permanently. I couldn't let that cancer spread. It was time to cure it.

"Alright, everybody, hang up the phone," I said. Crystal gasped as if escaping a torture chamber. Gary and Julie put their receivers in the cradles. "Here's what we'll do. I must prove to you it's not the territory. Yes, I'll agree it's not as responsive as our other territories, but it's not as bad as you are imagining it to be. If I can't convince you of this tonight, it will destroy all the training I have given you. I'm going to prove to you I'm right. Decide and choose who has the very worst strip of numbers."

For the first time that night, their eyes lit up. They came together as a team to choose the worst numbers. After deliberating like spunky chipmunks, they handed me a sheet.

"This one is the worst," Barry said. "Not one single sale on it. Those people are mean."

"Yes, that's right," Julie said. Crystal nodded.

"Thank you." I took the dreaded number sheet. "Now we have forty minutes until nine, when we have to stop calling, and we have barely more than an hour before Steve must quit delivering. So, here's the plan: I'll sell and repeat the information out loud. Crystal, you'll write them on tickets. As soon as I get four sales, Steve, you'll leave to deliver, then call back in. By then, Barry will dispatch more tickets to you. I must spend every minute selling. Here we go."

I closed my eyes and whispered, "Sheena, help me connect and concentrate." I knew how powerful that technique was. I picked up the phone and called the first number. A lady answered. I talked with her and she agreed to buy it. I repeated the information. Crystal filled out the ticket. I hung up and made the next call. The next three people purchased. Steve took those four tickets and left. Every three minutes, I got a sale. No one rejected me. I needed to prove a point and I needed to prove it in such a way that my crew couldn't deny the evidence. By the time nine o'clock came, I had made twenty sales, $1,200 worth of business in less than an hour. I hung up the phone at nine o'clock and sat in my chair.

"They won't deliver," Barry said. He smirked as if he'd be overjoyed to verify the area stinks.

"Barry, they will. They feel wonderful about their purchase," I said. "I want you all to wait for Steve to return." We waited until 9:40 when Steve walked in the door. His big smile stretched his face like a rubber band.

"So, how'd it go, Steve?" I asked. Steve threw the stack of tickets with checks and cash onto the table. Barry sat straight up, drawing his feet under his chair. Julie's and Crystal's mouths hung open.

"Every single one of them delivered," Steve said. "Every stinking one." Steve stepped back and leaned against the wall and crossed his arms as if he had just beat Superman.

"Everybody, listen. In the future, no more excuses about bad numbers. Is that understood?" I asked.

"Yes," everybody said. Steve took a long draw on his cigarette and grinned. Gary shook his head, still staring at the pile of tickets and money. After we chatted for ten minutes, we closed the office and went home.

I estimated that we had two weeks' worth of numbers before we would run out. The next morning, I woke up with an idea and called Harley.

"Hey, Harley, this is Tim."

"Yes, Tim."

"What if you gave us three of the phones in Whitehall?"

"I don't think Tony would be happy about that."

"Well, we can use the back room. Stay out of his sight."

"He won't give up any of his territory."

"He's lost so many salespeople, he can't call them all. He has empty phones. Ask him to give us their worst area."

"Alright, I'll talk to him and see what he says."

"Thank you, Harley." I hung up and drove out to Newark to open the office. After the morning crew finished, I walked across the street with my portable phone to have lunch. Thirty minutes later, the phone rang.

"New Day Marketing," I answered,

"Hey, Tim, where are you?" It was Harley.

"I'm in the Newark office."

"No, you're not. Where are you?"

"I'm across the street in the café. Come on over," I said.

I watched Harley walk across the street from the office. He stopped as a blue Chevrolet crossed. He dodged the next car and came in with a big grin on his face.

"Your brother said I'm confined to the office because somebody might call. I can answer the phone here." I handed my menu to Harley.

"I talked to Tony," Harley said. "He's not happy about giving you three phones, but I told him he had little choice unless he could pull off $15,000 this week." Harley smiled at the server as she came over to our table.

"Hello darling, would you like to order?" She asked him.

"Just coffee, please." Harley handed the menu to her, connecting with her gaze.

I waited for Harley to finish flirting and then asked, "How much has Tony been doing? When your brother called last week, he said I did $1,000 more than the top office and I did eight grand last week."

"He's lucky if he breaks $5,000." Harley shook his head.

"I did 13,000 and your brother canned me. Why's he letting Tony stay?"

"Tony's from New Jersey."

"Oh," I said. I looked out the window and wondered what New Jersey did for job security. "We'll finish Buckeye Lake in two weeks. I'll break the news. What territory did Tony decide to give us?"

"Pataskala. The entire crew believes that it's the territory from Hell."

"Really? Did Brett complain about it?"

"I'm sure Brett started it, but everybody agreed, including Tony. He thought it was hilarious you'd have to work in that area. He said it'll put you in your place."

"Well, I have faith that my crew will shine." Harley and I relaxed and talked for thirty minutes.

"Well, I gotta get going. Keep up the good work," Harley said.

"I will. Don't tell your brother that I'm sitting in the café."

Harley waved back at me as he left. Five o'clock came around and my crew came in.

"Alright, everybody. I've got a special treat for us. I had told you we'd be out of work until January. However, I've made a deal for us to work in the Whitehall office. We're going to dial the Pataskala area."

"Pataskala?" Crystal asked. "Is that a good territory?" I gave Crystal a stern look.

"Oh, right," Crystal said, "of course it is."

"That's right Crystal, you got it." I gave her a thumbs up. "We'll kick ass and we're selling holiday wreaths along with the lightbulbs so we can make double sales to everybody, maybe even triple."

"That sounds great to me," Steve said. "I love dropping off multiple boxes at a stop."

"We're only getting three phones." I paused and looked at everyone. "But we'll rotate so all four of us can work. It'll be fun and you'll get lots of breaks. And we'll still kick butt."

"We believe you, Tim," Barry said. That was a lot coming from Barry; he was Mr. Cynical USA in the 1985 pageant.

"Thanks, Barry," I said.

"Wow, high praise from Barry," Crystal said. She patted Barry on the back. Barry leaned away. The others laughed.

Chapter 16

TWO WEEKS PASSED, AND we met for our first Monday in Whitehall. Harley moved my inventory to our back room. No door protected the boxes, however, and I worried about keeping track of it. Tony didn't come across as one-hundred percent trustworthy. Tony had twelve phones up front, we had three in back.

Our fifteen feet by fifteen-foot room was next to the bathroom and the rear door exit. Anyone from Tony's crew that needed use of the facilities would traipse through our space. I posted a map for dispatching, plus charts for bonuses and goals on the blank wall. I brought our gourmet coffee and Mr. Coffee machine, which tempted Tony's crew with the aroma. Tony's crew had a ten-gallon pot with day-old burned coffee to pour from the spout.

I filled a white cardboard box with snacks for my crew that emptied faster than usual, as Tony's crew would snag them as they walked back from the bathroom. Occasionally, they'd beg for a cup of our gourmet coffee. It was ok with me as I expected it to build goodwill.

"Alright, everybody," I stood in front of my crew. "We beat every office in the company on four phones. We can crush them with three, right?"

"Yes," my crew said. Crystal high fived Julie and gestured to Barry, who lifted his hand halfway to meet hers.

"Alright, let's get started." I handed out strips of numbers for Pataskala. Pataskala was in the country and twenty minutes from our office. Steve couldn't return to the office as often as he did in Newark, so we crammed his car full of boxes. He drove out to the small town to prepare for our sales.

The routine I came up with was a twenty-minute break per person per hour. My theory was correct, our sales did not decrease, they increased.

Our average sale in Newark had been forty dollars. The company's average sale was twenty-five, but now we had Christmas Wreaths for thirty-eight bucks we could add to every light bulb sale. Our average sale went to seventy-five dollars because of the double and triple sales with Christmas wreaths. I kept track of the numbers religiously, as I always did. We were closing fifty percent of everyone we called, and these weren't previous customers. This was cold calling. The highest ratio I personally obtained for cold calls had been one sale for every three presentations. The average for other salespeople was one in ten. All four of us were now closing one in two.

After the time I had trained my crew in Newark, they were now a fine-tuned Ferrari. Our first day we did two-thousand dollars in sales. Tony did eight hundred.

We had enough sales to empty Steve's inventory mid-day. To aid him, I loaded my car with inventory and met him in Pataskala to maximize his delivery time. While I was delivering to Steve, my crew stayed on the phones without breaks.

The next morning, I heard Harley and Tony in the back alley. Tony was loud and not a happy camper. I moved closer to the door where I could see Harley and Tony holding their cigarettes.

"Those sales come from my office," Tony said. Tony stood with his black overcoat flitting at his feet. His fedora tipped forward as he stared at Harley. He flicked a spent cigarette onto the gravel and reached in his side coat pocket and slipped out a pack of smokes.

"That's the Newark office. You have nothing to do with it," Harley said.

"Those should be mine. I should get paid for it." Tony raised his voice higher. He lit his cigarette and waved it at Harley.

"Half your twelve phones are empty. He's kicking your ass with three. You don't deserve to get the manager's commission on that," Harley said.

"You'll give me my commission, or I'll take it. Your choice," Tony said. He lifted the cigarette to his mouth and glared at Harley. Harley flicked his cigarette onto the ground and walked toward the door. I stepped into the bathroom to hide.

On Saturday night, Harley came to close me out. We pulled off $11,575 for the week in sales. My cut was right at $1,800 including commissions on my personal sales. I needed this for Christmas and to fix the Phoenix. Three weeks of that and I'd be flush, plus, I could add to my carpet cleaning company fund.

"Okay, Tim, it's time to count the inventory," Harley said. Harley moved and counted it.

"Tim, you're $1,200 short of inventory."

"What? That's inconceivable. You know my inventory always comes out perfect."

"I don't know what to say. I counted it twice."

Tony was at his desk toward the front. He had a cigarette dangling from his lip. He had a smirk as he looked at me, leaning on his desk. I knew where the inventory went.

"Harley, Tony had to have taken that inventory," I said. That was nearly ten percent of my sales, a manager's fee.

"It was your driver," Tony said. He crossed his legs and arms. His blue wool pinstripe suit blended with his dark polished shoes. He pushed his fedora to the side.

"My driver's honest and works for his money. He doesn't steal. Harley, this isn't fair. I'm guessing Tony did $1,200 less in sales than usual, right?"

"It's hard to say with Christmas wreaths and such. There's nothing I can do." Harley left. Tony laughed as Harley passed, partly at me and partly to goad Harley.

I paid my crew their commissions. I was planning on giving them each a bonus, but I couldn't afford it after that loss.

"Hey guys, we'll come back next week and kick butt again, right?

"Right," Barry said with a reserved response.

"Right," Crystal said. She gave me a pitiful smile. I could see they felt sorry for me, but I didn't want that to affect our team.

"Have a great weekend, have fun. I'll see you on Monday," I said.

Everybody left through the front door. Tony locked up. I paused in the parking lot to enjoy a breeze kissing my face. Steve's car came to life with a pop and squeak. He turned the headlights on and, as he drove by, he and Crystal honked and waved. I waved back. The parking lot was dark and I waited there wondering what the hell I was going to do.

As I stood in the quiet night alone, my hairs prickled on the back of my neck. I felt a heavy presence, but when I slowly turned full circle, I could see nothing. There was a dim light from the Brass Rail next door, but it barely lit the pavement. Either I needed to head to the Brass Rail, or I needed to get into my car. I opted for my car. I fished for my keys in my pocket as I walked and dropped them. I leaned over to pick them up and I saw two feet standing by my car door.

"Hey, Timmy," I heard. I stood, clutched my chest, and held my breath. It was Dale. He stood there, motionless, covered with a dark hoodie sweatshirt. His arms dangled beside him and one of his tiny hands was doing its best to hold on to a brick. He took a step forward and stumbled slightly, catching himself. I smelt alcohol. The brick must have come from the flowerbed outside the Brass Rail.

"Why do you hang up every time I call you?" Dale asked.

"Because I don't want to talk to you, Dale. I don't want to talk to you now, either. Shouldn't you be in Dayton?" Dale stumbled forward to me and put his finger three inches from my nose.

"I know you're cheating the rest of us. How is it you're getting so many sales off three phones? You're beating my Dayton office and I have ten."

"Guess I'm just that good, Dale."

"No, you're not, you're cheating somehow. I'm going to destroy you. Dagger hates you. As soon as Harley's gone, you'll have nobody to watch your back." Dale pushed his finger into my cheek. I stepped back.

"What do you mean, 'when Harley's gone?' Are you going to hurt him?" I asked. I slipped my keys between my fingers to form a brass knuckle.

"He'll not be around here long. I'm going to see to it. I'm supposed to have his territory."

"Dale, it seems you're supposed to have everybody's territory. Why don't you make sales with what you have?"

Dale stood quiet and I could feel a dark cloud of vaporized evil swarming around me. I shuddered and took a deep breath. This man was smaller than me, but he terrified me. I turned to walk away.

"Don't walk away from me, you son of-a-bitch. Get back here!"

I kept walking until he followed me. I then ran back in a half circle toward my car and tried to put the key in the lock. My hand shook, and the key wiggled outside the keyhole. Dale started stumbling toward me and the key finally opened the door. I got into my car and backed out of my parking space. As I drove past Dale, he threw the brick at my driver's side window. The glass sprayed over my body, but I kept driving.

When I got home, Colin was helping Candy decorate our Christmas tree. Music was playing. Candy stretched Christmas lights and extension cords over the table in a queue to go onto the tree.

"It looks so beautiful, honey. I love the smell of pine in the air."

"Did you make a lot of money so we can get presents?"

Chapter 17

"I MADE EIGHTEEN-HUNDRED BUT Tony stole twelve-hundred of it. I'll make it up next week and the next."

"How'd he steal it from you?" Candy walked behind the tree as she threaded a string of lights.

"He moved inventory from my pile to his."

"What if he steals it next week?"

"I've got a plan to fix that." *Just as I had a plan to stop your stealing,* I thought. I went into the kitchen and opened the fridge. Candy had eggnog in there. "Candy, thanks for getting eggnog."

"There's rum for yours. Would you pour one for me?"

"Candy, I'd love to." I put a shot of rum in my drink and poured a virgin eggnog for Candy. I walked to the living room and sat to watch Colin toss tinsel at the tree with his pitching arm. Candy picked them up and hung them on the branches.

"Are you enjoying Christmas?" I asked Candy.

"Yes," she said. Colin pulled a handful of tinsel and threw it in the general direction of the tree.

"Candy, I think it'd go easier without him, but it's really nice you're letting him help."

"He's having fun. And the baby's kicking. I think she's having fun too."

"She?" I asked.

"Yes, she feels like a girl."

"How do you know?"

"It just does, women's intuition." I wouldn't doubt her intuition; she had proven to me she was reading my mind or had x-ray vision to find my money. I stood and placed my hand on her baby bump.

"Can you feel her?" Candy asked.

"Yes, that's so cool. What do you want to name her?"

"I always liked the name Sapphire."

"That's a good name. Reminds me of a little girl that used to ride the church bus when I was working in Cheyenne. Her name was Sapphire. She was six years old. She had blonde hair and was small as a pixie. Every time she got on the bus she'd say, 'I'm going to marry you someday.'"

"Oh, that's so cute," Candy said.

"I know. I always told her that by the time she grew up, she'd change her mind. I remember when I was six years old, I was in love with my first-grade teacher. I wanted to marry her when I grew up."

"How'd that work out?" Candy laughed.

"Well, she wasn't in our church, so they wouldn't have allowed me to, anyway."

"It's time to put the angel on top of the tree. Do you want to do it, Tim?" Candy picked it out of the box and its tissue bed.

"Colin, do you want to put the angel on the tree?" I asked.

"Yes," Colin said. He jumped with his arms stretched.

"Okay, hand the angel to Colin." I picked him up. Candy handed him the angel, and I lifted him to the top of the tree. He slipped it over the top branch.

"Good job, Colin," we said. I sat him on the floor and he bounced around the tree. Candy and I watched him and smiled. A child's energy at Christmas was precious.

"I'm going to play Christmas music," Candy said. "Will you turn down the lights and light the tree?" I switched on the tree and dimmed the lights. Candy sat with me on the couch. Bing

Crosby was singing "White Christmas" and Colin jumped onto my lap. I gave him a hug and he put his head against my chest. I raised my glass and toasted Candy.

"My eggnog is virgin, right?" She asked.

"Yes, Candy." I took her hand, and she squeezed mine as "Silver Bells" played on the stereo.

Monday morning at eight o'clock, I called Harley.

"Harley, this is Tim."

"Hey Tim, what's up?"

"I want you to inventory my stock every night."

"Why's that?"

"Do you even need to ask? Would you do that for me? I'll keep making you guys money if you'll protect mine."

"Sure, I'll do that for you," Harley said.

When my crew came in, I explained the plan to do nightly inventories. They agreed that it was a good idea. From their expressions on Saturday's closeout, I could tell it upset them that Tony stole from me. I wanted their mind on sales, not my troubles.

I had Christmas cookies, candy, and chocolate on plates for my crew. Candy had prepared snack trays of vegetables, meats, and dip. I kept the gourmet coffee brewing. I wanted my crew in a holiday mood. In a sales mood.

Berta walked back from the bathroom and snatched a cookie. I looked at her over the top of my glasses. She was part of Tony's crew now. Not mine.

"Berta, would you like gourmet coffee?" I asked.

"Sure," Berta said. I grabbed a foam cup and poured one for her.

"It's not fair you guys got our best territory," Berta said. She took the cup and poured cream into it.

"Berta, I offered to take the very worst town you had. Harley said the entire crew agreed Pataskala was terrible."

"You did?" Crystal asked. Her voice tipped up, showing concern. I looked at her with my eyes half closed. "Oh, right," she said.

Berta sipped her coffee, then looked at Crystal. "I never said it was bad. Everyone else did."

"Berta, it doesn't matter which town you gave us. We'd kick ass," I said. Crystal smiled. Berta walked back up front.

That week, people were in the holiday spirit and wanted Christmas wreaths. We even suggested they buy light bulbs as gifts for their family and friends. Our average sale went up to one-hundred dollars. We closed out with $12,000 in sales for that week. No inventory came up missing. The following week was better, and it was time for Christmas break.

"Hey, you guys, do you want to take off between Christmas and New Year's? Or do you want me to open the Newark office?"

"A vacation would be wonderful, and we certainly can afford it, thanks to you, Tim." Steve said.

"How about you, Barry? Julie?" I asked.

"Yes, we're up for a break," they said.

"I'm happy to take a vacation. Candy is at her due date; we could have the baby any day now."

Crystal gave me a hug. "We're so happy for you!"

"Thank you. I'm glad you guys manage your money well. I have gifts. Candy picked them out. I suggested what you may like. And a gift to her was to let her shop for them. She loves shopping."

"Tim, we all went in on a gift for you," Steve said. He handed me a gold wrapped box.

"Thank you, everyone." I got tears in my eyes. I set the box near my stack of gifts. "Steve, this is your gift."

"Thanks buddy," Steve slapped my back.

"Oh, come on, Steve. Give me a hug," I said. Steve put his beefy arms around me and squeezed.

"Barry, this one's for you," I said. I handed him his gift.

"Oh, thanks." Barry grunted. "I prefer not to hug."

"That's ok, Barry. Julie, this one is yours."

"Tim, thank you," Julie gave me a hug. "And thank you for teaching me to sell."

"It was my pleasure, Julie," I said. Julie sat to open the gift. I turned to Crystal.

"Crystal, this one is yours." She hugged me and sobbed. "Don't cry, Crystal," I said.

"Thank you, Tim." Crystal said. She kissed my cheek.

"You're welcome, Crystal. All of you are a great crew. You did a great job this year. I appreciate your work."

"We appreciate you," Crystal said.

"Merry Christmas, everybody," I said. We patted backs and hugged again, except Barry. They helped me clean the room. I picked up my gift, we turned out the lights and went home.

I drove up to our townhouse and parked at our front door. It had a red door. The building was brick. A strip of window next to the door showed Candy had the lights low and the Christmas tree lit. I opened the door and walked in.

Candy waddled out from the kitchen to see me. "Merry Christmas, Candy. How are you feeling, honey?" I asked.

"I'm feeling like a Sherman tank."

"I'm surprised you even know what a Sherman tank is?"

"My dad talked about Sherman tanks and all kinds of stuff."

"Well, I wouldn't say you're a Sherman tank." I poked her baby bump gently and leaned in to give her a kiss.

"I'm so excited about this baby." Candy patted her belly.

"Me too. Hopefully, Colin will have a friend to play with."

"Hopefully Colin will calm down around her."

"Yeah, I kind of doubt that." We both laughed.

"I made an appointment for a sonogram next week at two o'clock on Wednesday. Can you come with me?"

"I can be there. The crew and I took a vacation until Jan 2nd."

"Oh, that's nice. I feel better having you near. I'm so close to my due date. I'm so big this time, I don't know why."

"You'll go back to normal, you still look beautiful, anyway."

"I wish I could believe you."

We never made it to Candy's sonogram appointment, because on Tuesday, December 27, 1987, our daughter was born. She came into this world quietly. Too quiet. I thought she was stillborn. The doctor said she was fine and patted her butt. Sapphire gave a little squeak. She entered the world with blonde, curly hair and a quiet, sweet personality.

Chapter 18

THE TREES WERE FROSTY as I drove east on 16 toward Newark. It was January 4th, 1987, Monday. The traffic crawled to a stop at a red light. I was twenty cars back in line, waiting for it to turn green. That part of 16 had open fields on either side with businesses sprinkled every half mile or so. The air was just below freezing, but the road was dry.

The light turned green and, like a heavy snake, the cars in front stretched until it was my turn to accelerate. Soon, the outskirts of Newark came into view. It was a peaceful town, mostly. The people were more country folk than Columbus, nearer to Sheridan, Wyoming. It made me feel at home. I exited 16 onto 79 and then took the first exit onto West Main Street. I waited at the light. When it turned green, I turned left.

My office was on the right. I parked behind the building. My car door squeaked from the cold as I pushed it open.

There was a musty smell as I opened the door to the Newark office. No one had breached it in six weeks. I set my briefcase next to the desk and flipped on the lights. The coffee pot was dusty, so I washed it, then put grounds into the filter and let it brew. My crew arrived at nine.

"Did y'all have a great Christmas break?" I asked.

"Very enjoyable," Julia said.

"It was ok," Barry said.

"You bet," Steve said. He slipped a silver cigarette case from his front shirt pocket and flipped it open. His thick fingers lifted a lone, slender smoke and he placed it between his lips.

"Nice case, Steve," I said. Steve closed it and showed me his name engraved into the metal.

"It's a Christmas gift from my beautiful wife," Steve said.

"Very nice, Steve." I took it in my hand to examine it.

"I wish you could've visited us on New Year's Day," Crystal said. "Steve cooked a turkey that was to die for."

"Oh, Crystal, I'm sure you wouldn't want your boss showing up on your holiday."

"We think of you as family. You'd have been welcome."

"Thank you, you're kind. It would have been nice to visit you, Crystal, but the new baby kept us busy."

"I'm so excited for you. Thanks for calling and sharing the news with us," Crystal said.

"I've got a cigar for you," Steve said. He handed me a Macanudo. "I know that's your favorite."

"Thanks, Steve, but the father hands out the cigars."

"Too bad," Steve said. "I don't like cigars." I laughed.

"Well, we have our first territory to call, and we have previous clients to call back. We call them taps. There's a unique script to use for taps. I'll show you how," I said.

"Yay," Julie said. She poured coffee and plopped three sugar cubes into the cup. Crystal and Gary sat, and I took out a bundle of taps.

"Everybody, here's the new script." I passed one to each salesperson. "As usual, you'll concentrate on your prospect and picture yourself in their living room talking to them. But the difference is, first you're going to thank them for their purchase six months ago. You must be sincere and they need to feel appreciated. Don't fake it, they can tell. You should hear feedback that shows they believe you. The last part of the script is a short reminder, of our offer. Are you with me so far?"

"Yes," Crystal said. She was looking at the script. The others nodded.

"Now," I continued, "you should close nine out of ten. Half of your sales should be double packs. Your income will triple over cold calling. You all just got a raise. I'm going to listen while you call and give you pointers until you get this down. I know you will."

We got to work and I listened and coached them. As I expected, they got the hang of it quickly. At once, everybody took their break. After the room emptied, I stretched out in my chair and closed my eyes.

"Timmy," a booming voice said. I sat up abruptly. Dagger and Harley walked through the door. I stood and stuck out my hand.

"Hello. What a surprise," I said.

"That's what I do. Keeps you on your toes," Dagger said. He picked up and examined a stack of taps.

"Yes, sir."

"We've come to talk to you," Harley said.

"Last time I saw you two together, you fired me. Is that what's happening?"

"Not firing, we want you to take back the Whitehall office." Harley sat at my desk and tapped his cigarette box on his hand.

"You fired me from Whitehall. Why would you want me back there?"

"You're doing better now, you've proven yourself," Dagger said. He leaned against the wall and crossed his arms. He had a navy-blue baseball cap pulled over his dark hair that stuck out like it was trying to escape.

"I'm doing better in Newark. I don't believe I could run Whitehall, it's too big for me."

"I'm sure you can make it work now," Harley said.

"Well, I love my Newark crew and the territory. I make more money than I did in Whitehall. I'm afraid I'm not good enough to run Whitehall. It overwhelmed me."

"You'll make more money in Whitehall on 15,000 in sales," Dagger said.

"Not much more, considering I'm one of the sales crew here. I can't be a salesman if I run Whitehall."

"You're taking Whitehall. If you don't take Whitehall then you're fired from Newark," Dagger stood forward and placed his hands on his hips.

"Are you serious?" I asked.

"You go where I tell you. This is my business." Dagger's jaw tightened.

"What happened to Tony? Wasn't he going to show me how to do it?"

"Look, ass wipe, don't get smart with me." Dagger pointed his finger at me.

"Sorry, sir." I sat to diffuse his anger.

"So, do you want Whitehall or nothing?" Dagger asked.

"If that's my only choice, I'll take Whitehall."

"Alright then. Who do you recommend replacing you out here?"

"I'd recommend Steve, he's the driver."

"Steve can't drive and remain in the office," Dagger said.

"He doesn't need to stay in the office. This crew is a well-oiled machine. Steve's very reliable. The office will always be open and making money."

"Can't happen. Drivers can't be a manager," Dagger said.

"You could make Crystal the manager. You'd have to ask her what she thinks about it."

Dagger looked at Harley. "Women can't handle it."

"Crystal could handle it. But if you're that concerned, let Steve and Crystal work together. The money goes in the same pot, anyway. Crystal could help with anything that needed managing while Steve was out delivering.

"So, you're saying to make Steve and Crystal co-managers?" Harley asked.

"Seems like a good idea to me. As long as they're happy with it."

"Okay, you do that, I want you in Whitehall tonight," Dagger said.

"Tonight? I need time to prepare the crew."

"Alright, tomorrow then," Harley said. "I'll run Whitehall tonight."

"Where did Tony go?" I asked.

"He's gone," Dagger said.

"Gone, where?"

"Where people that fail me go." Dagger glared at me.

Shit, I thought. *Did he kill him?* I decided not to press the issue.

Harley and Dagger left, and I walked across the street to get lunch. I guessed I'd give my portable phone to Crystal and Steve. I wondered what "gone" was. I shivered.

At five o'clock, the crew reported for work. I stood and faced them.

"Everybody, I have news." Everyone looked at me. "I'm being transferred to the Whitehall office. Steve, Crystal, would you like to be co-managers for this office?

Crystal looked at Steve. Steve looked at Crystal. He took a drag on his cigarette.

"That sounds perfect to me," Crystal said.

"Steve?" I asked

"Sounds good to me," Steve said.

"This office should continue to do well. You're all motivated and excellent salespeople. Steve will get your stuff delivered. Crystal will be helpful to you. Barry, Julie, what do you think?"

"As long as I keep making money, I'm okay," Barry said.

"Fine with me," Julie said

"Okay then. Steve, Crystal, you'll want to hire another person, maybe two. I'll help get an ad in the paper. I'll coach you on how to recruit and train. I think you know everything else."

We finished out the evening and I handed the keys over to Steve.

"Good luck buddy, good luck Crystal," I said. Crystal gave me a hug.

"I'm going to miss you so much. Thank you so much for teaching me to be a salesperson and promoting me to manager. Thank you so much," Crystal said. She stood back and wiped her eyes.

"You're very welcome. If you guys have any problems, call me, okay? I'm not your supervisor, but I'm willing to help you if I can. And Steve, I know you're not intimidated by Dagger, so maybe you should try to protect Crystal from him?"

"Not a problem," Steve said.

"I wish it wasn't a problem for me. Dagger scares the shit out of me."

"Don't let scary people control your life," Steve said.

"Yes, yes. You've given me that excellent advice before. I wish I could accept it."

"Oh, Tim," Crystal said. She stood and took my hand. "My birthday party is this month, on the sixteenth. Would you and Candy come?" Her enormous eyes waited for my answer.

"I'm sure we'd love to, Crystal. I'll see if we can find a babysitter. I'm not sure Candy will want to leave the baby yet."

"We'd love you to be there. It's a costume party." Crystal winked.

"Yeah, wait till you see her costume," Steve said. He wiggled his eyebrows. I felt my face redden.

"Oh, well. Okay, I'll see if Candy wants to come. I don't want to come without her, you understand?"

"Yes, of course we do," Crystal said. We stood around and chatted for twenty minutes and then I left. As I sat in my car and looked at the door of the office, I could feel the office now had a thriving, happy, and beautiful soul. I smiled, then drove out of the parking lot and headed toward home.

Chapter 19

"HONEY, I'M HOME," I said as I walked into the townhouse. Colin ran to me and grabbed my pants.

"Hi Daddy," Colin said. I picked him up.

"How are you, Colin?"

"Look at my truck," Colin pointed at his toy on the floor. I set him down so he could bring it to me.

"That's really cool, Colin. Can you show me what it does?" He set it on the floor and pushed it around, making car noises.

"Guess what, honey? I'm coming back to Whitehall," I said.

"Really? Is that a good thing?"

"There's no difference in my income, but I'll be closer to you guys and see you in the afternoons again."

"Well, that's nice," Candy turned and walked back into the kitchen. "Do you want some dinner?"

"That'd be nice."

"I made macaroni and cheese. I was in the mood for it and Colin always loves it." Candy brought a Pyrex serving dish and set it on the table.

"Darling, that sounds good." I sat and Colin jumped onto my lap with his truck.

"See daddy? This is a good truck." Colin said.

"Yes, that is a cool truck."

"Vroom," Colin swished the toy into the air.

"Candy, Steve and Crystal invited us to her birthday party on the seventeenth. I told them I didn't know if we could go. You know, Sapphire being so young, and us not having a babysitter."

"Oh," Candy said. She pulled out her chair and sat. "Which ones were Steve and Crystal?"

"Steve is my driver. The big man. You've met them. Crystal is his wife."

"Oh, the hot one," Candy said. She wrinkled her nose.

"They are both nice people. I don't care how they look."

"Well, it would be nice to attend a party. We haven't done that since we left Columbus."

"What about a babysitter? And do you feel okay leaving Sapphire so early?"

"Arlene would babysit, and I trust her with Sapphire."

"Arlene? The lady you visit down the alley?"

"Yes. Colin and her boy get along great. We've become good friends. I trust her."

"So, should I accept the invitation?"

"Yes. Go ahead. Tomorrow, I'll ask Arlene to babysit."

"Crystal says it is a costume party."

"What kind of costumes?" Candy sat her fork on the plate and looked at me. I didn't know the answer. And Steve's comment about Crystal's costume worried me. If it made her look sexier, I'm sure Candy wouldn't be happy.

"Candy, I don't know. I'll find out. Probably just anything. Maybe we could go as a pair."

"I could sew something for us."

"Okay, honey," I said. We enjoyed our dinner and evening together. It had been a long week. I was ready to relax. Poor Candy, she needed rest, too. The baby and Colin ran her ragged.

Monday morning, Harley met me at the Whitehall office. The parking lot had a thin fresh coat of oil which made the painted white lines pop against the black. Not thick enough to cover the cracks or pocks. Hmph. Cheap landlord.

Harley was inching out of a red Stingray Corvette. He stood and patted the top and smiled.

"Nice Vette, Harley. What year is it?"

"It's 1980. I got it yesterday." Harley walked around the car, admiring its lines. I looked inside at the leather seats.

"Can I sit in it, Harley?" I felt the smooth handle and opened the door, hardly waiting for an answer.

"Sure, Tim. Go ahead." Harley and I chatted about the fine craftsmanship and listened to the motor. After ten minutes, it was time to open the office. Harley handed me the key, and then followed me inside.

The soul of the office had been damaged since I was evicted from it. It was still strong and alive but hurt. I took a long slow breath as I entered and felt its sadness. I was there. I'd help the soul of Whitehall heal and thrive again.

"Hey Tim, we're going to need a manager for our Cincinnati office. Keep an eye out for somebody with potential," Harley said.

"Sure. I'll keep an eye out."

"I'll stop by later this afternoon with payroll."

"Thanks, Harley."

Harley wandered out the door, circled his Corvette once, mounted the cockpit, and roared away.

By nine AM, Don, Kwame, Vernon, Cheryl, Kenny, and Gabriel had arrived. They all high-fived me and said they were happy I was back.

"Hey, where are Gary and Johnny?" I asked.

"Tony fired Gary," Kwame said.

"What why?"

"Because he snapped back at his nasty remarks to the crew. Tony didn't like that. He said it was disrespectful."

"What the hell? What about Johnny?"

"He's probably on a bender. He hasn't been here in a week," Don said.

"Didn't Tony cut him off after he made 400 bucks for the week?"

"No, Tony, let him make as much as he wants," Kwame said.

"I explained to Tony not to let Johnny earn more than $400. When he does, he goes on a bender. Last time, he was gone for three weeks."

"I don't think Tony cared too much about that," Vernon said.

"I'll call and get them back." I opened the drawer of applications. Tony had covered them with banana peels and cigarette butts. I pulled out the papers and shook the trash off. I dug through them and found Johnny and Gary's and called the phone numbers. Both played a disconnected message.

"Hey, you guys, their phones aren't working. When you see them, tell them I want them back."

"If we see them on the bus line, we'll tell them," Gabriel said.

"Thanks guys. Did Tony recruit any new people?"

"No, he didn't recruit anybody. He sat behind his desk, smoking and making sarcastic remarks." Don said.

The phone rang and I answered, "New Day Marketing."

"I'm calling about your cash paid daily ad. Do you guys take taxes out?" The man asked.

"No, but you sign a receipt daily. We'll give you a 1099 at the end of the year. I can tell you how much to save for taxes."

"Last week, the guy said we didn't have to pay taxes."

"Everyone has to pay taxes. That was Tony. He's gone."

"What's your address?"

"3872 East Main St. in Whitehall. We'll be here till nine."

"My name is Jack, I'm coming in."

"Okay, Jack see you." I hung up the phone. By the time the evening shift came around, we still had seven phones open. Before Dagger fired me, the phones were crowded.

"Hey, everybody, tell your friends to come back to work."

"You betcha, Tim," Vernon said. He pumped his fist. I spent the evening encouraging the eight faithful salespeople and dispatching. The room exploded with energy and sales.

The next morning, the brakes on the bus squeaked as it came to a stop in front of our office. Pressured air pushed the doors open and three of my missing people came off the bus. Their clothes were filthy and their hair unkempt, as they were when I first met them. They had cleaned up over the time they worked with me. They must have become homeless again.

"Hey, guys," I said.

"Tim, we're glad you're back. That Tony was a jackass," Jaime said.

"Yeah, I've heard."

"Are there sandwiches?" Jaime asked.

"Always, in the fridge."

"Tony didn't have any. He told us if we wanted to eat to make more money."

"Well, my opinion is, that if you're hungry, it's hard to make sales. Help yourself," I said.

They headed toward the coffee machine and fridge. Jaime inhaled a sandwich in three bites, then grabbed a second. The phone rang again.

"New Day Marketing," I answered.

"Why are you in the Whitehall office?" I heard Dale's voice crackle. I held my breath for five seconds.

"Hello?" Dale demanded.

I exhaled. "Dagger and Harley put me here."

"You shouldn't be running the flagship office. Wasn't that already proven? I should run that office, not you."

"Goodbye Dale." I hung up the phone and sat. Blood rushed through my ears, and I felt faint. I closed my eyes to relax, but a heavy presence filled my chest. I had pondered how Dale could conjure this dark energy. I wondered if he did it purposely or if it followed his actions of its own accord. *Dear God, Sheena, ghosts, please help me,* I thought. I hoped they could understand the unspoken words. After five minutes, the air felt clear. I went back to my work.

I walked over, waiting for Kwame to hang up the phone. Kwame had a positive attitude. Nothing seemed to deter him from sales. I admired him for that. He finished his call and looked at me.

"Kwame, follow me to the back." We walked near the alley exit so no one else could hear.

"Am I in trouble?" Kwame asked. He squinted; his eyebrows pushed together.

"No, no, Kwame. Harley needs a new manager at the Cincinnati office. I think you've got the temperament to do that. What do you think? Would you want to move there?"

"I'd be up for that. How much is the manager's pay?"

"It's ten percent of the sales."

"Can I make sales myself?"

"No, it's a twelve-phone office. It must be five or less for you to do sales also. You'll commit your time to recruiting, training, dispatching, and motivating. I'll teach you how."

"What do I do now?" Kwame straightened his shoulders.

"I'll talk to Harley. He told me to find somebody and if he's good with it, I'll start training you."

"Thanks, Tim. I appreciate it." Kwame shook my hand.

"You've always been trustworthy. Everyone likes you, and you can sell. I think you'll do just fine." I walked up to my desk and called Harley. He answered.

"Hey, Harley, this is Tim. I got something for you."

"Oh, what's up?"

"I got a solid person who's interested in Cincinnati. I'm thinking I could start a manager training program here. Did you know Tony didn't recruit anyone?"

"Yeah, we saw that."

"I recruit more salespeople than I need. I could focus on training the best ones to be a manager. How many rooms are you guys going to open?"

"We need to replace six of our ten managers, then we'll expand to other states. We'll open enough offices to keep up with you."

"Geez, I can do that for you."

"What do you want in exchange?" Harley asked.

"All I want you to do is keep your promise. You said that if I helped you guys get your system going, I could be the owner of a state."

"We'll stick to that."

"When you guys fired me, I figured you were breaking your promise."

"That was out of my control."

"Yeah, I worry about that. When would you want Kwame in Cincinnati?"

"We could have used him yesterday."

"If you want my stamp of approval on a trainee, I need two weeks with him."

"Alright, get on it then."

"Harley, maybe one more thing."

"What's that?"

Chapter 20

"CAN YOU GET DALE off my ass? That guy has got it out for me. I haven't done shit to him."

"Dale's a bitter little man. I'll talk to him."

"Thanks. I'm going to work on an outline for the training program. I'll talk to you later." I hung up the phone and gave a thumbs up to Kwame. He was talking to a prospect on the phone. After he finished, he strolled over to me.

"So, what's the story?" Kwame asked.

"I'll give you training for two weeks and then you can go to Cincinnati."

"Great, when do we start?"

"This afternoon," I said. The phone rang again.

"New Day Marketing," I answered.

"I'm calling about your ad in the paper. I called last week, and the guy said that you weren't hiring. Why's the ad in the paper?"

"We got rid of that guy. We're hiring, come on in."

"I'm on the way," he said. As I hung up the phone, a lady with dark red hair and black roots walked in the door.

"Hello," I said. "Come on in. What can I do for you?"

"I'm here to make sales. I'm Sammie."

"Oh, nice to meet you, Sammie. Have you done telemarketing before?"

"Oh yeah," she drew the words out slowly. "I'm Dagger's mother-in-law. I've worked in his other rooms."

"Oh, okay, I didn't know he was married. But you're welcome to work here."

"Well, they're not married, but they live together."

"Yeah, I think I met her in Colorado. She came in with Dagger once and I thought it was his daughter. Harley told me later she was his girlfriend, and for God's sake, don't ask if she's his daughter."

Sammie rolled her eyes. "Where do you want me to sit?" She looked around the room.

"Pick any place that's open. Coffee is in the back."

"Yeah, I know the routine," she said. I watched as she shuffled back to the coffee. I wondered if Dagger had sent her to spy on me. Not that it mattered. I wasn't doing anything wrong. After she sat her coffee next to her phone, she walked over to me to get numbers. She drew on her cigarette and the smoke wrapped around her leathery face.

"Sammie, here's your numbers. Do you know how to mark them?"

"Yeah, I do."

"Alright, blank tickets and your script are on the table. Do you want me to go over it with you?"

"No, I'll read it a few times, don't worry." She shuffled back to her area and sat. She reclined in her chair, looked at the ceiling, and shook her head. I think she was having a conversation with herself. She took a long drag on her cigarette, leaned forward and started reading the script. After five minutes, she laid it on the table and picked up the phone. As she waited for the person to answer, she held the phone between her shoulder and ear and took another draw on her cigarette.

Someone answered the phone, and she quickly sat up. After three minutes, she hung up the phone and brought me a ticket.

"I got one," she said.

"Good job, Sammie."

"I'm taking a break now."

"That's fine, but somebody may grab your phone while you're on break."

"I don't care."

Sammie went outside, leaned against the glass, and lit another cigarette. Don grabbed his crutches and swung out the door to stand next to Sammie. Larry saw Don talking to Sammie and he shuffled out to join the conversation.

Kermit arrived in his '79 Bonneville. He waved his arms as he sauntered toward Sammie, Don, and Larry. Kermit would take a step and his body would follow shortly thereafter. His perfectly combed, parted, and feathered hair fluttered in the breeze. His designer jeans were tight and his silky shirt billowed. I walked outside to see what all the hubbub was. Kermit was talking about his car.

"Kermit, your Bonneville looks great. Did you just get it painted?" I asked.

"Sure did, buddy. Great job, don't you think?" He snapped his gum.

"Yes, beautiful. Is this your delivery vehicle?" I walked behind the car to admire his mud flaps and stenciled designs.

"Yeah, I can haul lots of boxes." Kermit opened the back door to show me the interior. He ran his hand over the velour seat.

"Yes, I remember it has lots of space. Aren't you worried about gas mileage?"

"Oh, I get great gas mileage with this thing."

"Really? Alright. Well, I got a bunch of deliveries ready for you." Kermit shut the door and we took a last lap around his painted beauty. He followed me into the office, waving and smiling at the salespeople. Kermit was walking energy, waiting to be released. One reason he was a good delivery man, he kept moving.

The phone was ringing and I picked it up. Kermit walked to the map to pick his tickets.

"New Day Marketing," I said.

"This is Johnny." I could hear traffic and sirens on Johnny's end.

"Hey, Johnny, this is Tim. I hear you left a week ago?"

"Yes. Not on purpose. I was calling to see if they fired me. I want to come back to work."

"Sure, Johnny, come on in. I'm in charge now."

"That's good news! That Tony was a jerk."

"Yeah, I've heard. What's that racket behind you?"

"Oh." Johnny paused as a siren drowned out our conversation. "I'm downtown. I'm at the bus station. I couldn't find liquor in Utah, so I sobered up. A couple of Mormons there purchased a bus ticket for me to get home. Real friendly people." Johnny said.

"How did you get to Utah?"

"I don't know. Last, I recall, I was at the Brass Rail. I'm on the way." Johnny hung up.

"Johnny's coming back?" Kermit asked. He plucked ten tickets in a tight bunch.

"Yes," I said.

"That's great. That guy's tickets are solid. They're always happy customers." Kermit walked away toward the inventory.

"Kermit, take these three tickets."

He snapped his gum twice. "Give them to the other guy, okay?"

"Come on, Kermit, fair is fair. You take those," I said.

"Okay, buddy." Kermit laughed. I handed him the other three.

That evening, I had all the telephones full. I kept Ralph and Kermit busy with deliveries. I even had Johnny back to work. By Thursday, I was on track for a $15,000 week. Johnny had written $2,000 in sales, which was $400 in commissions for him. I gestured to him. After he finished his sale, he purged through a smoke cloud to come to my desk. The simple room had brown paneled walls. I remembered a lighter cream color when we leased the office. The brownish hue must have been from cigarette tar.

"Johnny, you've got four hundred bucks for the week, so you're done."

"But it's only Thursday?"

"Do you want to work next week, Johnny?"

"Yes, I do."

"If you make too much, you'll do a Houdini and vanish."

"Yeah, you're right. I guess I can relax until Monday."

"You're welcome to hang out here." The phone rang. "New Day Marketing," I said.

"Hey Tim, this is Steve."

"Hey Steve, how's the Newark office going?"

"We're doing good, we'll hit eight grand this week."

"Eight grand? Wow, that's pretty good considering you lost your best writer, me, ha ha."

"Yeah, we got a couple of good people recruited. Crystal's been training using your system."

"Tell Crystal she's doing a good job."

"I will. Anyway," Steve paused, "I'm calling about Dagger. He keeps calling and screaming at me and Crystal. It freaks Crystal out."

"I know he does that. I don't know how the hell he believes that motivates sales people. What's he hollering about?"

"He wants us to do two thousand dollars a day."

"He expects that from four phones? The only time we did that was one week during Christmas."

"Yeah, I know." I heard Steve sigh. The telemarketers in the office filled the background while Steve paused for a minute. "He doesn't bother me. I answer the phone when I'm in the office. While I'm delivering, Crystal takes the assault. I hate that."

"I know. I feel bad for her. Tell Crystal she needs to let him rant, agree, and ignore it. I know that's difficult to do. Have her call me this evening after work and I'll give her relaxation tips. I'll talk to Harley, but I doubt it'll do any good. I'm really sorry. I'm the Dagger filter for my crew. You guys didn't know he screamed at me. I didn't want to demotivate you. Unfortunately, now you're the filter."

"Okay, Tim. Thanks," Steve said.

"You're welcome. Good luck." I waited until Steve hung up the phone to make sure he finished.

At 5:15, Sammie walked in when the phones were packed. She came to my desk, looked at the full telephones and puffed her smoke.

"I need a phone," she said.

"When somebody takes a break, you can take the phone. If you want a guaranteed phone, be here by five," I said. Sammie turned and shuffled outside toward the Brass Rail Pub next-door. I tacked tickets on the wall map and listened to my crew. I could tell from Vernon's voice he had a sale. I walked to look over his shoulder. He was writing 3022 Broad St. I went back to my map and put a pin on 3022 Broad.

Two minutes later, the phone rang. "New Day Marketing," I answered.

"Why the hell didn't you give Sammie a phone?" Dagger yelled. I held the phone away from my ear.

Chapter 21

"**S** IR, SHE CAME IN late. I told her she could have a phone when somebody takes a break."

"She doesn't wait. When she comes in, you give her a phone immediately."

"That's not fair. Everyone will get pissed."

"I gave you an order. You do it without question." Dagger screamed so loud the salespeople stopped calling and looked at me. My knees weakened; my breath increased. Adrenaline exploded my mind with fear. I hated those assaults.

"Alright, I'll put her on."

"You better, you goddamn idiot." He hung up. Sammie strolled back in to see me. She leaned up against the desk and crossed her arms, her cigarette precariously close to burning her fingers.

"Thanks for calling the dogs on me, Sammie," I said. Sammie shrugged.

"Who's ready for a break?" I asked. Don raised his hand.

"Don, Sammie wants to take your phone." Don pulled himself up on his crutches and swung outside. He leaned against the window to watch Sammie, drew out a cigarette and lit it. I closed my eyes and imagined my favorite place in the Big Horn mountains. When I lived in Sheridan, I would spend days camping and hiking among the evergreen trees. A stream trickled along a winding base of a hill of boulders. Watching it relaxed me. It had become one of my favorite relaxation techniques after Dagger's attacks.

I was hoping Sammie would do her usual one sale and then quit. After ten minutes, she got a sale and handed it to me.

"Thanks, Sammie. Are you done?" I asked.

"Yep," Sammie said. She walked outside to talk to Don. Larry jumped up to join them. Looked like a love triangle was forming. Larry and Don were about Sammie's age, forty, I'd say. Larry stood with them, not talking. His eyebrows lifted.

At closing time, I locked the office door and scanned the dark parking lot. The Brass Rail lights barely lit our spaces. Ever since Dale ambushed me, I inspected every shadow. Every three steps, I'd freeze and look behind me. I made it to the car without incident and drove home.

"Daddy," Colin yelled as he ran across the floor to grab me. I scooped him up.

"Hey, buddy, how are you?" I gave him a hug. "Candy, how are you doing?" Colin giggled and kicked over my shoulder as I patted his butt.

"I'm okay, but the baby and Colin wear me out."

"Would you want dinner at Bob Evans?" I put Colin down and picked up Sapphire from her carrier. I put a blanket on my shoulder and cradled her.

"That'd be nice. I'm frazzled."

"I get that. Colin by himself is a handful. I have some good news too."

"What's that?" Candy asked.

"I'll tell you at dinner. Let's get in the car." I placed Sapphire back in the carrier, took Colin's hand, and went to the car. Candy turned out the lights and locked the door. We buckled the kids in and drove through the parking lot toward Main Street. I looked in the rear-view mirror at the kids. It felt good to have my family together. Candy closed her eyes and I turned on the wipers as rain drizzled. The smell of negative ions from the rain would relax Candy. In smoke damaged homes, I used a commercial size negative ionizer. It was so strong it made you nauseous. But just a small amount from rain made you relax. After we arrived at Bob Evans, the hostess seated us. The server poured coffee and took our order.

"Could you bring Colin some chocolate milk while he's waiting for the dinner?" I asked the server.

"Certainly," the server said and walked away carrying the menus.

"What's your good news?" Candy asked. Candy moved the blanket away from Sapphire's face and unbuckled her. She brushed Sapphire's blonde hair with her hand. That child was born with curls.

"I'm creating a manager training program. I'll let them run the office without me a few hours every day."

"How's that good news?"

"I get more time with you."

"Oh, okay. Well, that's nice." Candy didn't look that excited about the prospect of seeing more of me. I opened the carton of crayons for Colin.

"Here, Colin, take this crayon and fill in this duck." Colin scribbled all over the paper. "Well, that's an artistic expression, I guess," I said. Candy laughed. We had a wonderful dinner and went home.

The next morning, my crew showed up at the office. Gary was among them. He came up to my desk. Gary had mostly gray hair that hung on his shoulders and a beard to match. His clothes were mismatched, and boots untied. I wondered how he got that job at McDonalds.

"Tim, I have a question," he said.

"What is it, Gary?"

"I want to go full time with you, give up my McDonald's job."

"Gary, you're doing good, but I'm concerned about you giving up your other income. I mean, you could have a terrible week and not make any sales here."

"I'm sure I could do it," Gary said. He pulled his hair from his face.

"How much do you make at McDonald's?" I asked.

"Minimum wage, so for forty hours, I bring home around a hundred bucks after taxes."

"I'll tell you what, Gary. Make $200 weekly for three weeks, then you can be full time. I'd feel guilty if you struggled here with no backup."

"That sounds like a reasonable challenge. I can do that." Gary smiled and went to his table. Sammie came in and grabbed some numbers.

Fortunately, there were already a couple of phones open, so I didn't have to kick anybody off. Three salespeople walked to me with their mugs to get first dibs on the fresh coffee I was brewing. We had the ten-gallon stainless steel pot, but everyone preferred my Mr. Coffee drip maker. I'd rotate among gourmet coffee flavors on each batch.

The phone rang and I answered.

"Let me talk to my mom," a kid's voice said.

"Who's your mom?" I asked.

"What, are you stupid? There's only one woman there."

"Sammie, your kid's on the line." Sammie came over and took the phone.

"What do you want?" Sammie asked her kid. "No, you can't do that. (Pause) No, give it back to him. (Pause) If you can't get along, one of you leave the house." Sammie put the phone down, rolled her eyeballs, and went back to her table.

The phone rang again.

"Let me talk to my mom," a different kid's voice said.

"Sammie, your kid is on the phone again." Sammie came over. I frowned and handed her the phone.

Sammie put the phone to her ear and looked at the ceiling for a minute. "I told him to tell you if you can't get along, one of you has to leave the house. (Pause) I don't know which one. (Pause) You guys have to work it out." Sammie hung up the phone.

"Sammie, I can't have your kids calling during work hours. I need to use it to dispatch the drivers," I said.

"Yeah, well," she said. She went back to her desk.

I walked over to Kwame. "Hey, see me when you take a break." He followed me over. "I didn't mean you had to do it right now."

"No, that's fine what you got to show me," Kwame asked.

"This is how we dispatch the drivers. I pin the ticket's corner on the map coordinates. This gives us a visual to dispatch an efficient route. Kermit will call in next and I'll read him this bunch of tickets." I moved my finger over a row of tickets. "And when Ralph calls in, I'll read him this group." I pointed. "Does that make sense?"

"Yes, that makes sense." Kwame put his hand on his chin and studied the map. "What about this far away ticket?" He pointed.

"It's thirty minutes old. We have to have them delivered within two hours. I'll wait an hour to see if we can get another sale close by. If not, I'll give an extra three dollars to the driver."

"Okay." Kwame nodded. "I can do this."

"Okay, come listen to me dispatch when a driver calls in. The next time you'll do it, okay?"

"Sure."

"Good, go back to work. I'll let you know when the driver calls in." Kwame walked back to his desk and picked up the phone.

Over the next two weeks, I trained Kwame to my satisfaction. I taught him to answer classified advertisement calls. I showed how the tone of his voice reveals his character. People want a competent and upbeat boss. Recruiting would be crucial in their new office. I also taught him how to take care of his money, make payroll, and keep the salespeople motivated and generating sales.

"Kwame, do you live alone?" I asked.

"Yes."

"Hide your payroll in the office overnight if that changes."

"Okay, why?"

"Experience, my man. I learned that the hard way."

On the day before he was to leave for Cincinnati, I took Kwame outside. "Kwame, you'll be an excellent manager. If you have questions when you're in your new office, call me, okay?"

"Yes, I will." Kwame smiled.

"So, here's one last thing. Dagger will probably make random drive-by phone calls to you."

"Drive-by?" Kwame asked.

"He won't actually drive to you. I was comparing it to a drive-by gang shooting. He'll call on the phone, scream and put you in a rotten mood. I hate it. The best advice I have is to listen and say 'yes, sir.' If it bothers you, take a quick break and relax. Keep Dagger's negativity away from your salespeople. It'll kill your sales."

"Bullies don't intimidate me," Kwame said.

"Well, you're better than me. He scares the crap out of me."

"Okay, Tim. I'll do my best for you."

"I know you will, Kwame."

Chapter 22

IT WAS SATURDAY EVENING, January 17th, 1988. Candy and I were riding to Newark for Crystal's birthday party. Arlene was watching the children. Candy needed this break. She hadn't had one day's rest without children since we left Denver.

I had discussed with Crystal about the type of costumes to wear. She said anything. Just have fun. Candy decided it would be fun if she wore a cocktail waitress outfit. I didn't see the fun in that, but it made her happy.

She chose a tight bodice with billowing sleeves and a plunging neckline. Her bra lifted her bosom to form eye-popping cleavage. Her skirt was short, the hemline above her knees, to show a garter belt. She accented her legs with black stiletto heels. Candy's costume surprised me. She looked good. Real good. I never thought she'd wear something so provocative. I wondered if she was competing with Crystal. Or trying to prove that she, too, was hot.

When we arrived at Steve & Crystal's house, cars clogged the driveway and the curb along the street. We found a space one hundred feet from the front door. Candy took my arm as we walked. She wasn't used to those stilettos. She had put her hair up in a French braid with an enormous bow on top. With that and the shoes, she towered six inches over me. It was a brisk

January night, cold but dry. I had worn a jacket, but Candy refused one. Said it wouldn't go with her costume.

Candy wanted me to dress as a barkeeper. I instead was a pirate. I did my portrayal of the character with a lone eye patch and Colin's plastic sword.

"I wish you had dressed up more," Candy said. I helped her step over the curb and through the grass onto the sidewalk.

"I think you dressed enough for both of us. You look hot, by the way."

"Thanks!" Candy smiled and forgot about my costume.

When we approached the door, we could hear music and voices inside. I pushed the doorbell. Within a minute, Crystal opened the door and squealed, "It's Tim and Candy!" She bolted forward first to hug Candy, and then me. Crystal had dressed as a cat. She had velvet ears in her puffed-up red hair and a short tail. More like a rabbit's tail. I guessed that was cuter. She had black mesh stockings showing her toned legs and, like Candy, accented with red stiletto heels. She had a sheer black lace bodysuit that showed her nipples, full breasts, and a gold ring on her belly button. Mascara and eye shadow manifested cat eyes with long dark lashes.

Her costume visibly unnerved Candy, but Crystal's immediate hug had disarmed her. Candy looked at me with her mouth open. I shrugged, then escorted her through the door with my palm on the small of her back.

Cheerful people filled every one of the five couches and five overstuffed chairs. I realized why Steve and Crystal had so much furniture. There were ten ladies standing near the kitchen holding drinks and laughing. Crystal grabbed Candy's hand and led her over to the group. She introduced Candy, and the group squealed and touched Candy's costume. I could see that Candy loved the spotlight.

Steve was behind a table he had transformed into a bar holding five kinds of vodkas, three types of schnapps, Jack

Daniels, red and white wine, and a cooler of ice filled with Bud and Coors. He sat with his fingers interlaced and resting on his belly. I walked over to greet him.

"Hi, Steve. Nice party you got going," I said.

"Thanks. Candy looks hot," Steve said. He looked toward the group of giggling ladies in the corner.

"Yes, thanks. So does Crystal."

"Don't you know it." Steve laughed. "What's your poison?"

"I'll have a shot of peppermint schnapps and a Coors Light. Candy surprised me with that costume. I never dreamed she'd wear something like that."

"Grab the beer," Steve said. He grabbed a shot glass, unscrewed the schnapps and poured it.

"Thanks," I said as Steve handed it to me. "This is fun. It's great to see you two outside of work."

"Crystal was jabbering all day about her birthday party tonight. She was ecstatic you were coming." Steve lifted a shot glass to toast mine, and we guzzled it, then slammed the glass down on the table.

"I should see if Candy wants a drink. I'll be right back." I had a swig of my beer and sat it on the table.

"See if Crystal wants one," Steve said.

"Sure buddy." I turned sideways to squeeze through five people talking. I nodded and smiled to be polite. When I reached Candy, she was listening to the other ladies' chat. A lady with stilettos and long blonde hair was the center of the conversation. She towered over the other ladies. She wore a Wonder Woman costume. It was a wonder she squeezed into that narrow outfit. Her breasts were so tight I expected them to pop a button and put someone's eye out.

"He was under my sink, squirming. I couldn't stop watching," Wonder Woman said. The ladies laughed. "I wanted to help with that big greasy pipe. But not under the sink." More laughter.

I tapped Candy on the shoulder. "Would you like a drink?"

"Yes, red wine, please," Candy said. "How about you, Crystal?" Candy asked her before I had a chance.

"Yes, Steve knows what I want." Crystal winked at me. Candy laughed. I squeezed back, sideways, to Steve.

"Hey Steve, red wine for Candy, and Crystal says you know what she wants."

"Yes, but she'll have to settle for a drink," Steve said. We both laughed. I took the drinks to the ladies. I stood for a few minutes next to Candy, but she and Crystal were talking and touching each other's shoulders. I didn't want to impede the budding friendship. I walked back to Steve.

"Crystal and Candy are getting along," I said. I picked up my beer and looked back at Candy. The music seemed to get louder.

"Do you guys swing?" Steve asked. I opened my mouth and nothing came out. I wasn't expecting that question.

"No, no. Not us," I answered after my second attempt to speak.

"Okay. Just asking." Steve handed me another shot. I waited for him to pour one, clicked his glass and downed it.

"Steve, I know you guys do. I have to ask; how do you find other swingers?"

"Word gets around. Half the people here are swingers."

"They are?" I looked around with my mouth open. Suddenly I imagined half the room naked and groping each other. And then I imagined Steve in there, taking up the space of four people. I shuddered.

"Steve, I have to ask. You're a great guy. So, I don't mean to insult you, but—"

"How do I get women?" Steve grinned and took a swig of beer.

"Well, yeah. How?"

"It's the same thing you got. Power. Women love power." Steve sat the beer down and folded his arms. He looked around the crowd.

"I don't get it, Steve. What power?"

"Look at me. I'm like an enormous bear. Powerful. Women love that." Steve stood and put his hands on his hips. Sitting behind the table, I didn't realize what costume he had chosen. He wore a red T-shirt and red pants. A big smile of the Kool-Aid man was printed on the T-Shirt.

"Oh my God, Steve. That's hilarious." I laughed so hard I had to set my beer down.

"People like it if you can laugh at yourself. Especially women. Come on Tim, let me introduce you around." Steve waved me to follow him. The crowd was getting louder and friendlier. Some were dancing to the music.

"Hey Steve, what do you mean I have power?" I asked.

"You're a manager. That's power. Tim, this is Marty and Joy. Marty Joy, this is my boss. Also, a good friend." Steve lifted his palm up toward me.

"Pleasure to meet you," I said.

"Nice to meet you. What kind of business are you the boss of?" Marty asked. He shook my hand, and Joy leaned forward to give me a hug.

"We have a telemarketing company. We sell light bulbs."

"So, you're the people that call us, huh?" Joy said.

"Only twice a year," Steve said.

"Yes. Only twice a year," I agreed. I wondered if Marty and Joy were swingers. They weren't someone I'd want to see naked. Steve took me around to meet others. Several teased me about my lazy costume. Steve stood behind me for an hour as he brought me around to greet people. I was not a party guy, but I made people laugh. I couldn't remember a joke even at gunpoint, but I had good timing for off-the-cuff comments. Parties were usually a chore for me, but I discovered myself enjoying Steve and his friend's company.

"Tim, are you sure you aren't swingers?" Steve tapped me on the shoulder. I looked at him. He pointed to the couch in the corner. Crystal, thirty minutes earlier, had turned the lights lower. The corner was dark. After I squinted for ten seconds, I saw Candy on the couch. Batman had his left arm around her shoulders, leaning into her. Not the real Batman, someone faking it. I was sure Candy would tell him to move his arm, but as I watched with Steve, she didn't. She didn't flinch when he placed his hand on her exposed knee. She was laughing. Batman must have known a joke.

"Steve, no, we're not. At least, I'm not." My face flushed with fiery blood. My heart stopped. I felt despair overcoming me. Memories of catching Candy naked with that other man on our bed slammed into my head.

Steve pressed his hand on my shoulder. "Tim, let's go to the bar."

"Yeah, sure Steve." Steve led and I followed. I had one good eye patch to hide tears. I should have had two. But I kept it together. I sat at the makeshift bar and grabbed a napkin. I wiped my eyes. I looked at Candy on the couch. Crystal had joined them and she was perching on Batman's lap, kicking her legs in the air. Candy whispered into Crystal's ear and they both laughed.

"Steve, that doesn't bother you, seeing Crystal flirting with Batman?"

"No. Crystal and I don't keep secrets. It's normal to flirt."

"Well, I'm glad it works for you two. It won't for me. I just want one special woman to share my life with."

"There's nothing wrong with that either, Tim," Steve said. He poured me another shot. We chinked and drank.

"That's the last one for tonight, Steve. I need to drive home at midnight."

"I got Cola, if you want it."

"Thanks, Steve. Go have fun. I won't be good company the rest of the night." The floor was my focus. Candy was breaking my heart.

"I'm having fun right here with you, buddy." Steve patted my back. Steve was becoming a true friend.

At midnight, I told Candy we had to leave. She and Crystal hugged and danced. New best friends, apparently.

"Thank you so much for coming to my party, Tim." Crystal hugged me.

"You're very welcome. It was a great time. It was nice of you to invite me." Crystal gave me a kiss on the cheek and another hug. I blushed and turned away. I took Candy's hand and escorted her across the sidewalk, then the grass, to our car. She almost fell twice, but I held her up. It was a good thing she wasn't driving.

I wanted to talk to Candy about Batman. But she was drunk, and I was angry. My decision was to wait for another day when I could control myself. If I started then, I'd start screaming. Plus, Candy wouldn't even remember it.

Candy fell asleep and I drove in silence.

Chapter 23

B Y THE TIME KWAME was managing Cincinnati, I had two new trainees. I was recruiting new people every day. Two thirds of them would quit. It wasn't a simple job. Harley came through my door the following Wednesday.

"Hey, Harley, how're you doing?" I asked.

"Doing good. Your man in Cincinnati worked out. You did a good job training him."

"He took instruction well, he's competent, and he has a respectful attitude. I'm sure he'll make a lot of money for you." I shuffled strips of numbers and put a rubber band around them.

"Thanks Tim. I need someone to replace the Dayton manager." Harley looked at the busy room.

"Are you firing Dale?"

"No, Dagger's making him the district manager of Northern Ohio."

"Maybe he'll be too busy to bother me," I said. Harley smiled.

"I can have somebody ready in two weeks. I have two new trainees."

"I won't tell you how to train, since you obviously know what you're doing. I'll let Dagger know that you'll have someone available in two weeks," Harley said.

The next day, I hired a fresh man by the name of Rudy. He was tall and intelligent. He was interested in management, so I added him to my program, giving me three trainees. Over the next two months, I got enough managers trained to open Zanesville, a second office in Cincinnati, and two for Dale's district. I hoped to God Dale treated them better than he treated me.

Dagger opened Illinois and I sent Rudy to open the first office. The Zanesville office was being run by Jeff. Steve and Crystal had found him for me. I trained him in my office. He lived in Zanesville with a wife and six young kids. He wore western clothes and cowboy boots. Zanesville was a rural town with a lot of cowboys around it. Jeff was a good fit.

Harley came to my office in the afternoon. The phone room was empty save for two reclining salespeople. The sun filtered through the dingy plate-glass windows. I had a pro window cleaner visit weekly, but the cigarette tar would gunk it up before he returned.

"Tim, I need to talk to you." Harley put his hands on his hips and smiled at the napping sales agents, looked at me and shook his head.

"Sure, Harley." I stood to greet him. "They need the rest."

"I know. Step out back with me." I followed him toward the back door. The white tile wasn't so white. It needed a scrubbing as well. It was like working inside a chimney. The boxes were stacked far from the phones to avoid smoky products delivered to our customers. We stepped into the alley. Harley squinted at the cloud dotted sky and took a single cigarette from his shirt pocket. It was Hawaiian design, untucked, hanging loose to hide his belly. It looked good on him.

"What's up, Harley?"

"Tim, I'd like you to become the district manager of Southern Ohio. I've been doing the job, but I'm getting busier, and I need help. Dagger wants me to manage the entire state."

"If I'm the DM, I can't recruit and train managers for you." I lifted my hand to block the sun from my eyes. A truck drove past

us and stopped two doors down at the Trophy Store. Two
uniformed men exited the cab and lowered the tailgate.

"I think you still could."

"What's the pay?"

"Two percent."

"Right now, I'm making $1,500 a week. If I took that job, I'd
be making 800 bucks a week."

"How'd you know that?" Harley asked. He lifted his eyebrow
and cupped his hands around his lighter as he lit his smoke.

"Well, I trained all the managers. They talk to me, especially
after your brother rips them a new asshole. They'd do better if
he'd quit doing that." I observed the two men carry boxes into
the rear entrance. Blank trophies, I assumed. I could see the
boxes weren't empty but also not heavy by the way they carried
them.

"I know. I've told him he shouldn't do that, but he doesn't
listen to anybody." Harley turned to watch the men lifting the
boxes.

"He acts like he's a god. I just don't understand why he thinks
it's good business to do that."

"Anyway, if you're the district manager, the sales managers
will improve. You'll increase sales and make more money."
Harley crossed his arms and looked at me, holding his smoke
between his fingers.

"Why don't you let Jeff in Zanesville be district manager. I
mean, the job is just a glorified gopher, right? Picking up
closeouts at the end of the week, checking inventory and
delivering products when necessary?" I turned to avoid the direct
sunlight. The sun was at an angle that created shade next to the
building. A chain-link fence bordered the back of the alley.
Vines and bushes grew wild through it, creating a living wall. It
boxed in our alley behind the shopping center. One way in and
one way out.

"I need a district manager that can continue training the sales managers."

"Harley, I've already been doing that over the telephone. I can keep doing that. If I need to run errands, I can send Jeff to do it. He's only making five hundred a week now, so I'm sure he'd be happy to make eight hundred. And knowing his ego, he'd love to have the title of District Manager."

Harley exhaled smoke and thought for a minute. "We'll give that a shot. I'd appreciate it if you keep working with the managers and monitor Jeff."

"I will. I have a system. Want me to explain it to you?"

"No, It's working. That's all I need to know. I'll talk to Jeff. See you later, Tim," Harley said. Harley walked toward the trophy door instead of returning inside. I watched him stop and talk to the truck guys. They laughed about something. Harley could improve anyone's day. He had that kind of personality. I walked back into the office.

Two hours later, the phone rang and I answered. "New Day Marketing, this is Tim."

"Tim, this is Jeff DeWalt, out in Zanesville." Someone was laughing in the background.

"Hi, Jeff, how are you doing?" I asked.

"Harley was just out here. He said I'm the new district manager, and you recommended me."

"Yes, I did. Are you in your office?"

"Yes, why?"

"There's a lot of background noise. Is your crew working?"

"We were, but Harley had everyone in stitches with his jokes. We'll get back to work. Anyway, I appreciate you recommending me. He said you could have somebody out here to replace me?"

"Actually, I think Steve and Crystal have someone that lives in Newark. I'll talk with them and have somebody soon."

"Good. Thanks, Tim."

"You're welcome, Jeff." I hung up the phone and called Newark. Crystal answered.

"Hey Crystal, this is Tim."

"Hi Tim, it's good to hear your voice." Crystal was a sweet soul. She was soft spoken and kind to anybody she met. There was no reason Dagger should abuse her. I may have made the wrong choice to put her in that position, but I had believed she was a powerful person and could overcome the evil of Dagger.

"I love hearing your voice too, Crystal. Hey, you told me you had a manager trainee, is that right?" I asked.

"Yes, Kathy, I've been training her on how to run a small office."

"Do you think she'd want to run Zanesville?"

"I'm sure she would. That's where she lives," Crystal said.

"Why isn't she working at the Zanesville office, then?" Larry watched with a smile as I turned and pinned his new sale on the map. I gave Larry a thumbs up. He trotted back to his phone.

"She was, but Jeff wouldn't keep his hands off of her."

"Oh, that's not good. I wish somebody had told me that earlier."

"I didn't think you could do anything about it."

"I'm the wizard behind the curtain. I can do lots of things. Let me know next time. Jeff's going to be the district manager."

"So, he's in charge?" Crystal's voice increased in pitch.

"Well, he's more like my gopher. He'll do inventory closeouts and such. But don't tell him about the gopher remark, we'll just let him think he's the district manager. Please, let me know if he misbehaves and I'll take care of it."

"Make sure he keeps his hands to himself," Crystal said. "We deserve respect."

"Yes, I know you do, and I will, Crystal. Thanks for the alert. Is Kathy ready to manage an office?"

"She is."

"She'll be a working manager like you, making sales and managing. I appreciate you doing that. I'll take you and Steve out for steak to say thank you."

"I know she can do it. But, we'd prefer barbeque at your house or ours." Crystal giggled. It was nice to hear. I wished Dagger would leave her alone.

"That sounds better, we'll do that. Thank you, Crystal, I'll let Harley know." I hung up and gave Harley a call.

Chapter 24

"HARLEY, TIM HERE. KATHY in Newark will manage Zanesville. She actually lives in Zanesville."

"Why wasn't she working in Zanesville, then?" Harley asked.

"Crystal said Jeff had his hands all over her."

"Oh, that's not good." Harley groaned. "Geezus."

"Yeah, we'll have to keep a close watch on him."

"You do that, Tim. I'll drive out to Newark and Zanesville to get Kathy in place. I'll talk to Kathy to get her perspective on Jeff."

"Okay, Harley, I'll talk to you later." I hung up the phone. I turned to pin more tickets on the map. The board was filling up. The gourmet coffee pot was dripping. My salespeople were holding their mugs, waiting for it to finish.

That night, I let one of my manager trainees run the office from five to seven. I went home to have dinner with Candy and Colin. Afterwards, we took a walk to help Colin run off his energy. Well, Candy and I walked, Colin zipped back-and-forth taking the longest route possible instead of a straight line.

That night in bed, I was laying with my eyes closed. Candy's breathing was rhythmical. She had her hand on Sapphire's bassinet next to the bed.

I felt a smothering over my face. I couldn't breathe. I stood and grabbed my throat and struggled for air. The shadow in the room's corner became even darker until it formed a human shape. I recognized the misty, shimmering energy to be Dale. Maybe, his spirit had traveled to me from Dayton. Lack of air was making me dizzy, my knees weakened, and I fell to the floor.

"Please, please, please, Sheena, help me, please." The dark mist engulfed my neck, and I passed out.

I'm standing with Sheena at the top of the Leveque Tower in Columbus. The view of the breeze cools us. The view is hypnotizing. As far as I can see, the streetlights stretch in lines and curves.

"Tim, you haven't been flying. You need to fly," Sheena says. She touches the back of my hand and smiles.

"With the stress from Dale and Dagger, I forget to fly."

"It's important to fly every night."

"Okay, Sheena, I'll start again. I have to fly in the country. Somebody is killing flyers in the city."

"That's where we'll go," she said. Instantly, we are standing on the roof of a country church near a cornfield. I look around at the unfamiliar landscape.

"Sheena, Dale and Dagger both feel evil." I assume Sheena knows this, but I need the words to come from my mouth.

"Yes, they are."

"But they're different. Dagger's evil is oppressive, controlling, maybe even murderous. Dale's evil feels like it could consume my soul."

"Yes, they are both different evils. Different types than you've ever had to deal with before," Sheena says. She raises her arms to let the breeze flow over her sleeves. Her hair flutters.

"And I thought Ambrose would be the evilest man I'd ever meet."

"There's a lot of evil in the world, Tim. I explained there would be hard lessons for you to learn. These are important to you. But to survive, you need to fly daily." Sheena turns and looks at me with a serious look. But she smiles again.

"I miss sitting on my porch, looking at our lawn. The glass people were interesting and calming. And it was nice that Colin had space to run." I hear crickets in the corn and smell the sweet leaves. The dark sky is unspoiled by city light. It reminds me of the country in Sheridan. The country is my sanctuary.

"You're making enough money, Tim. Move to a house with a big yard. Leave your townhouse."

"I still have six months on my lease."

"I'll take care of that. Start looking for a new home, okay?" Sheena turns and puts her hands on my shoulders, looking me in the eye.

"Yes, Sheena, thank you."

"Now, Tim, you must fly. Every day." She frowns. She's serious. I wonder why flying is so important to her. I leave the roof and fly over the cornfield, touching the tips with my hands. It's calming. I love to fly.

When I woke, I was sprawled on the floor. It was still dark. I was breathing freely. The clock said I had been asleep for an hour. I stood and went to check on Colin. He had landed with his arms and legs stretched out spread eagle but was asleep. I pulled a cover over him. I came back and looked at Candy. She was resting. I looked in the bassinet at Sapphire; she was breathing peacefully. I lay on the bed and pondered the pattern swirled into the plaster ceiling. After ten minutes, I went to sleep.

In the morning, Colin jumped on our bed, waking us.

"Good morning, Colin," I said. He bounced on the bed. I stood and put on my robe and caught Colin. I held him sideways and gave him a raspberry on his belly. Colin laughed and curled up, holding his hands over his belly.

"Candy, I'm going to have my trainees watch the office this afternoon and pick you up to look for a house."

"Why?"

"Colin needs a yard so I can build him a play fort and swings. He needs space to run." I released Colin back to the bed. He clutched the blanket and rolled himself into a mummy.

"What about our lease?" Candy picked up Sapphire from the bassinet and laid her on the bed. She picked up a fresh diaper from our headboard shelf and stretched it out. She then removed the wet diaper from Sapphire, rolled it up, taped it and set it aside.

"Sheena said she'd take care of it."

"Oh, okay? How'll she do that?"

"I don't know, but I'll see you at one, okay?"

"Okay, Tim."

I prepared myself for work and left. When I arrived at the office, there were six Whitehall police cars and an ambulance with their lights flashing in the parking lot. They had strung yellow tape around the front of the Brass Rail Pub. An officer put his hand up as I entered the parking lot. I rolled down my window.

"Do you work here, sir?" he asked

"Yes, I manage that office." I pointed. The officer waved at a man in street clothes wearing a badge. He walked over to me.

"Detective, this man manages the telemarketing business," the officer said.

"Good morning, sir," the detective said. "What is your name?" He looked into my back seat, scouring every inch with his eyes.

"Tim Drobnick."

"What time did you leave your office last night?"

"I left at 9:30, that's when I finished the books and checked in the drivers," I said.

"Where did you go after that?" He flipped open a pocket notebook.

"Home. I took my wife, and two kids to Chi Chi's for dinner," I said. He made a note, then bit on the end of the pen.

"We need to talk to your employees. When do they come in to work?" He asked.

"The morning crew comes in at nine."

"Tell them not to leave until we speak with them."

"Yes sir, I will." The detective walked to the front of my car, copied my license plate number, I assumed, then came back, glanced in my back seat again, then patted the roof of my car and walked back to the Brass Rail Pub entrance.

I unlocked the office and prepared it for work. Kenny and Cheryl arrived first. Their eyes were drooping from sleep or the lack thereof. They stopped and examined the crime scene. He said something into Cheryl's ear, then walked inside the office.

"What's going on over there?" Kenny asked. His voice sounded as if he was struggling to breathe.

"I don't know, but the detective wants to talk to everyone in our office. We need to stay until he does."

"We did nothing wrong." Kenny looked at Cheryl. She looked at her toes. Kenny's wheezing increased. He wiped his brow with his sleeve.

"Then you have nothing to worry about," I said. The detective came in and asked me to step outside. I followed him to the middle of the parking lot.

"How long have you been the manager?" He flipped through his notebook, licking his thumb to grab the paper. I wondered where his hands had been. He must have had a hell of an immune system.

"Three weeks, but I was also a manager last July."

"Did you go to the Brass Rail before you went home?" He found a page that pleased him and wrote on it.

"No, sir. My family was waiting for me."

"Did you notice anyone walking into the pub?" He pointed at the Brass Rail, as if I didn't know which pub he was referring to.

"No, sir. I did not," I said.

"Ok, send another person out," he said. He looked through the plate-glass window at Kenny and Cheryl and squinted. I walked back into the office.

"He wants to talk to one of you," I said.

"Which one?" Kenny asked.

"Probably both, but just one for now." Cheryl looked at Kenny with wide eyes.

Chapter 25

"I'LL GO," KENNY SAID. He walked out. We watched as he talked to the officer. Kenny shook his head several times, raised his hands in the air, and pointed down the street. The detective made notes. Then the detective pointed at the Brass Rail. Kenny shook his head repeatedly. The detective pointed at Cheryl and Kenny walked back inside.

"He wants to talk to you," he said to Cheryl.

"What did he ask you?" Cheryl asked.

"He wants to know what we did last night." Cheryl walked out, stopped, looked back at Kenny, then walked to the detective. We could see the detective talking to her. Cheryl covered her eyes and cried. Kenny stepped forward and clenched his fists.

"Kenny, don't go out there. Just wait," I said. Cheryl shook her head several times as she cried, never looking at the officer.

"He better fuckin' not upset her," Kenny said.

"What in Sam Hill is happening?" Don asked. He and Larry walked in.

"I don't know. The detective is asking everyone where they were last night. He said he needs to talk to everyone that works here," I said. Don swung over and pulled out a chair and sat, leaning his crutches against the table. He scooted the ashtrays out of his way. Larry stood next to me to watch Cheryl crying. After five minutes, Cheryl came back in, wiping her eyes.

"What did he say to you?" Kenny asked her.

"He wanted to know where I was last night," she said.

"Why were you crying?"

"Police scare me." Cheryl covered her eyes. Kenny put his arm around her. The detective motioned to me with two fingers.

"Go on out, Larry," I said. Larry moved like a walking bear, his front paws swinging. He talked little, but his face disclosed his feelings. He walked to the detective. We watched as he nodded and pointed down the street. He put his hands in his pocket and looked down as the detective talked. Larry shook his head. The detective took a picture from his folder and showed it to Larry. Larry looked and shook his head. The detective slipped it back into the folder. He motioned at me again. Larry walked back inside.

"What was that picture?" Kenny asked.

"It was a picture of a man. I didn't know him. It was one of those pictures when they book you into jail," Larry said.

"A mug shot, dummy," Don said.

Larry nodded, "Right. Yeah. a mug shot."

"Why didn't he show any of us the picture?" Kenny asked.

Larry looked up for a second. "He asked if I went to the Brass Rail last night. I told him I did. He asked if I saw that man in the picture."

"I told him that Cheryl and I didn't go in there," Kenny said.

"Same here," I said. Vernon and Gary came in.

"What's going on?"

"Murder, probably," Don said.

"You don't know that," I said.

"Maybe that guy in the mug shot murdered someone in the bar," Don said

"The bar closes at two AM. Wouldn't the police have been here earlier?" Gary asked.

"Maybe he killed the bartender," Vernon said.

"Look guys, we don't know what happened. Don, the detective, is waving. Go out and talk to him." Don hopped up on his one leg and grabbed his crutches. He swung outside to the detective. Don shook his head, then he pointed at the bus stop. He shook his head again. The detective pressed his pen against his chin and looked up, then he shook his head and waved Don away. Don came back inside.

"It's a shit show," Don said. "They don't know what the hell they're doing." Dale sat back at the table.

"You're next, Vernon," I said. Vernon took a black New Testament bible out of his pocket and walked out to the detective. Vernon shook his head. He raised his hand and looked at the sky, then started tapping his bible as he spoke. The detective looked at Vernon and squinted, then pointed at the Brass Rail. Vernon shook his head. The detective wrote in his book and waved Vernon away.

"Vernon is a religious nut," Don said.

Vernon came back in with his chest raised. "Praise be to God," he said.

"Christ, Vernon, what's wrong with you?" Don asked. Vernon ignored him.

Gary walked out to the detective. He shook his head. He pulled a paper out of his wallet and showed the detective. The detective took it and walked to his car. He grabbed a bigger notebook and wrote in it. He walked over to a uniform and spoke with him for a minute. Then, he went back to Gary. Gary nodded. The detective motioned him away and Gary came back.

"What did you show him?" Kenny asked.

"I told him I work at McDonalds at night. I showed him my pay stub and told him who my supervisor was," Gary said.

"Did he explain what's happening?" Larry asked. Gary shook his head. The detective motioned and I walked out.

"Are there more people that work here?" The detective held the larger notebook at his side. The smaller one was back in his shirt pocket.

"Yes, six other people work at night."

"When do they come in?"

"Five."

"Okay, tell them they need to be interviewed and not to leave. I'll be back." The detective turned and walked away. He lifted the yellow tape and went into the Brass Rail.

"What did he say?" Kenny asked when I went back.

"He said he'll be back to talk to the night crew."

"One of the psycho night crew probably killed the bartender," Don said.

"Don, you don't know that," I repeated.

"You're part of the psycho night crew," Larry said. Don squinted at Larry.

"Okay, everyone, let's get to work." I handed out the number sheets. At one, I drove home to get Candy, Colin, and Sapphire.

I drove into the parking lot in front of our townhouse. My neighbor was polishing his black Ford F150 truck. He sold parts to manufacturers. I pulled into the space next to him and got out. The doors on our brick faced houses were only twenty feet apart. The sidewalk allowed a five-foot space for landscaping against the wall. Someone forced the shrubs to be square and the trimmings on the ground showed they had recently assaulted them.

"Howdy, neighbor," I said. Michael glanced up from the chrome extended mirrors he was waxing.

"Hi Tim. You're home early."

"Yes, for an hour. Your truck looks great. Why do you need a truck? You just sell, not deliver, right?"

"Yes. Appearances mostly. When I'm seeing my customers, they don't trust you unless you're in a truck. They assume we can't move pipes and gears and such."

"Huh. weird. I'll talk to you later, Michael."

"See you later, Tim."

I opened the door into the ceramic tiled hallway. Colin spotted me and ran to grab my legs.

"Daddy!"

"Hi, son." I bent over to tickle his rib cage, which released his vice grip from me. I picked him up and threw him over my shoulder to pat his butt. I carried him into the living room to see Candy.

"Honey, my drivers told me about new homes in Gahanna. I've read that the Gahanna schools have an excellent reputation. Colin will be in kindergarten next year, I'd like to have him in those schools."

Candy was changing Sapphire's diaper. The not-so-subtle aroma of poop filled the air. She stood and handed me a rolled-up diaper.

"Get this outside. Baby girl had a blowout. I had to wash her entire body." I put Colin on the floor, and he followed me out to the trash.

"That stinks," Colin said. He pinched his nose.

"It sure does, son." We walked back inside.

"I'm ready to look at houses," Candy said. She had dressed Sapphire in a soft pink, clean one piece and was buckling her into the carrier.

Colin held my hand as I carried Sapphire to the car. Candy locked up the house.

We drove to Gahanna and found a construction site on Ashford Glen Drive. There was one two-story house with a concrete driveway leading to a two-car garage. The exterior was mostly tan stucco, but the builders accented the front with brick. A concrete pathway wound to a small front porch wrapped in neatly trimmed bushes. The front door was red with shiny brass hardware, including a kick plate. The yard had sod that still showed the separation from when they unrolled them. Posted in the grass was a for lease or sale sign.

The house sat as an oasis among brown dirt and gravel. There were twenty basement foundations holding frames for walls and roofs circling a common area left unused.

"This looks perfect," I said. "It looks like it has a Colin-sized yard. The center of the construction area looks like it'll be a park. Colin could go full blast here."

"That'd be nice. Maybe he'd take a nap then," Candy said. We laughed.

"And maybe, I'd see my glass people here."

"You haven't seen them since we've been here?" Candy looked at me.

"No. Maybe I need a large yard like we had in Denver."

"We don't have credit. How will we get a house?" Candy focused on the front door. It had twelve inches wide, door height windows on each side. It looked like a carved crystal. "I like that entrance a lot."

Chapter 26

"YES, THE ENTIRE HOUSE is nice. As far as credit, we didn't have it when we got the townhouse."

"Yeah, but that's because it was Saturday, and they couldn't check your credit."

"I know. Sheena whispered something in the realtor's ear and then she let us move in."

"Yeah, but it pissed her off on Monday, when she found out we didn't have any credit," Candy said. She shook her head.

"Well, I've always paid my rent on time. We're better tenants than the ones next to us. Not Michael, the other side of us."

"There's always a funny smell coming from there," Candy wrinkled her nose.

"I think it's the cooking. Ethnic food. There's twelve people living there. There's only supposed to be three."

"It'll be nice not to smell that food anymore, and they're awfully noisy. They wake up Sapphire."

"Do you like this house, Candy? The sign says it has four bedrooms. It's got a two-car garage. It's brand new."

"I do like it; I'd like to live here." Candy nodded. "But why is only one house finished?"

"They probably use this as a model to sell the other ones. Alright, I'll call the realtor this afternoon." We went to Denny's for lunch and then drove back home. I returned to the office at four and called the agent.

"Eastern Real Estate, this is Brian Williams," a man answered.

"I'm calling about that house you have listed on Ashford Glenn. It's a new building," I said.

"Yes, that's for lease."

"Do you have an option to buy?" Don hobbled to me with a ticket. I smiled and winked at him, then pinned it on the map.

"If you sign a two-year lease, we'll give you an option to buy."

"That'd be great. I'm sure within two years, I could arrange financing. How much is the lease?"

"Twelve hundred a month."

"My wife and I would love to have it. We have a four-year-old son and new baby."

"Did you see we're building houses around it?" Brian asked.

"Yes. Are you building a park in the middle?"

"Yes, it'll be a common area for all the homes. We'll grass it over."

"That's perfect for us. Am I allowed to put a play set in the backyard?" I asked.

He paused, then said, "You can build wooden ones from professional kits. We don't want an eyesore. That's in the lease."

"That's not a problem. I'll do that. What do I do now?"

"Well, as I was saying, you see we're building around that house. So far, no one wants to live with the noise."

"Yeah, I've been in construction. I know how that is. I think we can handle the noise."

He paused again. "The work crew starts at seven AM sometimes."

"We can deal with that." Kenny brought me a ticket for the map. I nodded and smiled.

"Alright, come to my office to sign the lease."

"Can I come by tomorrow afternoon?"

"That'll be fine. We're at 630 Morrison Road, suite 310."

"Thank you, sir." I hung up and called Candy. "Honey, the realtor said to come over and sign the lease tomorrow afternoon."

"Did he ask you about your credit?"

"No, he didn't."

"He's probably going to check it and we won't get the house."

"It doesn't hurt to try."

"I won't get my hopes up. What about the lease on our townhouse?"

"Sheena said she'd take care of it."

"How?"

"I don't know. She didn't say anything. I'll talk to you later, honey, I love you." As I hung up, I saw the detective in the parking lot. He was looking at license plates and writing in his notebook. He finished and walked inside to see me.

"I need to talk to everybody I didn't talk to this morning," he told me.

"Sammie, the Detective wants to talk to you outside." Sammie had just hung up her phone and turned to look at me. Then she looked at the detective.

"What'd I do?"

"Somebody murdered the bartender next door," Don said.

Sammie's eyes widened and she looked at Don. "It wasn't me," she said.

"Shut up, Don, nobody said anybody was murdered," Larry said. Sammie followed the detective outside and talked to him. I was too busy to watch. As the evening went by, he routinely took each person out to interview them, then he left.

Larry, Michael and Vernon came up to my desk and asked, "What's that detective up to?"

"I don't know any more than you guys do," I said.

"Don says someone murdered a bartender next-door."

"Don's just guessing. He doesn't know. Maybe it'll be on the ten o'clock news tonight." They straggled back to their tables.

I finished the workday, closed, and went home. I turned on the news. I told Candy why I was watching it. Halfway through the news, they finally had a breaking story from Whitehall. A murder at the Brass Rail Pub. Dang, Don must be psychic. Somebody murdered the bartender at about one AM. He wasn't discovered until this morning by the owner.

"Do you think it was one of your people?" Candy asked.

"God, I hope not," I said. I scanned through my salespeople in my mind.

The next afternoon, I took Candy and the kids to the leasing office. We pulled into the parking lot of a three-story brick building with tall tinted windows. The rows of spaces had lines of trees on raised landscaping of black mulch and concrete curbing.

When we entered the building, the lobby sported a huge fountain. Colin released my hand and ran toward the pool. I let him put his hand in the water. To be safe, I held the back of his shirt. That kid would dive in if the spirit moved him.

We took the elevator with dark wood, chrome accents and oriental designed carpeting to the third floor. There we stepped onto shined marble, followed the numbers, and found suite 310. A lady was at the reception desk.

"Hello, I'm Tim Drobnick. I'm here to see Mr. Williams."

"Yes, he's expecting you. I'll take you back to his office." She stood and we followed her down a brown carpeted hall to an open door. She stopped, faced us, and put her hand palm up toward a man seated at a grand mahogany desk. "This is Mr. Williams, please go in."

"Thank you, Ma'am," I said. I let Candy enter first and then followed. Mr. Williams stood to greet us and reached out his hand. I shook it.

"Hello Mr. Williams, I'm Tim Drobnick. I talked to you on the phone about leasing the home on Ashford Glen Drive yesterday. This is my wife, Candy."

"Yes, Mr. Drobnick, have a seat," he pointed to the chairs by his desk.

"You can call me, Tim."

"You can call me, Brian."

"Thank you, Brian." I set Colin on a chair next to me so I could catch any quick escapes. I set the baby carrier between my chair and the one Candy sat in. Candy unbuckled Sapphire and picked her up. "Brian, my credit is new. We're leasing a townhouse right now. I don't have credit cards or anything yet to show you, but we've been paying our rent on time and I have a good management job."

"Oh, I see." Brian leaned back and put his hands together, forming a tent with his fingers. He paused for a minute, but it seemed like an hour. "Hm, we're having a hard time getting somebody in this place because of the construction noise. If you give me an extra thousand dollars on the deposit and your current landlord gives you a good written recommendation, I'll let you in, okay?"

"Oh, that's great, thank you, yes and the extra thousand's not a problem." I smiled at Candy. She frowned.

"I need to see your IDs for the lease. If you want to wait in the reception area, Julie will get it prepared and then we can sign it. If you write a check today, the lease will go into effect as soon as the check clears and you bring me the written recommendation from your landlord."

"Yes, we can wait. How long will it be?" The volcano that was Colin would explode if he sat too long. I looked at him. He was wiggling and had his eye on expensive things on the shelves.

"Julie should have it ready in thirty minutes." Brian said.

"Okay. I think we can control this little guy that long. Thank you, Brian." We stood and walked out into the reception room. Julie was the administrative person as well. She took our ID's and opened a file on her word processor. We sat as she typed.

Plants adorned the corners. Shelves on the walls held awards and pictures of buildings. In one corner was a model house. It looked like the one we were moving into.

"Daddy, can I play with that house?" Colin spotted it. Of course.

"No, son, that's not a toy. But it's pretty cool, huh? We can look at it." We walked over and I held his hands that could move at the speed of light if something sparked his interest.

We kept Colin entertained until Julie finished. Candy and I signed the lease and I wrote a check. We shook Brian's hand and went home.

Chapter 27

A S WE ENTERED OUR living room, Candy was humming. "I can't wait to get the keys so we can look around inside. Maybe we should've looked inside first," Candy said.

"No, the iron was hot. I was going to strike. I'm sure it's beautiful inside, it's brand new. We saw the outside. It has four bedrooms and a full basement. I'm allowed to build a play set in the back for Colin and it's got a park attached to it. I think we're set."

"You're right," Candy said. "What if we can't get a recommendation letter from our landlord? Then we lose the house?"

"Sheena said she'd take care of this. I believe her."

"Well. Okay." Candy pursed her lips together.

"Alright, I'm going to be home at 9:30 for dinner. Is that okay with you?"

"Yes, I'll cook us something special to celebrate." Candy's smile came back.

"That'd be great, baby." I leaned in for a kiss, she kissed me back. After work, I came home, and Candy had dinner ready for us. We sat at the table.

"I made pork chops," Candy said. She set a hot plate in the center of the table.

"I love these, baby, thank you." I rubbed my hands together and leaned forward to smell the sizzling aroma.

"And I made mashed potatoes." She brought in a bowl from the kitchen. She sat it next to the pork chops. "And gravy." I took the gravy boat from her and set it next to the potatoes.

"Candy, this meal looks delicious." As Candy sat, I saw something odd. "What is that?" Something wiggled on Candy's plate. Candy looked at it.

"Oh my God, what is that?" she said. She jumped up and pushed back from the table. I grabbed her plate. It was the size of a quarter but dark. And oblong. I held it closer, and I saw antennae and legs.

"Oh my god, it's a cockroach," I said. I sat the plate down quickly.

"Where did it come from?" Candy asked.

"I don't know." Another fell into the mashed potatoes and made tracks as it squirmed. Another fell into the pork chops. Two more into the potatoes. They started falling onto the table like dirty rain. I looked up at the ceiling beam above the table. It was swarming with cockroaches invading us from the cracks.

"Tim," Candy screamed. She started picking cockroaches off Colin and Sapphire.

"Tim, look." Candy pointed to the ceiling. A flood of cockroaches squeezing through the space next to the ceiling were coming from our stinky neighbors. The rain of cockroaches became a hailstorm landing on our hair and arms, crawling down our shirts.

"Oh, my God." I grabbed Colin. "Candy, grab Sapphire, let's get out of here."

Candy was breathing heavily and talking in a treble voice, "This is a nightmare. Where did those come from?" We stood outside and batted the roaches off the kids. Colin cried.

"It's okay buddy, I'm getting them off you."

"They're wiggling in my pants," Colin cried. I unsnapped his pants and slipped them off. I picked him up and wiped them off his legs. Candy had undressed Sapphire and was knocking them off her. I stomped on them as they scurried away. Some scurried back toward us. After stomping and batting and combing for twenty minutes, we were rid of them.

"They're obviously coming from the family of twelve people. None are coming from Michael's side," I said. Candy and I got the kids in their car seats and then sat, panting, in the front seat.

"I'm going to get roach spray." I started the car, and we drove to Kroger. The parking lot was half full and well lit. I pulled into a spot near the front between two other cars. We sat quietly, recovering from the shock we had.

"Candy, look." I pointed. Candy looked. "People returning to their cars on each side of us. A reminder my ghosts are here."

"Why did they let the cockroaches attack us?" Candy asked.

"Their job isn't to make our life easier. Although often, they do."

"What is their job?"

"Honestly, I don't know. I know they have protected us many times. And guided us. Let's go inside." We walked inside the clean supermarket and relaxed. We went to the delicatessen. Candy and Colin ate ten-cent hot dog specials and a cookie. I got four cans of roach spray and three cans of roach foam. After we followed Colin around the store for half an hour, we returned home.

"Candy, why don't you sit in the car while I go inside to spray. I don't want the poison to hurt you or the kids," I said.

"Okay, I'll sit out here. I locked the car doors, then walked inside. When I looked at the ceiling, I jumped back. There was a dark cloud of roaches moving across it. I held a can up to spray them and roaches fell around me. Several landed on my shoulders and hair. I flung them off and ran back to the front door. After the ceiling was clear, more roaches invaded. I climbed on a chair holding the can of bug killer. I pushed the nozzle into the cracks, releasing the foam. I filled all the cracks along the top of the ceiling. Then I worked on the beams that crossed the room.

When it seemed I had stopped the invasion, I started vacuuming the furniture and the floor to suck up the dead carcasses. The vacuum filled quickly, and I emptied it into the trash, then continued vacuuming. After being inside for forty minutes, Candy knocked on the door. I opened it. She was holding the baby and Colin's hand.

"Colin needs to go to the bathroom," Candy said.

"Take him upstairs, don't look in the living room. I'm still cleaning." Candy walked upstairs. I filled and emptied the vacuum bag of carcasses three more times. Each time I dumped them in the outside dumpster.

"Candy, it's okay to come down now." Candy walked down the stairs, holding the baby.

"What are we going to do? This place needs to be disinfected." Candy said.

"I know. Let's go stay in a hotel tonight. I'll call management first thing in the morning." Candy packed a small bag for us and we drove to the holiday express. The next morning, I called management.

"Metro Real Estate Management, this is Marjorie," the lady answered.

"Marjorie, I need to talk to the manager about our townhouse."

"Is it something I can help you with?" Marjorie asked.

"I don't know. We had an invasion of roaches last night," I said.

"Oh my, I'll patch you back to Dorothy." I waited for a minute.

"This is Dorothy," she answered.

"Dorothy, this is Tim Drobnick, we're one of your 5322 Great Oak Drive, Whitehall tenants. Last night, we had a horrible invasion of roaches coming from our neighbors. The ones that have twelve tenants."

"What unit are you in?"

"Unit B."

"We don't have any units with twelve people," Dorothy said.

"Well, you may not know about it, but they do. They park several of their taxi cabs out front and there's always a funny smell coming from them. Whatever they're doing over there is breeding cockroaches. I vacuumed up three bags full of them. I used up eight bottles of roach spray. Our place needs to be sanitized before we can live there. We were in a hotel last night."

"Sir, I will call and check with them."

"What's there to check?"

"I'll see if your neighbors are having roach problems."

"Does it really matter? We're having the problem either way."

"Sir, I'll call you back." Dorothy hung up the phone. Well, that didn't sound promising.

"Candy, do you want to stay here in the hotel today? I'll call her back after I get to work." I hugged Colin and let him fall back onto the bed with a bounce. He laughed.

"Yes, we can enjoy the pool and the cafe." Candy said. "God knows we can all use some peace of mind."

"That's a good idea. A mini vacation. I'll see you guys later. Call me if you need me." I left for work. At one o'clock, I called Dorothy. I didn't see how she was going to call me back; she didn't have my telephone number.

"Hello, Dorothy, this is Tim Drobnick again."

"Yes, Mr. Drobnick, I called your neighbors on each side of you. Neither of them has a roach problem."

"Of course, Michael in Unit A doesn't have a roach problem because I stopped them all coming in from Unit C, the unit with twelve people. And Unit C won't complain because they don't want you to learn they've got too many people living there."

"Sir, there's no proof you have roaches. I can't do anything for you."

"You've got to be kidding me," I said.

"I'm sorry, Mr. Drobnick, there's nothing I can do for you." Dorothy hung up.

Crap, I thought.

Chapter 28

I CHECKED ON OUR townhouse. The roaches were back. They had tiny little picket signs saying, "Poison or no, we won't go." I rushed over to the drugstore and grabbed a disposable camera with a flash. I returned and took a dozen pictures. I held up a newspaper to prove it was today. Then I ran over to the one-hour photo shop to get them developed. As soon as they were ready, I called Dorothy.

"Dorothy, I have photos of all the roaches that are back today. Come see the roaches. If you prefer, I can bring the pictures to you."

"Mr. Drobnick, sir, I told you there's nothing we can do."

"Will you come here, or should I bring the pictures to you?" There was a long pause.

"I'll come over," Dorothy said.

"Can you be here within an hour? I have to get back to work."

"Yes, I'll be right over." I sat outside in my car, waiting for Dorothy to show up. An hour and a half later, she arrived.

She stepped out of her dark blue Honda Accord Sedan. Glistening beads on the hood showed she had her car washed on the way to see me. She had business clothing, a mid-length dark gray dress and sports coat with sensible low heel shoes. Her thin and stern face had the slightest shade of red lipstick.

"Are you Dorothy?" I asked.

"Yes, I am. I presume you're Tim Drobnick?"

"Yes Ma'am. Please come inside." I opened the door and entered before her. My usual rule was to allow guests and ladies to enter first, but I wanted to see her face when I flipped the lights to reveal my grazing herd of roaches. Although most seemed happy to graze in the light, anyway.

"Dorothy, I'm going to turn on the light. Many of the roaches will scatter. Look at the ceiling." I pushed the switch, lighting the room. The ceiling was moving like a sea of brown water. When the light hit, the sea became a roiling storm.

Dorothy slapped her hand to her chest and screamed, dropping her satchel.

"See, I wasn't lying to you." I pointed at the roaches scrambling into the crack toward the stinky neighbors.

Dorothy sputtered some words, but I didn't understand them. She picked up her satchel with two fingers and ran out the door. I followed her. She stood in the parking lot breathing heavily and knocking roaches off her sleeve.

"That was a dirty trick, Mr. Drobnick." Dorothy stomped her feet and looked over her arms and legs for any bugs refusing to leave.

"You didn't believe me. What else could I do? Just live with the roaches?"

"You must have garbage attracting the roaches. It has to be you because your neighbors are roach free."

"Michael's roach free because I kill them before they get to him. They're coming from there. I pointed at the stinky neighbors. Knock on the door. You can look inside." Dorothy walked to her car and opened the door, throwing the satchel into the passenger's seat.

"Aren't you going to investigate?" I raised my arms. "Isn't it possible I'm telling the truth?"

Dorothy slammed her door shut and glared at me. She walked stiffly to the door and knocked. No one answered. "Nobody's home," Dorothy said.

"Yes, they are. Look at their taxicabs." I banged on the door with my fist without stopping. The door opened. I stepped back and let Dorothy approach.

"Your neighbor has a roach problem we're checking to see if you have one," Dorothy said.

"No, no roaches here." The man shut the door.

"You're right. There are many people inside." She hesitated, then knocked. The man opened the door.

"Sir, too many people are residing here. Your lease allows three people," Dorothy said.

"They visiting. Be gone in hour," the man said.

"They're here around the clock," I said. "And there are foul smells. I see the roaches coming in from their unit through the cracks."

"May I come in?" Dorothy asked. She tipped her nose up and sniffed.

"No," the man said. "You give twenty-four hours' notice."

"Fine," Dorothy said. She went to her car and came back with her clipboard. She wrote a note and handed it to him. "Here's your twenty-four-hour notice. I'll be back tomorrow to inspect." The roach king shut the door.

"That's all I can do for now." Dorothy straightened her sleeves and blouse. A last check for roaches, I assumed.

"Will you sanitize our place after you fix the roach problem?" I asked. "We're living in a hotel right now."

"Mr. Drobnick, that is not in your lease."

"Dorothy, having roaches isn't in my lease either."

"We'll talk about it tomorrow, Mr. Drobnick. If there are no roaches in your neighbors' unit, then you'll be the one paying for damages."

"I won't pay you to fix this, it's not my fault."

"We'll sue you then."

"Lady, that can go both ways," I said. Dorothy said nothing and crawled into her car and left.

The next morning, I saw an exodus of ten people next door. They got in their taxis and left. Dorothy met me at three PM.

"They all left, ten of them, this morning. See, only one taxi here today." I pointed.

Dorothy took a quick look but mostly ignored me. She went to their door and knocked. I stood with her.

"You're not allowed to come inside with me," Dorothy said.

"That's fine, I'll wait here."

"I'm here for the inspection," Dorothy said when the door opened.

"Come in," my neighbor said. She walked in. My neighbor frowned at me, then shut the door. After ten minutes, I heard repeated screaming. Dorothy busted out the door with her eyes wide, gagging and covering her mouth with her hand.

"What did you see in there?" I asked.

Dorothy bent over, putting her hands on her knees. I picked up the clipboard she dropped and walked up to her.

"Are you okay?" I asked. She was hyperventilating. I waited for her to calm down. After two minutes, she stood up and faced me.

"I went to the kitchen to inspect. It was clean. Even the oven appeared unused. Their microwave was spotless. I noticed the smell of strong food you mentioned. But there's no rules against that."

"Why were you screaming then?" I asked. Dorothy took a moment to breathe.

"I went to inspect the living room and looked at the ceiling crack between your buildings. The one that your roaches were coming from. Or going through. There were a few bugs, but not a lot. I assumed this meant the problem was from your side. But then I noticed a fifty-five-gallon rubber trash can by the back sliding doors but inside the living room. I thought that was unusual, so I lifted the lid. That's when millions of roaches and a putrid smell poured out. That's when you heard me scream."

"So, do you believe me now?"

"Yes. I can see they are the source of the infestation, not you. There were only two people inside, however."

"They left this morning. They knew the inspection was coming. What are you going to do?" I asked. Dorothy knocked on the door. The man opened it.

"Sir, we will have to fumigate your place and penalize you for the roaches," Dorothy said.

"Roaches come from him." The man pointed at me.

"No, they're not. If I had roaches, both my neighbors would have them," I said.

"We will fumigate," Dorothy said. "But someone is paying a penalty."

"So, I have to live in a hotel even longer? Are you going to sanitize our house?"

"No, we'll have it fumigated and that's it."

"No, I'm not happy with that. I can't bring my family back to this place before you sanitize it. If you won't, then I need you to let me out of my lease so I can move."

"That's all I can do. We're not letting you out of your lease." She turned and left.

I kicked at the gravel in frustration, placed my hands on my hips, and gazed at the sky. This wasn't over. I got in my car to return to the hotel.

I walked through our hotel room door. "Candy, Dorothy saw the roaches. She said they're going to fumigate the place, but she won't sanitize it. And she won't let us out of the lease either."

"What are we going to do now?" Candy asked.

"I don't know."

"Colin's been complaining that his ear is hurting the little poor guy," Candy said.

Colin was lying on the bed. I sat by him. "Which ear hurts, son?" He pointed at his left ear. I peered inside, but he cried when I touched his ear. "We can't leave him like this. I'll call the pediatrician and see if we can get in there today." I called, and they told us to come in.

We traveled to the medical office. We sat in the waiting room, Colin on my lap. He was whining and leaning his head on my shoulder. After twenty minutes, we met with the pediatrician in an examination room. He bent down to look through his auto scope into Colin's left ear. He shook his head.

"What's wrong, Doctor?" I asked.

Chapter 29

"THERE'S SOMETHING IN THERE," he said. "Mr. Drobnick, hold his head still for me." He picked up long, thin tweezers and slid them carefully into his ear. He pinched then pulled out a one-and-a-half-inch long roach.

"Oh my God," Candy said. She covered her mouth.

"What is it?" Colin asked.

"Nothing, Son, nothing," I kept his head turned away. The doctor put the wiggling roach into a plastic bag and sealed it.

"What's going to happen to him?" Candy asked.

"He'll be just fine," the doctor said. The doctor looked in Colin's ear for a minute. He walked to the cabinet and grabbed a glass bottle and put three drops into Colin's ear.

"Doctor, would you write a note about this? I'm trying to get out of our lease. The neighbors caused this. Our house is infested with," I looked at Colin, then back at the doctor, "this. They won't do anything to help us. We're living in a hotel."

"I'd be happy to write a note," he said. The doctor laid the auto scope on the stainless-steel table and turned the wheeled stool to his desk. He took out a prescription pad and scribbled. We took the note, thanked the doctor, and left. When we got back to the hotel, I called Dorothy.

"Candy, cover Colin's ears. Dorothy, this is Tim Drobnick. We took our son to the doctor and he pulled a big roach out of his ear. I have a note from the Doctor. I'll sue if you don't let us out of our lease. And I also want a recommendation letter for our next landlord."

Dorothy was quiet for thirty seconds, then said, "Yes, Mr. Drobnick, we'll release you."

"I'll be there in thirty minutes to pick it up." I hung up the phone. My next call was to Eastern Real Estate.

"Hi Brian, this is Tim. I have a recommendation letter from my current landlord. I could bring it to you within an hour and a half."

"Good, Tim. Bring it to me," Brian said.

"Can I pick up the keys today?"

"Yes, you may."

"Thank you, Brian." I hung up the phone. Candy was looking at me. Her smile showed her teeth. She squealed and hugged Sapphire to her shoulder.

"Candy, I'm going to go pick up this release and the recommendation letter. Then I'm going over to the realtor's office. Do you want to come with me?"

"I think I should stay here and let Collin rest."

"I think that's a good idea. I'll get new mattresses and some utensils for the house. Sunday I can take our clothing to the laundromat, so we don't bring roach eggs with us. I'll run the dishes in the dishwasher."

"Okay, that'll be an enormous relief. Sheena did what she promised. She got us out of our lease," Candy said. "I wish she would have thought of an easier way to do it."

"Yeah, she says we have lessons to learn. At least we're out."

"What would the lesson from this be?" Candy asked.

"I have no idea." I shook my head. "But I'm not going to complain."

The next morning in my office, I was at my desk. I heard a voice behind me.

"Hey, Timmy, I'm here to do a spot inventory." I turned around to see Jeff, our new district manager. He had arrived from the back door, his snakeskin boots clopping over the tile. He had a toothpick hanging out of his mouth and a western cut shirt with shiny snaps.

"Jeff, first of all, really? And second of all, call me Tim, not Timmy."

"Dagger told me your name is Timmy." He pulled the toothpick out of his cheek.

"It is not. I consider that demeaning and I have told him so. He says it to be an ass."

"Fine. I'm going to do an inventory. That was Harley's instructions." Jeff plucked his cowboy hat off and laid it on a table.

"I understand, go ahead." I turned back to my desk. Jeff took an inventory sheet from my desk drawer and walked to the piles of inventory. I glanced at him as he tapped the boxes to count them, then went back to my business.

"Now, I need the inventory you gave your drivers," Jeff said. I pulled a clipboard from the wall and gave it to him. I watched him count. At least the guy could do math.

"Everything's fine. So how are sales today?"

"Good as usual, Jeff."

"But how much?"

"We're at $800." I turned and leaned against my desk to give Jeff my attention.

"That doesn't sound like much." Jeff walked to the whiteboard where I wrote the names of my salespeople and tallied their sales.

"It's only ten AM." I shook my head.

"I'm looking at your roster, isn't Johnny supposed to be working today?" Jeff scanned the roster with his finger.

"He made four hundred bucks, so I cut him off."

"When did you cut him off?"

"Last night." I turned my back to Jeff to take sales tickets from three salespeople. "Good job," I told them.

"He made four hundred bucks by Wednesday?" Jeff asked.

"Yeah, he's an ace."

"I bet if you let him work all week, he'd make twice as much." Jeff popped the toothpick in his mouth and grinned like he invented a genius idea. He placed his hands on his hips and looked at me.

"You're probably right, but then we wouldn't see him for two weeks." I walked to the map to pin tickets for the drivers.

"Why's that?" Jeff raised one eyebrow.

"Because if he earns more than $400, he goes on a bender. He needs about four hundred bucks to pay his bills and have some extra for beer and gambling."

"Well, that's just stupid. You need to let him work." Jeff shook his head and took the toothpick out of his mouth again.

"No, I won't let him work. I'd rather have money from him every week than once a month. Plus, it's not good for him to go on those benders."

"Well--" Jeff paused. "Stay on top of things. I'm going to the next office."

"See you later, Jeff," I said. I watched as he aligned his cowboy hat, one hand on the front, the other on the back. He walked out the front door to his car. That made me wonder why he had entered from the rear. I needed to check the alley, I noted to myself. The phone rang and I answered.

"Tim, this is Kwame in Cincinnati. I'm almost out of lightbulbs."

"Alright, hold on, I'll have Jeff bring some down to you." I ran outside. "Hey, Jeff," I yelled.

"What?" Jeff was backing out but stopped and looked out his window at me.

"Kwame needs light bulbs. Take some of my inventory to him."

"I wasn't going to Cincinnati."

"Well, where are you going?"

"That's none of your business."

"Kwame is out of inventory. If you want your district to make money, you need to keep our rooms stocked."

Jeff parked the car, slammed the door, and walked back in. His cowboy boots clipped across the tile. He grabbed a two-wheeler and stacked boxes on it.

"After you finish loading, I need a receipt for those," I said.

"You know you're not my boss, right?" Jeff sat the two-wheeler upright and looked at me.

"You know I'm responsible for the inventory, right? I need a receipt," I said. He snatched the receipt book from my desk, filled it out, then threw the book on my desk. Then he walked out, shaking his head.

I called Kwame. "Kwame, I'm sending fifty boxes to you. I'll talk to Harley about getting more inventory shipped."

"Thanks a lot Tim."

"You're welcome. Kwame, sounds like you have a busy room, how's it going?"

"I have the phones full. Not bad for the morning shift." Kwame sounded extra perky. His productive energy was producing a productive sales force.

"Kwame, I'm proud of you. Keep kicking butt. I'll get the inventory supply under control."

"Thanks, Tim."

My next call was to Harley. "Harley, this is Tim."

"Hey Tim, how's it going?" I could hear laughter and glasses clinking in the background.

"I just sent Jeff to Cincinnati with fifty boxes of lightbulbs. Kwame's completely out. We need to get accurate shipments. The managers keep running out of inventory. Who's ordering the inventory?"

"I've been doing it." Music started blaring in the background.

"Harley, you got a party at your house?" It was too early in the morning for a party, even for Harley.

"I've got a few friends over. Come on over if you want to." I knew Harley's friends were probably women. Women getting naked in his pool. Harley liked to party a little too much, in my opinion.

"I appreciate the invitation, but I have a sales crew to take care of. About the inventory, what if I calculate shipments needed weekly, and send you the count?"

"Better yet," Harley said, "I'll give you the fax number. You can put the orders in yourself."

"That works. Thanks a lot Harley." Harley was happy to give me his chores. I was happy because it gave me more control over my destiny.

After two minutes, Harley returned to the phone. "Okay, the number is 614 555-2315. You need to put account #59235 on it."

"Thanks, Harley."

"No, thank you Tim." Someone squealed. Harley hung up.

Chapter 30

I PUT TOGETHER A spreadsheet that calculated how much inventory each office needed, based on the previous three weeks' sales. I faxed an order to be delivered on the following Monday. Then, I called the offices and told them to expect regular inventory deliveries on Mondays. I'd make sure they wouldn't run out from now on. They needed to call me every Monday with the inventory count from Saturdays.

My next call was from Dagger. "Timmy," he said. I didn't hear any background noise. No Harley parties or phone room buzz.

"It's Tim, Sir, and what can I do for you?"

"Why are you letting Johnny work half a week?"

"I let Johnny work until he makes four hundred bucks and then I cut him off for the week."

"Why would you do that? We're making more money if he's there all week."

"No, we're not because if he makes more than $400, he goes on a bender, and he's gone for weeks."

"You let him work."

"Sir, that is not a good idea. It's not good for us and it's not good for him."

"This is an order. Put him to work." His voice increased slightly in volume and muffled like he had his teeth clenched.

My knees shook a bit.

"Okay, but it's not a good idea." Dagger hung up. Crap, if I let Johnny work, I'd lose him for a week or more. If I didn't, Dagger would come into the office, scream at me, and demotivate the crew. An hour later, Johnny came in to get his pay.

"Johnny, I don't think it's a good idea, but Dagger ordered me to let you work all week."

"Oh yeah, I could use some extra money," he said.

"Johnny, if you get more than $400, you go on a bender. It's not good for you. I think you're better off not working the rest of the week."

"There's a new VCR I wanted to buy. I could use the money for that." Johnny looked at me with hope in his eyes. I wanted him to see my point on this, but I couldn't force him to agree without Dagger wreaking havoc on my other salespeople.

"Okay, how about you let me hold your extra money and then when you get enough to get the VCR, I'll give it to you? Then, you show the VCR to me to verify how you spent your money?"

"That seems fair to me." Johnny smiled and his eyes widened.

At seven-PM, Jeff walked in the front door. Every phone had a salesperson and sales were plentiful. At that instant, everyone had a prospect. The room carried a unique buzz when everyone was simultaneously pitching. When that happened, the smoke cleared somewhat. When a salesperson was dialing or listening to the phone ring, they would puff away on their cigs. But when they started talking to a prospect, they set it aside. The smoke continued to rise from the ashtray, but not as fierce. I knew that buzz would bring a slew of tickets to the map. The last thing I needed was a distraction from Jeff. Jeff walked over to me.

"What's the big idea calling all the managers?" He asked.

"What are you talking about?" I asked.

"They told me you'd called and told them inventory was coming in on Monday. And to call you every week with their

close out count. That's not your job." Jeff's toothpick bobbed on
his lip as he talked. I wondered what oral fixation he was
substituting for that thing.

"It's not my job to order inventory, or it's not my job to call
the managers?"

"You're not to talk to the managers. That's my job."

"Jeff, I'm helping you do a better job. You're going to make
more money. What's wrong with that?"

"I'm the district manager. You work for me. You do what I
say." He turned and stomped out the door. Several salespeople
noticed the commotion. I waved with my hands to the side and
shook my head. My crew understood that to mean to just ignore
Jeff. They did. Jeff was going to be a problem.

The next night, Jeff arrived at eight. He stopped and observed
the telemarketers. They were busy and making sales as usual. He
walked back to me.

"Who's the new girl?" He had taken his toothpick out of his
mouth and stood with his tongue hanging next to his lip and his
eyes wide open, gazing at the woman.

"That's Janet. I just hired her today. You can't call women,
'girls.'"

"She's hot."

"Okay."

"Hook me up with her." Jeff tugged on his belt to straighten
his pants, smoothed his western shirt sleeves, and kicked his
boots against my desk. My guess is that he was preening in a
bizarre cowboy ritual.

"What?" I frowned.

"I said, hook me up with her, I want to go out with her."

I stopped pinning tickets and turned to Jeff, "I thought you
were a married man."

"I am, but everybody likes a little strange, right?"

"Jeff, number one, I'm not your pimp. Number two, it's
against our company policy to date people we manage."

"I'm your boss and you'll do what I say." Jeff touched the front of his hat, then crossed his arms as he glared at me.

"Jeff, I'm regretting recommending you to be district manager."

"You had nothing to do with that. I was the best man for the job, that's why Harley picked me," Jeff said. He put his fists on his hips.

I turned back to the map. *I'll just ignore this clown*, I thought. Jeff hung around until nine. After everybody hung up their phones, he went over to talk to Janet. He leaned over. He positioned one hand on the table next to her and the other on his hip. He flashed his teeth. Janet edged over in her chair, away from him. Jeff was saying something, to which she smiled and shook her head. It appeared she shot him down in flames, which was good, but I didn't want us getting into lawsuits over sexual harassment. After Jeff left, I gave Harley a call and told him what happened.

"I'll call my managers and tell them to keep an eye on him, but he's going to be a problem for us if he doesn't straighten up," I told Harley.

"I'll talk to him," Harley said.

"Harley, would you prefer to call the managers?" I could hear laughing and music at Harley's house.

"No, you do it."

"Thanks, Harley."

The next day at noon, Jeff stomped in. He clenched his fists and mouth. He stepped up to me and pointed. Three of the salespeople were filling up their mugs from the gourmet pot. Don and Larry were outside on a break, talking about something amusing. Don was waving his cigarette in the air as he told a story. Larry had a half smile but laughed. I had the front door hanging open since the day was warm. Fresh air was a luxury for me and I'd take it whenever I could.

"Follow me, I need to talk to you," he glowered and stomped his boots toward the back. I followed him into the alley. His lizard skins crunched on the gravel as he turned like a hurricane to face me. I observed his fists, wary of what he would do with them.

"What the hell is wrong with you, talking to Harley behind my back?" Jeff took one step toward me, his jaw clamped.

"Oh, you mean about when I said you're not allowed to date employees and you did it, anyway?"

"I didn't take her out."

"Only because she turned you down. We can still get sued just for asking her."

"You're not in charge of me." Jeff took another step toward me. I stepped away from him.

"I don't want this entire company to go under because you get us sued for sexual-harassment. Everybody loses their job. So, I don't care if I'm in charge of you or not."

"If you ever talk about me again, there'll be consequences. I'll fire you." Jeff pointed his finger, tapping it on my chest. I backed up again.

"Okay, Jeff. I have a job to do." I went up front. Jeff left the alley to walk around the building.

I called my office managers and told them that Jeff asked a female out on a date and to keep an eye on him. If he does that in their office, let me know. I knew Jeff was a loose cannon and I was concerned he might hurt me, but I didn't sense evil in him like I did Dale or Dagger. He didn't scare me. The managers agreed to alert me to his misbehavior.

The phone rang. I answered, "New Day Marketing."

"Hello, is this the owner?"

"No, I'm the manager here."

"I'm calling from the Geraldo Rivera Show. Have you heard of him?"

Chapter 31

"I HAVE NOT HEARD of him, what does he do?" I asked.

"I can't believe you haven't heard of his show. He interviews entertaining guests."

"I don't watch TV, I'm too busy."

"I'm inviting you to be on the program."

"I'm not that entertaining."

"You don't need to be. I want you to come on and talk about your telemarketing company."

"Why would I want to do that?"

"To be on TV. You want to, right?"

"No."

"Everybody wants to be on TV."

"Not me."

"Well, how about the owner? Would he come on the show?"

"I can't imagine why he would."

"Give my number to him and tell him to call me, okay?"

"I'll do that." I hung up the phone.

I called Dagger, "Dagger, this is Tim in Whitehall."

"Hi Timmy."

"It's Tim, sir. Somebody called from the Geraldo Rivera Show."

"Really? What did they want?" Dagger's voice became friendly. Excited even.

"They want you to go on the program and talk about your telemarketing company."

"Oh, I'd love to do that. Wouldn't that be great?"

"You're kidding. Why would you talk about our company on TV?"

"Don't you want to?"

"No. Here's his phone number to call." I gave it to Dagger and hung up.

"What was that about?" Sammie asked? She set a sales ticket on my desk.

"That was your father-in-law."

"No, he's my son-in-law."

"Whatever. Geraldo Rivera wants him to go on the show."

"Really?" Sammie's eyes widened.

"Yeah, I don't know what the show's about."

"You've never seen the show?"

"No, I don't have time to watch television."

"It's pretty crazy."

"What do they talk about?"

"They bring all kinds of crazy people there. A woman accuses another woman of cheating on her with her husband. Then they bring the husband on and they fight about it."

"On TV?"

"Yeah."

"Do people actually watch that?

"It's one of the highest rated shows on TV."

"Oh my God, what's this world coming to?" I asked. Sammie shook her head and moved back to her phone. She groaned as she sat in her chair. Don moved the ashtray toward her so she could flick her ashes.

"Hey, Tim," Kenny said. He walked up to my desk. Cheryl was always right behind him. Kenny's three-day beard and shaggy hair gave him an aura of *I don't give a damn*. His clothes gave an aura of *Please wash me.*

"Hey, Kenny, what can I do for you?"

"I'm in desperate need of money. Can you give me an advance?"

"If you get a couple of sales, I'll give you an advance. If I give advances on no sales, I'll be broke and nobody will work."

"Okay, boss." Kenny went and sat by Cheryl and picked up the phone. I noticed he wasn't enthusiastic. I wasn't hopeful about his chances of getting sales.

"Uh oh," Sammie said. She was handing me a ticket and looking out the front door. "Here comes that detective."

"Maybe, they found out you were the murderer," Don said.

"Yeah right," Sammie said.

I walked over to the detective and stuck my hand out. "Hello Detective."

"Top of the day to you sir, I need to speak with two of your employees, a--" he pulled out his little flip notebook and looked at it, "Kenny and Cheryl Artiside."

"Yes, actually, they're here now, Kenny, Cheryl?" Kenny turned around.

"This detective wants to see you again."

"Detective Tallridge," the detective said. He looked at each of the telemarketers.

"Yes, sir, Detective Tallridge wants to speak to you." Kenny stood from his chair, looking at Cheryl. Cheryl looked down at her shoes and stood.

"Please follow me outside," Detective Tallridge said. He signaled with his index finger and walked through the door.

Everybody watched out the window after they finished their calls. The detective talked. Kenny shook his head vigorously while looking at the sky. Cheryl was looking at her feet and crying. A police cruiser arrived. Two uniformed officers got out and stood by the car.

"Jesus, what's going on?" Gary asked.

"They murdered that bartender," Don said. Don sat on the side of the table, leaning on one crutch. His cigarette hung between his fingers; the half inch ash ready to fall.

"You don't know that, Don," Larry said.

"Geez, he was right about the bartender being murdered. I hope he's not right about this one also," I said. Everyone became quiet and continued to watch. Kenny put his arm around Cheryl, who buried her face in his sleeve.

The detective pointed at the cruiser and one officer opened the door. Kenny and Cheryl got inside and the officer shut the door. The detective went over to his car and started talking on his radio. After thirty minutes, he came back over and talked to the officers. They opened the door and let Kenny and Cheryl out. And then they left. Kenny and Cheryl returned to our office.

"Geez, what was going on? Michael asked.

"He wanted proof of our whereabouts the night of the murder," Kenny said.

"Did you give it to him?"

"We told him we were at our hotel. They called our manager who said he saw our car there that night, but he didn't see us. He told us not to leave town."

Kenny walked over to me. "I could really use twenty bucks right now."

"Kenny," I said, "go make a couple sales and I'll give you twenty bucks."

"We've had nothing to eat today," Kenny said.

"There're sandwiches in the fridge. Grab a couple for you and Cheryl."

"I don't want sandwiches."

"Then you're not that hungry." Kenny clenched his fist and glared, then turned and went back to the phone. Cheryl sat by him. He started making calls. Cheryl never made calls herself; she just sat with Kenny while he worked.

"Okay, everybody, the show's over. Either go to work or leave. Come back for the evening shift. Everybody except Gary meandered outside. Gary put his hands in his pockets and looked at me.

"I still can't work on the evening shift," Gary said. "I have to work at McDonald's."

"Gary, come over here," I motioned. Gary walked over and I patted him on the back. "Congratulations, you did it, three weeks of making at least $200 each week. You can quit McDonald's now."

"Can I work the evening shift tonight?" Gary lifted his eyebrows and pulled his hands from his pockets.

"I'll squeeze you in," I said.

Gary made a single clap of his hands and walked to his table. He dialed the phone, then I heard him say, "Jim, this is Gary. I'm not coming in tonight. (Pause) No, I want to pick up my last paycheck. (Pause) Yes, I'm quitting. (Pause) Because I got another job. (Pause) Okay, talk to you later." Gary had a gigantic smile on his face as he hung up the phone. "Thanks, boss," he said. He walked out for a cigarette break. Unlike the others, Gary was always polite about smoking outside. He knew I was a non-smoker. It made little difference, however, as we usually had a cloud of smoke inside.

I left my trainees in charge and went home. After lunch with my family, I returned to my office at 4:30. At five, the phones were full, Vernon came in at 5:15.

"Tim, I need a phone," Vernon said. He looked around the room. He had his new testament with black leather cover in his hand. The gold edge and red silk page marker accented his dark suit.

"Well, they're occupied, but if somebody takes a break, I can let you use their phone."

"Why is Gary here tonight?"

"He's full time now."

"He's got my phone then." Vernon turned away from the telemarketers to frown at me.

"No, Vernon," I paused, "your phone was available at five and when you didn't show up, I gave it to someone else. Not necessarily Gary."

"But I'm a great writer. You should kick somebody else off."

"Vernon, you know my rules. I'll hold the phone for you till five o'clock. After that, if you're not here, I give it to somebody else. These phones need to be making money, not sitting idle."

"Why are you picking on me?" Vernon scowled at me and clenched his bible.

"I'm not picking on you."

"Did you take anybody else's phone away today?" Vernon shook his bible at the other workers.

"No, everybody else was on time," I said. Vernon stormed out of the room. Ten minutes later, he came back and talked in murmurs to Ron. Ron listened but shook his head. Vernon motioned him to follow him. Ron shook his head. Then Vernon walked over to Gabriel and whispered in his ear. Gabriel held the phone receiver against his chest and looked at Vernon. He shook his head. Vernon said something else. Gabriel shook his head. Vernon turned around and left while waving his bible.

It was Friday night and Johnny had earned enough money to get his VCR. I called him up to the desk.

"Alright, Johnny, here you go." I handed him his cash. "If you're going to get your VCR, go get it now. It's eight o'clock and the stores close in an hour. You're going to buy it tonight, right?" I asked.

"Yes," Johnny said.

"Alright, show it to me in the morning, Okay?"

"I sure will," Johnny said. He shoved the money in his front pocket and walked out the door. We finished out the night and I closed the office. I was alone and the parking lot was dark. I stood by the door scanning the cars, looking for anyone hiding.

After five minutes, satisfied I was safe, I walked to my car and drove off.

Chapter 32

"CANDY, I'M HOME," I said as I walked in the front door. Colin ran and jumped into my arms. I crossed my legs to fend off a kick to the groin and pulled him over my shoulder.

"Hi Tim, I'm in the kitchen," Candy said. She had the baby in a carrier sitting on the floor.

"How are you liking our new house?" I hung Colin upside down and ticked him. He wriggled and laughed.

"It's wonderful. I can't wait for Colin to have a playset to burn off his energy."

"Yes, I'll do that on Sunday. The company is delivering the kit on Saturday. It has a fort with a canvas roof, slides, ladders, and swings."

"I got some lawn chairs for us today they're out on the back patio," Candy said. "If you like, I can bring our dinner out there."

"Yes, I'd like that. Let me take Sapphire for you." I gingerly took the precious package from the carrier. "Colin, let's go outside." Colin jumped down the stairs to the patio and rocketed through the grass. I sat on one of the plastic chairs Candy had purchased. This was nicer than the townhouse. Sans roaches helped.

"Thank you, Sheena, for helping us get here," I said. A breeze kissed my face as if Sheena was saying, "You're welcome." Candy came out with a plate of food for me. I placed Sapphire in her baby carrier. I took the plate and Candy sat in the other chair. She brushed her blonde hair back from her face and sighed. She smiled as she watched Colin zooming over the common park.

"Candy, thank you for fixing dinner for me. I sure appreciate it. And thank you for getting these chairs." I lifted the plate to smell the food.

"You're welcome, and thanks for getting us this house." Candy sat her plate on her lap and looked at the sky. I could see she was relaxing.

"You're welcome, I had help."

"Sheena, huh?" Candy asked.

"Yes and I assume the other ghosts. And probably God."

"Why don't you know the other ghosts' names?"

"They never told me."

"Did you ever ask them?"

"Not that I remember. They're always around, but Sheena's the one that usually interacts with me. Remember that day we rescued that lady from the car pile-up on the icy highway?"

"Yes, I'll never forget that." Candy took a bite of peas.

"All three of my ghosts pushed that van. It wasn't just Sheena."

"I thought you and that lady were going to die."

"Yeah, me too, that van stopped only two feet from us."

"I wonder how she's doing?" Candy said.

"Hopefully, she's got a healthy child and is living a good life. And staying off the ice," I said. Candy laughed.

"I love this enormous area between the houses. Look at Colin run. It's like having the house we left in Denver, only this one's even better," I said.

"It sure is," Candy said. I stood and took her empty plate and carried it inside to rinse and put in the dishwasher. I walked back outside and sat by Candy. I reached over to grab her hand and she let me hold it.

"Candy, do you think you'll feel like making love soon? I miss us being together. I loved the intimate time we had on our vacation."

"Maybe soon." Candy said. We sat silently for five minutes.

"These floodlights are really bright. It'll let the kids play out here longer than normal," Candy said. No more mention of my request. We watched Colin run and scream. Fortunately, we had no neighbors yet.

"Candy, I see the glass people."

"You do?"

"Yes. Maybe, they only appear when there's a large yard."

"That's interesting. I wonder what they are?"

"I don't know. But it's very calming when I watch."

"What are they doing?" Candy asked.

"Looks like it's people walking down by the skyscrapers. Going and coming from work, I guess."

"Are there any colors yet?"

"No colors. The only color I ever saw was that yellow rose."

"I remember that. That's when you found out Rose was pregnant."

"Yes. Oh wait, I see yellow again. Looks like two men in yellow raincoats and a hood."

"What are they doing?"

"Just walking along with the other people."

"If I didn't know you better, I'd think you're crazy, you know."

"Yeah, I know. Maybe I'm schizophrenic. Seeing things that don't exist."

"But what you see comes true. How would you explain that?"

"Yeah, I hope I'm not crazy." I watched for thirty more minutes and then they left.

"The mosquitoes are coming out, let's go inside," Candy said. "Colin, come on, we're going inside."

After we had Colin asleep in bed, I asked Candy to sit with me in the living room.

"Candy, I have been wanting to talk to you about Crystal's birthday party. There is something bothering me."

"What is it?" Candy frowned.

"That guy dressed as Batman. You were letting him keep his arm around you. He was squeezing and hugging you, he even put his hand on your knee."

"I was just being polite, Tim."

"Candy, that bothers me. You should have been playing with me." Candy crossed her arms and clenched her teeth. She had a short fuse sometimes. I didn't want to fight, but I had a strong desire to explain my feelings.

"It was nothing. We were just having fun."

"Well, it wasn't fun for me. It hurt my feelings."

"I'm going to bed." Candy stood and went upstairs. My heart was beating harder. Candy upset me. It was useless to talk to Candy about it.

The next morning, which was Saturday, I opened the office and Johnny showed up with his new VCR in the box. He opened it up and pulled it out for me.

"Good job, Johnny. I'm very proud of you," I said.

"Thank you, I'm going to work this morning, okay?" Johnny asked.

"I worry about you getting too much money. Can you control yourself?"

"Yes, I can. I went and bought this, didn't I? I feel confident."

"Alright, Johnny, maybe it's a new steppingstone for you." I let Johnny work until I closed the office at one PM.

The next Monday night, at 5:15, Vernon appeared late again.

"Do I get a phone?" Vernon asked. More of a demand than a question. I suspected he was purposely arriving late to be contrary.

"Yes, Kenny's not here. If you get here by five, I'll guarantee a phone for you. Not after," I said. Vernon walked to his table, slapped his bible next to his phone and sat.

I worried that Johnny hadn't shown up for the morning or the evening shift.

"Has anybody seen Johnny since Saturday?" I asked the room.

"He was over at the brass rail drinking on Sunday," Don said.

"Oh, great." I imagined him getting drunk, blacking out, and disappearing. I didn't let him earn too much extra money. Only on Saturday. He shouldn't have had enough for a drunken safari.

The buzz from salespeople on the phone increased. Kenny and Cheryl sauntered in the front door. They were late. Kenny surveyed the room like he was taking count at lock down. Cheryl stood behind him, concealing her eyes from me. When Kenny moved, she would shuffle next to him.

"Kenny, I haven't seen you all day. Is everything okay?" I asked.

"We just assumed they arrested you for murder," Don said as he dropped a sale on my desk

"Don, you're the only one that thought that I didn't. Nobody else did." Don walked back to his desk. Kenny stepped up to me and opened his coat. "What's up Kenny?" I asked. Kenny said nothing. He had layers of clothing, at least two flannel shirts and some kind of t-shirt underneath them. His coat was made of heavy canvas with eyelets that tied shut. The strings hung free as he opened his coat and looked inside. On his chest was a holster that held a bowie knife. The knife was large enough to be intimidating, which I assumed was the point.

"I see you have a knife strapped inside. What's this about Kenny?

"Give me twenty dollars," he said. His wheezy voice was weak but audible. His eyes were sunken and bloodshot.

"Kenny, you don't have any sales." He tapped his knife with his left hand, while holding his coat open with his right hand. He focused his eyes on me.

"I said give me twenty," Kenny said.

"Kenny, are you saying this is a stickup? Are you threatening me with that knife?" I put my tickets on the desk and looked Kenny in the eye. He squinted.

"I said give me twenty dollars." Kenny tapped his knife again and nodded toward it.

Sheena whispered in my ear, "Jump on the desk, grab his collar and scream." A picture of myself acting like a crazed criminal came to my mind. Immediately, I jumped on top of my desk, reached down, grabbed his coat collar, and pulled him up as far as I could toward my face, and started screaming.

"Are you robbing me Kenny, are you robbing me, tell me, are you robbing me? I'm not giving you any money unless you tell me you're robbing me." Kenny's eyes widened and Cheryl stepped back. Everyone in the room stopped talking to look at me. Kenny's arms flailed as his feet lifted from the floor. Insanity played on my face. My voice portrayed a homicidal man.

"Yes, I'm robbing you," he said. Immediately, I loosened my grip on his collar, letting his feet hit the floor, relaxed my face, became quiet, and stepped off the desk. I took twenty dollars from my pocket and handed it to him as if this was a simple ordinary transaction.

As I gave him the twenty with my left hand, I picked up the phone receiver with my right hand. "Alright, Kenny, let's see if you're faster than the Whitehall police." I dialed 911. Kenny turned and pushed through three salespeople to reach the exit. Cheryl followed and they ran out of the room. Within five minutes, the Whitehall cruisers came howling into our parking lot. I already had Kenny's address written on paper for them.

"I was just robbed. His name is Kenny Artiside. He was with his wife, Cheryl. This is where they live. They left about five minutes ago on foot." The police jumped in their car and took off.

"Jesus, what happened?" Larry asked.

"The murderer robbed Tim," Don said.

"Yes, he robbed me. You don't know he's a murderer," I said.

"I'll bet he is," Don said.

"Alright, everybody, calm down. Back to work," I said. Within minutes, the incident was forgotten. Or so it seemed.

At nine o'clock, when everybody was finishing, I said, "Hey, does anybody have a small TV they can bring in tomorrow?"

Chapter 33

"**I** DO," GARY SAID. "Why?"

"I want to watch Dagger on the Geraldo Rivera Show, tomorrow afternoon."

"Geraldo Rivera? Why the hell would he do that?"

"I don't know, I've never seen the show, but I heard it's wacky."

"Wacky ain't the word for it," Sammie said.

The next afternoon, I set the TV up where we could watch. Geraldo Rivera came on and said, "We're going to talk about telemarketers." Sure enough, there sat Dagger on the stage, with a big cartoon smile.

"There was only one telemarketing company owner that would come on the show today. His name is Dagger Stone," Geraldo said. "Mr. Stone, tell us about your business."

"Mr. Rivera, you can call me Dagger. Is it okay if I call you, Geraldo?"

"Sure," Geraldo smiled into the camera. The crowd laughed

"Well, we sell lightbulbs and we give away part of it to a charity. We provide jobs for unfortunate people others will not hire," Dagger said. Just then, the phone rang and I answered. It was Kermit needing tickets.

"Hey guys, let me know what happens. I have to read tickets to Kermit."

"Okay," they said. When I hung up the phone, everybody was laughing.

"What's so funny, guys?" I asked.

"Geraldo made Dagger look like a total idiot," Michael said.

"Yeah, that shouldn't be too hard," I said.

"Is he coming back on?" I asked.

"No, they went to a commercial. It's over," Gary said.

The next day, Dagger arrived, having driven back from New York. He walked into the room, holding his chest out as proud as a peacock.

"Hey everybody, did you see the show?" Dagger asked.

A few people said "yes," quietly.

"Well, what did you think?"

"Oh, you were great," Don said.

"Thanks," Dagger said. He came over to me. "So, what did you think?"

"I was on the phone dispatching Kermit when they were interviewing you, so I missed it," I said. *Thank God I missed it*, I thought.

"I showed him a thing or two. I had Geraldo running in circles. He didn't know what hit him," Dagger said. He put his hands on his hips.

"Okay, Dagger, I'm glad you had fun."

Dagger went around the room, asking everybody what they thought. Most of them said they didn't see it. The others said he was great. They've seen him scream at people. Dagger wouldn't get an honest answer.

The next night, at 5:15, Vernon came in late. All the phones were full.

"I need my phone, Tim," Vernon said. He stood looking at me with his feet spread. Like a challenge. I was certain that was his ploy. Purposely coming in late so he could challenge me.

"Vernon, I gave it away. I only held it until five for you." I turned toward the map to pin tickets.

"Why are you picking on me?" Vernon stepped over so I could see him. He wanted my attention.

"You asked me that before. I told you, I'm not picking on you, it's the same rules for you as everybody else. There's not a separate set of rules for Vernon."

"I want my phone, or I'll teach you a lesson." Vernon crossed his arms and glared at me.

"Well, like, what kind of lesson? The kind that Kenny taught me?" I looked at Vernon. He opened his mouth, then shut it. Vernon had been there for my crazed performance. I knew people were saying not to mess with Tim. Tim can go crazy. Tim's a good boss, but don't steal from him. I knew Vernon was mulling this in his head.

"You can have a phone as soon as someone takes a break," I said.

"I'm not staying here, I'm leaving." Vernon waved his bible at me, then trudged out.

The next afternoon, Ron came up to me. "Tim, I need to talk to you." Ron looked around the room. I assumed, to see who was listening.

"Sure, what's up, Ron?"

Ron stepped close to me and spoke just above a whisper. "Vernon was telling me you're prejudiced and that's why you won't give him a phone."

"Ron, how do I treat you?" I looked Ron in the eye and tilted my head.

"You're always good to me." Ron straightened his shoulders.

"Do you show up at five o'clock for an evening shift?"

"Yes, always." Ron looked up as he pictured this.

"And do you always get a phone?"

"Yes, I sure do." Ron smiled.

"Do you think you'd get a phone if you showed up at 5:15?"

"Only if one was open or someone took a break."

"And that is exactly how I treat Vernon. Is that prejudiced?"

"It's not. Yeah, you're right. He's trying to recruit us to sue you for discrimination."

"Did you guys agree to go on it?"

"No, we don't see that you're treating him differently from anybody else."

"Thanks, Ron."

The phone rang. "New Day Marketing," I answered.

"I'd like to speak with Tim Drobnick." It was a professional and serious voice.

"This is he."

"This is Attorney Isaiah Sheldon; I'm representing Vernon Jefferson."

"What can I do for you?" My blood pressure rose slightly, speculating why Vernon had an attorney.

"Mr. Jefferson has asked me to bring a discrimination lawsuit against you. I want to discuss a settlement before taking it to court."

My heart slammed against my chest wall. I imagined a million-dollar lawsuit taking all my income, leaving me unable to support my family. I moved the phone away from my mouth so the attorney couldn't hear me hyperventilating. I didn't speak for ten seconds.

"Mr. Drobnick, are you there?"

"Yes. Yes, I'm here." I paused for more time to think. He should visit my office. I was certain that would change his mind.

"Mr. Sheldon, why don't you come into the office and we can talk about it. It's hard for me to get out of here." Again, I paused, waiting for his reply. After ten seconds, he broke the silence.

"I'll stop next week. Is any time better than another?" Mr. Sheldon rustled papers.

"Come in the evening between five PM and nine PM. That might be the most helpful, or come on Saturday from nine AM to noon."

"I'll see you soon," he said. I heard more papers rustling and then he hung up the phone. *Geez, my life sucks,* I thought. *Vernon is suing me, Kenny may want to kill me, Dale harasses me, and Dagger screams at me.*

At six o'clock, the room was full. I was dispatching tickets over the telephone to Ralph. The other line rang.

"Hold on, Ralph, someone's calling on the other line. I'll be right back. New Day Marketing," I answered.

"Let me talk to Sammie," the youthful voice said.

"Who is this, please?"

"You know who this is, you imbecile."

"I'm on the other line with the driver, you'll have to hold." I put him on hold and went back to my driver. The line rang again. "Hold on, Ralph." I switched to the other line.

"Why did you put me on hold? I said I need to talk to Sammie," the child's voice said.

"I told you, I'm dispatching a driver, either call after nine or hold until I'm finished." I put him on hold, finished dispatching, and hung up. The phone rang again.

"New Day Marketing," I answered.

It was Dagger. "You son of a bitch, when my family calls you, do what they command you." I held the phone away from my ear. My heart bumped into overdrive. Dagger's attacks were always worse when they were unexpected.

"Dagger, I was dispatching tickets to a driver." I sat in my chair to steady my wobbly knees.

"I don't care, when they call, you jump."

"So, if my sales decline, you won't call and scream about that?

"Do you want me to come tell you in person?" Dagger reached full volume.

"I'd rather not, sir. I'll have Sammie call her kids back. Is that okay?" I asked. Dagger slammed the phone. I hoped he wasn't coming to see me.

"Sammie, call your kids," I said.

After work, I went home. Candy sat with me on the patio for dinner. Colin pretended to chase the road runner and I held Sapphire.

"Tim, you look nervous. Are you okay?" Candy asked.

"I'm trying to be. I had a rough day." I wanted to tell her I feared a nervous breakdown, but I didn't want to worry her. The glass people appeared, and I took a deep breath and stretched back in my chair to watch. I held Sapphire on my chest and patted her back. After thirty minutes of watching the glass people, I relaxed.

We tucked Colin into bed, put Sapphire in the bassinet. Candy and I got into bed. I set up to read while Candy fell asleep. When my eyes drooped, I turned out the lamp and slid under the covers.

Then, I felt a heavy energy. It felt like Dale. I sat back up and looked at a dark floating mass. It looked like Dale. My heart started beating heavily and I hyperventilated. The shadowy figure moved toward me and engulfed my throat. My breath stopped. I contracted and expanded my throat muscles, repeatedly trying to breathe. I could not. I jumped to my feet with my hands around my neck. I didn't know what to do. Slowly, I passed out.

Chapter 34

I'M ON TOP OF a skyscraper in downtown Columbus. I want to fly. I jump off the top to dive, gathering momentum and turning it into forward motion with my arms. The wind rushes past me. Soon, I'm on a productive flight and I fly out of the city. I worry about getting killed. Someone has killed many other flyers. As I fly over a crowd, I see two men wearing yellow raincoats and hoods. They look like the ones I see among the glass people. I fly until I'm in the country.

I find the country church where Sheena and I meet and land on the roof. Sheena is waiting for me.

"Hi Sheena, I need a hug." She hugs me. Her hair tumbles over my face and I feel pure love.

"Sheena, I don't know if I can handle all these lessons. Dagger screams at me and scares me. Now I've got Vernon suing me and I'm afraid I'll lose all my money. Sammie's kids are making my life Hell. Kenny might be a killer. Dale attacks me at night. It's too much." I release her hug and look over the cornfield. I inhale the sweet smell of night, corn, and stalks.

"You can do this, Tim." Sheena smiles and faces the cornfield.

"Sheena, I don't think so. I really don't think so. I had a bad day. I can't handle many days like this."

"If you keep flying every night, you can do this." Sheena places her palm on my cheek and smiles.

"Why does Dale hate me so much?"

"Some people hate just because it's what they do."

"I haven't dealt with two evil men simultaneously."

"You'll be okay, Tim."

"Okay, Sheena, I'll believe you." We stand silently, looking at the landscape.

"Sheena, sometimes I can't tell if I'm dreaming or if I'm awake. You told me this is another reality, not a dream. Sometimes I wonder if I have schizophrenia."

"If you had schizophrenia, Tim, how would you have helped many people?"

"I know. I don't really believe I am, but it's confusing to know which reality I'm in. Sometimes things happen here that I swear happened in the other one."

"Create a clue so you know which reality you're in."

"Something different?"

"Yes, like a unique name."

"I like my name."

"Call yourself Timothy in this reality. You could even choose a different last name."

"Will that work?"

"Yes. Introduce yourself as Timothy in this reality. People will call you Timothy. When people call you Tim, you'll know you're in the other reality."

"I wonder what my last name should be?"

"How about Tibb, with two Bs? Timothy Tibb. Timothy translates to honor God, and Tibb means bold. You are bold. But, you haven't let it manifest yet. While you're in this reality, you can develop your belief that you are bold."

"Timothy Tibb? I love how that sounds. And I love what it means."

"Keep flying Timothy Tibb, okay?"

"I will Sheena. Thank you."

I woke up. I was lying on the floor and breathing easily. I looked at the clock. I had been asleep for two hours. I remembered that I had two names. Maybe that would solve my confusion. And maybe I could become bold.

The next afternoon, I got a call from Steve in Newark.

"Hey, Tim, this is Steve."

"What's up, buddy?"

"Dagger just ripped us a new one on a tirade over the phone. He fired me and Crystal."

"For what? Your numbers have been fantastic?" I asked.

"I chewed him out for abusing Crystal. He didn't like that."

"Good man. I'm glad you're brave enough to do that. He shouldn't treat Crystal like he does."

"And I won't let him. He says we can't work on the phone in any of his rooms. We don't know what to do."

"Oh my God. Let me give Harley a call. I'll call you back." I called Harley. "Harley, this is Tim."

"Yes, Tim."

"Your brother just fired Steve and Crystal. That's a good earning office. They're honest and steady. Dagger said they can't even work the phone anywhere. Can you do something about it?"

"I can't right now. I was at Dagger's house when he fired them. He thinks Steve insulted him," Harley said.

"Steve was defending his wife. Can you blame him? I seriously doubt Steve insulted him. He just doesn't bow down to him like Dagger wants."

"Yeah, you're probably right, but Dagger is extremely angry right now. Maybe, I can reason with him after he cools down."

"Where can they work now?"

"I don't have an answer for you. They're not allowed in any offices. If you get an idea, let me know."

"Dagger makes it really hard to run a business, you know that?" I asked.

"Yes, I know," Harley said. "But there's another side to him."

"I wish he'd show that side instead." I hung up the phone and called Steve back.

"Steve, this is Tim. Harley says Dagger's too angry to deal with right now. But don't worry, I'll think of something for you and Crystal. Give me until tomorrow to figure it out, okay?"

"Thanks, Tim. We appreciate you," Steve said. I hung up.

My knees felt weak and I sat in my chair. I felt panic coming. I needed to ward off panic so it wouldn't start my depression. My head was swimming. There was too much to comprehend. Maybe, I should have quit. Sheena said I could handle it, but it didn't feel like I could.

"You okay, Tim? Your face is white," Gary asked. He laid a ticket on my desk.

"Thanks Gary. I think I'll be okay. Dagger fired Steve and Crystal. I want to keep them working. They're good people and good workers." I grabbed a napkin and wiped my brow and leaned back.

"Have them come work here."

"Dagger says they're not allowed to work anywhere."

"That guy is a total ass."

"Yeah, I know."

"I heard Vernon is going to sue you for discrimination," Gary said. He leaned against my desk and crossed his arms.

"Yeah. That's what I'm told. His attorney called me."

"Well, I don't see that you treat him differently than anybody else."

"I don't, but sometimes you must understand another man's point of view. I'm sure he's experienced lots of discrimination and the slightest thing makes him think I am too." I stood and walked out the front door. Gary followed me. I looked at the cars passing by. I wondered how many of them were having a bad day. The light at the intersection two-hundred feet from our office turned red. Cars lined up to wait, showing their brake lights.

"I wouldn't be that forgiving with Vernon. I'd just tell him to go pedal the pavement." Gary shook his head.

"I won't fire him. I just want him to follow the same rules everybody else does. Of course, if he takes all my money in a lawsuit, I can't work here, anyway. What would be the point?"

Don walked over. "Are you guys talking about Vernon?" He leaned on his crutches and lit a cigarette.

"Yeah, he's going to sue Tim," Gary said.

"Yep, I heard that scuttlebutt. Also, Kenny's going to kill Tim," Don said.

"Don, you don't know that. Quit saying that," I said.

"Dagger fired Steven and Crystal," Gary said.

"For what?" Don asked. "I don't think I even know them." Don leaned against the plate-glass window.

"They're good salespeople and managers in Newark. Honest and hard-working. But Steve told Dagger to quit screaming at his wife. Dagger considered that to be disrespectful, so he fired him." I looked at a loose piece of asphalt and kicked it away. It tumbled and came to rest against the building.

"That's why I agree with whatever he says," Michael said. "Seems like the type that would fire you for no reason. That's why I said he looked great on Geraldo Rivera."

"Be careful what you say. Sammie is his mother-in-law," I said.

"Oh yeah, we know that," Don said. We all stood for five minutes without talking. Don puffed on his smoke. Michael crossed his arms and leaned against the window next to Don.

The rest of the day, I tried to keep my mind busy, but I'd panic when I paused. Finally, it was time to go home. I called Candy.

"Candy, I'm coming home. If you haven't fixed dinner, would you like to go to Denny's? I need time to think."

"I haven't started yet. I'd be happy to go to Denny's. What's wrong?" I could hear Colin making jet plane sounds in the background.

"Everything. My entire world is falling around me. I don't want to stress you out. I need to relax."

"We'll be ready for you when you get here."

"Thank you, Candy." I locked up and stood alone in the parking lot. I searched the shadows for Dale. I saw nothing move. I didn't feel his evil energy. I hurried to my car and drove home.

Chapter 35

AFTER THE HOSTESS GAVE us our booth at Denny's, and I had Colin drawing with crayons, Candy asked me, "So, what's going on Tim?"

"I hate to tell you all my troubles, but the biggest one is that Dagger fired Steve and Crystal." Candy smoothed Sapphire's hair and wiped her mouth with a damp napkin. She took a jar of Gerber creamed peas from the diaper bag and opened it.

"For what?"

"Dagger said Steve was disrespectful. I don't think he was. I think Steve doesn't take shit from anybody. That's one reason I needed to come here and think. Dagger banned them from all our offices. I need to help them. I feel responsible for them."

"Could they work in another telemarketing business?" Candy sipped her Diet Coke. She sat it on the table and dipped a rubber covered baby spoon in the baby peas and put it up to Sapphire's mouth. Sapphire kicked her legs and waved her hands and opened her mouth. Candy slipped the spoon in and pulled it out against her lip.

"Not any good ones." The waitress brought our food. I placed my napkin on my lap and waited for Candy to take the first bite. Then, I cut into my fish. As I chewed, I looked up and was thinking. *Another telemarketing room.*

"Maybe I can open my own business. My own telemarketing room. Steve and Crystal could manage it."

"Can you do that?" Candy asked. She wiped Sapphire's mouth and gave her another spoonful.

"I don't have a non-compete contract. All we have is a scary guy threatening us."

"Would you sell light bulbs?"

"No. I'd sell something different. It'd be hard for Steve and Crystal to sell light bulbs since our company is doing such a good job of it. I wish I had my own products I could manufacture. I'd decide who sold what and where."

"It seems like a good idea," Candy said. She picked up a fork.

"Yeah. If Dagger found out, I don't know what he'd do. That's the part that scares me."

"You said your entire world is falling down. What else is going on?" Candy asked.

"Well, for one thing, Sammie's kids call and harass me while I'm trying to dispatch drivers. If I don't give the phone to Sammie, they'll call Dagger. Then, Dagger will call and scream at me."

"Well, that's rude." Candy took a bite of mashed potatoes. She put the fork down and gave Sapphire another bite of peas.

"Yep, it sure is. And there are other things. I'll get them figured out. I don't want to worry you."

"Should I be worried?" Candy raised her eyebrows.

"No, honey, I'll take care of it one way or the other." But, I thought to myself, *I'm not positive I can get everything taken care of. And, I sure didn't want to scare Candy with Dale's evil energy attacking me at night.*

I thought about my new name for the other reality, Timothy Tibb. Sheena picked it for me because she said I was bold. Not in this reality, I guess. I remember doing bold things before. Heck, just moving out here to Columbus was bold. Standing up to Kenny was bold. Why can't I be bold with Dagger?

I put Colin's grilled cheese sandwich to his mouth to distract him from his crayons. He took a bite and kept coloring.

"You know, honey, when we were in Denver, one sales room I looked at was selling coupons for Kodak film. It was a pretty good deal. If you used that processing company, they'd give you a free roll of film every time you got one developed. Maybe I can sell those."

"Sounds honest." Candy stabbed her roast beef.

"It's a good deal. I'll make calls tomorrow to see if I can find the wholesaler. I'm not sure I can. The library has Yellow Pages from other cities. That may help."

At bedtime, I turned out the lights. I could feel Dale's oppressing energy. I turned slowly to look behind me. I saw nothing, but I could feel him. I walked into the hall. I opened Colin's bedroom door. I saw nothing. I went into the bathroom. I saw nothing. I opened the closet door. I saw nothing, yet I still felt him. I walked to our bed. Candy and Sapphire slept. I lay on the floor to look under the bed. I saw nothing. I stood and peered into every dark shadow. I saw nothing. I went to bed and closed my eyes. I counted to three as I inhaled. I exhaled as I counted to three. I repeated until I fell asleep.

I'm flying over the cornfields. It feels good to fly. I see Sheena standing on top of the country church and I land by her.

"Sheena, I'm happy to see you." I hug her.

"I'm always around, Timothy."

"Oh, right, Timothy, I'm in a different reality than a moment ago. Timothy Tibb. Bold."

"You are bold, Timothy. Think of all the bold things you've done. You left Sheridan with your young family and moved to Denver. You left the guaranteed income at Genie to go on straight commission. You built a solid business at ServiceMaster, then left when you were cheated. That was bold."

"I know. I don't know why I'm so afraid of Dagger. I'm not always bold. Sheena, I have a solution, I believe, to save Steve and Crystal. I can start my own telemarketing room and let them run it. Kodak coupon books are an excellent product. But I don't know the wholesaler."

"Do you like this idea, Timothy?"

"I do, except I'm afraid of what Dagger would do when he finds out."

"Timothy, tomorrow, you'll have your answer. Tomorrow you will be bold. Let's fly now."

"Thank you, Sheena."

"You are welcome, Timothy Tibb."

The next morning, I was in the office when the phone rang. "New Day Marketing," I answered.

"Hey, you were the guy on the Geraldo Rivera show, right?" The voice asked.

"No, that was the owner. I'm the manager."

"This is Marco. I saw him talking about his telemarketing company and he gave the name, so I looked you guys up on 411. I have something I'd like to talk to you about."

"Okay, what is that?"

"You guys are selling light bulbs, right?"

"Yes, we are."

"You can increase your sales by adding another product. Have you considered doing that?"

"I have, but the owner's not open minded to new products," I said.

"Maybe you could bring these to him and convince him and I'll give you a cut of the sales, okay?"

"It doesn't hurt to try, what's your product, Marco?"

"We have coupon books for Kodak film," he said. Immediately, I felt energy surging through my ears. My knees became weak and I sat and dropped the phone. I leaned over to pick it up.

"Hello, hello, are you there?" Marco asked.

"Yes, yes. Marco. Sorry, I dropped the phone. Give me your phone number. We can work together."

"My phone is 614-555-2758. I'm Marco Bullstein, last name is spelled BULLSTEIN."

"Oh, so you live in Columbus?"

"Yes. The company is based in Denver. I'm their rep for Ohio."

"That's handy for me. Thank you, Marco. I'm busy right now but I'll call you between two o'clock and four o'clock this afternoon, is that okay?

"Sure, if you like, we could meet for lunch."

"That's even better. Meet me at Denny's on East Main by I-270 on the east side."

"See you there at two o'clock?" Marco asked.

"Yes, see you there." I hung up the phone. Sheena said I'd have my answer that day. That must have been it. It was a miracle. Sheena could still surprise me. But what would I do about my fear of Dagger?

I stared out the window. Dagger could fire me at any time. Dagger could kill me. If he is a killer. I wasn't sure. I needed to quit worrying about Dagger and make plans to protect my income and my future and my family. We could lose the company because of Vernon's lawsuit, or a lawsuit for sexual harassment because of Jeff, my future with Dagger was built on sand.

I felt a surge of confidence welling up inside of me. I recalled many bold acts in my past. I was confident I could take care of my family and I did. I started a lead business by signing a lease on six machines. I was positive I could do that and I did. And when Kenny robbed me, I had no fear. Sheena was right. I was bold.

The last bit of fear released from my chest as ozone rising to the sky. I decided I wouldn't let Dagger scare me. He could do his worst. I'd do what I needed to protect my family and those that needed protection. I decided to open my own telemarketing company. I picked up the phone and called Newark. Steve answered the phone.

Chapter 36

"I THOUGHT YOU GUYS were out of there," I said.

"Harley's coming to close us out and then we are," Steve said.

"Steve, I have something for you. I'm going to start my own telemarketing room. We're going to sell Kodak film coupon books. They're an excellent product. I'll give you and Crystal forty percent for sales and another ten percent to manage the room."

"Tim," Steve paused, "I trust you. If you say it's good, I'm in." I felt gratitude welling up inside. Tears came to my eyes. Steve's faith meant a mountain of hope to me.

"This is good, Steve. What does Crystal think?"

"Hold on," he said. "Crystal, Tim is going to give us our own room selling Kodak coupon books. He says it's a good deal. What do you want to do?" I could hear Crystal saying something. "Tim, Crystal wants to talk to you."

"Okay," I said. Crystal came on the phone.

"Tim, we trust you." I sputtered as I held back my emotions. Tears flowed down my face and I wiped them away. I was grateful that I could protect Steve and Crystal. I was thankful for their faith.

"Thank you, Crystal. I'm going to get it set up today, okay? I'm meeting the wholesaler for lunch." I sniffed.

"Yes, Tim, thank you," Crystal said. "Are you okay?"

"Yes, I'm thankful for you and Steve. I got weepy."

"We love you too," Crystal said.

I arrived in the Denny's parking lot at two PM. A man in a dark suit and yellow power tie was standing by the entrance waiting for someone. He was holding a briefcase. I walked to him and he put his hand out.

"Marco," He said.

"Polo," I said.

"Oh yes, I never tire of that one," Marco said.

"I'm Tim. Nice to meet you, Marco. Sorry for the corny joke."

"It's okay. I'm excited about working with you. Should we grab a table?"

"Yes." We walked inside and let the hostess seat us. I scooted on the yellow vinyl bench and turned my coffee cup over. So many events in my life have involved Denny's. Starters and endings and wonderings. I sought refuge and relief from Ambrose on these yellow padded benches. I brainstormed new ideas and problem solving.

"Let me show you our product," Marco said. He brought my mind back to the present. He handed me an inch thick paper book with the Kodak color and logo on the cover. I flipped through it. This was the same product I had seen in Denver. It was the size of an index card and an inch thick. Delivery would be easy for these. We could fit a day's worth of inventory in a shoebox. Lightbulbs filled the entire vehicle. Some days drivers had to reload.

"This is exactly as I remember them from Denver." I sat the book down on the table and looked at Marco. He laid brochures on the table and pointed at them.

"This explains our pricing and sales policies. We don't guarantee territory, but the more you sell, the better pricing you get." Marco flipped over the page. "These are testimonials from our salespeople."

I picked up the colored flyer and read the testimonials. I knew I could sell these, assuming the customers had a need and desire. I wasn't sure of how they sold in Denver as I never worked at one of those telemarketing rooms.

"So, Marco, what's your top salesperson doing?" My standard question for every sales job I had applied for. This wasn't a job, but the question fit this situation.

"We have a room on the coast in California that sells $10,000 per week. Why do you want to know?"

"Because I know I can double or triple what your top people do. How many phones are in that room?"

"That one has ten if I recall correctly." Marco pressed his index finger on his lips and looked up.

"My room is selling $15,000 per week in light bulbs. Kodak coupons must be a hot product." I picked the coupon book up to inspect it again. Marco opened his briefcase. He peered inside for twenty seconds and dug through the pockets.

"Ah, here it is," Marco said. He handed me a blue bank check. The account number and name of the company were blacked out. It was written out to Barnes Sales Associates for $20,000. "That is a recent order from our top company. He makes an order every three months to get the biggest discount."

"Every three months?" He must have more than one sales office.

"Yes, he has two. May I ask, how many offices do you have?"

"Right now, eight. We have Columbus, Dayton, two in Cincinnati, Zanesville, Loraine, Parma, and Newark."

"How long have you been in business?" The waitress brought us menus and poured coffee. We thanked her.

"We started here eight months ago." I opened the menu. I knew what I wanted, but Denny's would have surprise menu items. None on that day. Just the usual.

"That is almost an office every month you have opened. How many offices will you open?" Marco's face was hidden behind his menu.

"About fifteen in Ohio. We'll go into surrounding states as well."

"Do you own part of the company?" Marco asked. I looked out the window.

"No. Sort of. I'm promised to have my own state after I help these guys get their business going." I raised one eyebrow and looked at Marco. "I don't have complete faith that it will happen. These guys have broken their promise to me more than once."

"If you get them to sell our coupon books, I'll give you a dollar on every book sold. It can be our secret. That way, you are making money off all of their company." Marco leaned forward and embraced his hot coffee mug with his palms.

"I thought about that," I said. "But I have another idea. Hear me out."

"I'm listening."

"Two of my best managers and salespeople, a husband-and-wife team, have been fired by the owner. No good reason. Dagger's ego was hurt and he's punishing them by banning them from the company."

"Okay."

"I want to start my own business. I will open a telemarketing room for your product. I will hire Steve and Crystal to manage it. We should make money from day one." I leaned back and looked at Marco. Marco frowned.

"Can you manage two businesses? Will you keep working for New Day Marketing?"

"Yes and yes. Marco, every sales manager we have was recruited and trained by me, save one in Zanesville. That one was recruited and trained by my husband-wife duo, who I trained to train. I still coach the managers and I order the inventory. Mostly, I'm running the entire business. All I need to do is keep recruiting and training for New Day Marketing. Dagger will fire more people, I'm sure. When he does, we will give them refuge in the Kodak sales room. Over time I will open businesses in many cities."

"That seems like a good plan."

"It is, and I can pull it off with no sweat. How many coupon books do I have to buy to get started?" I pointed at the price sheet. Marco picked it up and pointed at the chart.

"The minimum purchase is $500. That's for fifty books. You get graduated volume discounts of up to four thousand books. Your price at that level is five dollars per book."

"Put me down for a thousand dollars' worth. And, you can count on much larger orders soon." I looked at Marco. Marco stuck his hand out to me.

"Deal," he said. I shook his hand.

Next, I needed an office. I didn't want to be near a high crime area. Dagger's philosophy was to place offices near criminals because they needed cash daily and didn't have the willpower to save money. Not all our salespersons were criminals. Most, however, were desperate. I didn't need desperate people. I had Steve and Crystal. I drove to Bexley, an upper-class city. It was two miles from the Whitehall office on the same street.

At 2700 East Main Street, I saw a for-rent sign in front of a two-story brick building. It was small for office buildings, only five windows wide. The bricks were clean, and the postage-stamp-sized yard was groomed to perfection. Maintenance had trimmed the sidewalks. Cedar mulch surrounded the base of the building. Two doors away, there was a patio at an ice cream shop. There were several places for lunch within walking distance. Indeed, many people in business dress populated the sidewalks. I wrote the phone number on my yellow pad and then walked inside. I wandered the first floor, then climbed to the second. There was no elevator. The center room facing Main Street was empty and had the door open. I walked in. It was small, but big enough. The window brought in a good amount of sunshine.

There was no soul in this office. Yet. It was neutral, better than starting with a negative, as I had to do in Newark. I liked the feel of the space.

"Are you here about the office?" Someone behind me said. I rotated to see a gentleman dressed in a blue suit standing in the doorway. He wore a blue tie and a white shirt. His hair was plenty and dark and I guessed his age to be thirty.

"Yes, I'd like to lease this space."

"It's $250 a month. I need two months upfront plus a deposit."

"Am I allowed to put five telephones in here?" I looked at the phone plugs on the wall.

"Sure. What kind of business do you have?" He asked.

"I have salespeople selling Kodak film over the telephone."

"That seems like a respectable business."

"It is and I've got dependable people."

"If you got the money, I'll lease it to you." He stepped inside and extended his hand. "I'm Jason Wallowitz, I just purchased this building."

"My pleasure to meet you, Mr. Wallowitz. I'm Tim Drobnick. I'll write you a check right now," I said. *Dang, that was easy*, I thought. *Strike while the iron is hot.* I wrote the check and handed it to him. "There's a lease to sign, right?"

Chapter 37

"YES, BUT I WAS testing to see if you were serious. I see you are. Come to my office and I'll get your information and we'll sign."

"Thank you, Mr. Wallowitz."

"Call me Jason."

"Yes sir, Jason, call me Tim."

"I'll do that. Follow me."

After I signed the lease, I went back to my Whitehall office and gave Steve a call. There was no answer. I guessed they had left the office.

Next to call was the telephone company. I escaped to the back to avoid attention. I ordered three telephones to start to be installed within six days.

An hour later, Steve called me. "Tim, I thought I better call you since you can't reach us anymore."

"Good idea, Steve. We're all set. I have inventory ordered, I leased an office and the phone company will install phones within six days. It's a sweet little office, well-groomed landscape, in the middle of Bexley."

"Wow, you work fast," Steve said.

"Once I decided to be bold, nothing stood in my way. Can you and Crystal come to our house at 9:30 tonight? We can talk."

"Sure, we'll see you there. And Tim," Steve paused.

"Yes, Steve?"

"Crystal and I thank you." I heard him choke up.

"It's my pleasure, Steve," I said.

After I hung up, the phone rang and I answered, "New Day Marketing."

"Tim, this is Kwame."

"Hi, Kwame, what's up?"

"You told me to monitor Jeff. He's hitting on the ladies."

"What did he do?"

"He asks them out for drinks and he says nasty things to them. He actually took one of them out to a bar last night." Kwame sighed. "He's disturbing them while they should be working. It's distracting to the other salespeople as well." I could hear a siren in the background. We waited for it to pass.

"Thanks for the heads up, Kwame. I'll talk to Jeff about this. How are things otherwise?"

"Good. I have a fantastic crew. They work hard for me and we have fun."

"That shows you are an excellent manager. Keep up the good work." Another siren blared and I barely heard Kwame's reply. Then, he hung up.

As I hung up the phone, Detective Tallridge was walking in the door. He placed his hands on his hips, which pulled his sports coat back, revealing a pistol in a shoulder holster. He looked at my workers. I walked over to shake his hand.

"Hello, Detective Tallridge." I extended my hand and he shook it, then placed it back on his hip.

"Hello. Have you seen Kenny or Cheryl?"

"No. Did the Whitehall police catch them the night he robbed me?"

"No, they weren't apprehended. Their car is at the hotel but they're not living there."

"Well, they'll need money at some point. I'm sure he'll show up somewhere. Do you think they're the murderers?" I asked.

The detective didn't respond for ten seconds. He looked toward the back and at the coffee pot.

"I can't talk about an ongoing investigation." He reached inside his coat pocket for his tiny notepad, letting his coat fall free, hiding his gun. The detective wrote in his notebook. "Let me know if you hear anything," he handed me his card and walked outside. He stopped, faced the street, and put his hands on his hips again. He surveyed the parking lot, street, and buildings. Then, he moved on.

I hope they catch him before he kills me, I thought. As the detective was leaving, Jeff pulled up. He got out and watched the detective leave, then came inside.

"Was that the detective?" Jeff asked.

"Yes, he was asking if we saw Kenny and Cheryl."

"They didn't catch them yet?"

"Apparently not," I said. "Hey, Jeff, I need to talk to you in the back." I waved him to follow and walked away. Jeff's boots clacked across the floor as he followed me.

"Jeff, I'm going to report to Harley about you taking our employee out the other night. You're not supposed to be hitting on ladies in our offices or dating them."

Jeff shook his head and pivoted on the heel of his left boot. He put his hands on his hips and stared at the floor, still shaking his head. After ten seconds, he looked at me, his toothpick hanging on his lip. "You just don't seem to get it, do you, Timmy? I'm your boss. This is your second warning. If you ever scold me again, I'm going to fire you."

"Second warning? I think this is the third warning you gave me."

"Don't get smart with me," Jeff said. He tipped his cowboy hat back and snatched the toothpick out of his mouth.

"Jeff, I told you before, don't call me Timmy. I consider that demeaning. That's probably my third warning, FYI." Jeff pushed his cowboy hat forward and frowned.

"Jeff, if we get sued for sexual-harassment and they win millions of dollars, it'll close the entire company. Then none of us will have a job, so it doesn't matter if you fire me." Jeff stuck his finger three inches from my nose, pursed his lips, then turned and left the room. I watched him squeal his tires as he pulled out of the parking lot. Jeff was going to cause enormous problems for the company. Another reason to own a business again.

When I got home, Steve and Crystal were there waiting for me. Candy had served them drinks and was having a good time. She loved company. Our couch was bending under the weight of Steve's five hundred pounds. He sat forward; his legs spread to make room for his belly. He held a gin and tonic and sported a tremendous grin.

Candy had placed two of our dining table chairs in the living room. She sat on one and Crystal on the other, next to Candy. They both had their legs crossed, leaning toward each other and laughing. Each held a wine cooler. Those two seemed to be best friends ever since Crystal's birthday party.

"Steve, Crystal, I'm glad you're here," I said. "Hi, honey," I walked over and gave Candy a kiss on the cheek.

"So, what's up, Chief?" Steve asked.

"Good things are up," I said. I reached to shake Steve's hand. Crystal stood and hugged me. "I got lucky and found the wholesaler for Kodak coupon books. I saw them in Denver and liked the concept." I wanted to tell them how Sheena arranged the sales rep to find us on Geraldo Rivera. But I had strong concerns about creating a tsunami of people wanting help. That story would have to wait.

"Did you sell the coupon books when you were in Denver?" Crystal asked.

"No. I visited several rooms that were selling them, but their management didn't impress me. I wish I had. Then I'd know for sure if we can sell it." Candy walked from the kitchen and handed me a Coors Light and took her place again next to Crystal.

"Thank you, Candy." I smiled at her.

"Do you think we can sell it?" Crystal asked.

"Yes. I may have to adjust our script as we get used to the product, but yes, I believe we can. The rep said there is a ten-phone room in California selling $10,000 worth of coupons per week. It must be a product with a demand and desire."

"Tim, take a load off." Steve pointed at the overstuffed chair next to the couch. I was so into telling them about the new business I was standing and waving my arms.

"Oh, thanks, Steve. I guess I'm not at work now," I laughed. Everyone laughed with me. I leaned into the chair and sipped my beer and looked at the ceiling.

"This could be big. Huge. If Dagger fires a salesperson, we can give them a place to work."

"You mean 'when' not 'if'," Steve said.

"Yes. I'm sure you're correct." I looked at Steve. "There's no reason we can't open offices anywhere we want. We can build an extensive business."

"We're with you, Chief, as far as you want to go," Steve said. He sipped his gin and tonic.

"If you like, I can show you the new office tomorrow. It's nice. Inventory and phones will be here within six days. Do you guys need money to make it that far?"

"No. We were making good money in Newark, so we've got plenty saved up."

"That's an outstanding characteristic. You have the discipline to save money. Glad to hear that."

"So, who's the driver?" Steve asked.

"Well, I was thinking about you, right?"

"Actually, I've gotten great at sales. I'd do much better on the phone, especially at forty percent."

"Maybe we can hire a driver for four bucks a ticket. That's double what New Day Marketing is paying," I said.

"Maybe, Kermit would do both," Crystal said.

"No, I don't want to get Kermit involved. If Dagger fires me, I don't want Kermit caught in the fall out. Dagger already fired both of you, so he has no leverage on you."

"What if he fires you?" Candy asked.

Chapter 38

"WE'D BE JUST FINE. I'd start selling Kodak film from our office." I smiled at Candy.

"Yeah, but we'd still be the managers, right?" Crystal asked.

"Yes, if Dagger fires me, you'll be my boss if I come to work in the office," I said.

"Good," Crystal said. Everyone laughed.

"We should get together more often," Steve said. "We haven't seen both of you since you came out for Crystal's birthday bash in January."

"It would be nice to get together more often. How about Sunday? We can barbecue outside."

"That'd be great. I love your house, by the way," Crystal said. She squeezed Candy's hand.

"Thanks. It's great for our family." I wanted to explain the glass people, but I couldn't. "I'm putting up a playground for the kids on Sunday. Maybe, you can give me a hand, Steve? Or you can just have a beer and watch me?"

"I can help you hold things in place," Steve said.

"Hey, what about me?" Crystal asked. "I'm pretty handy with tools."

"That's a mouthful," Steve said. We all laughed.

The following Friday afternoon, the phones were in the new office. We had the inventory, but we didn't have a driver. Steve,

Crystal and I were at the Bexley office. I had filled the room with chairs and tables I purchased at Sam's Club. The tables had faux wood printed over press wood and brown metal frames and legs. The legs folded out. Steve helped me carry them up the stairs. The chairs had chrome legs and frames holding gray cushion seats and backs. That's how we furnished every telemarketing office. Sam's Club provided for us everywhere. For a fee, of course.

I positioned the iconic Mr. Coffee in the center with packs of gourmet coffee next to it. I had hung a poster on the wall that featured a sprinter celebrating with a jump and his fist in the air. Printed boldly at the top it said, "It won't be easy, but it will be worth it."

"Alright, you guys, I've written a script. I haven't tested it but let me know how it works. I might come over later, do some calls and tweak it," I said. Crystal picked up the paper and read it.

"I can sell this," Crystal said.

"I know this is scary. We don't know if we can sell this product. But if anyone can, it's you two." I smiled at them.

"We'll find out tonight," Steve said.

"I'm headed to the Whitehall office. Steve. I guess you'll have to do the deliveries tonight in between sales."

Steve leaned back in the chair and put his arms behind his head. He looked at Crystal.

Crystal said, "We'll handle it. But please get us a driver so Steve can be full-time sales."

"I'll work on it. I'll place an ad if I need to. Well, gang, this is it. Do or die."

"We'll do, not die," Steve said. He raised his hand and Crystal gave him five. I nodded and smiled.

I walked to the hallway and looked at our office. It wasn't a neutral, empty room anymore. It had a soul. It was alive and full of good energy. We took something dead and brought it to life.

Crystal was pouring coffee and talking to Steve. Hope filled my spirit, and I waved away the caution of failure. The stairway led me outside and I stopped again to look at the center window. Steve stood, looking out the window. I waved. He smiled and waved back.

I drove back to the Whitehall office. They had propped the front door open. I entered stale smoke. Three salespeople had their legs propped up on the table as they napped. My trainee, Jenks, was at the manager's desk dispatching tickets. I walked over to see his choices. They were good. I gave him a thumbs up.

I took a quick glance at the inventory. I did a mental count, it looked accurate. I pushed some aside to check for empty spaces. One of my trainees had the bright idea to pull out inventory from the middle and re-stack it to hide the missing boxes. That trainee was a permanent salesperson now. No management opportunity for him. Jenks finished and walked over to me.

"Jenks, you're doing good. Go take a break before the evening shift," I said.

"Thanks, boss. I will." Jenks picked up his Cincinnati Reds ball cap and walked outside. The phone rang and I answered, "New Day Marketing."

"Hey, Tim, this is Scott over in Dayton. I was the driver here."

"Hi, Scott. I haven't seen you since I sent you over to Dayton. What do you mean you were the driver?"

"Well, Dagger fired me today."

"Why'd he do that?"

"Oh, he was here today. He didn't like my humor. I was just kidding. I was calling to see if you need a driver."

"No, I actually don't in this office. However, I have a small office I can put you in. But keep quiet about it. You remember Steve and Crystal, right?"

"Oh, yeah, I go to Newark and party with them."

"Well, I'll give you four bucks for a delivery. The office is in Bexley. How soon can you be there?"

"I'll be there in an hour, the way I drive," Scott said, laughing.

"Great, I'm sure they'll have work for you tonight. But don't get a speeding ticket. Here's the address, 2700 East Main St. Bexley," I said.

"Hold on." The phone was muffled. "Okay, I got my pen and notepad, give that to me again."

"2700 East Main St. Bexley."

"Alright, I'll head over there."

"Thanks, Scott."

I picked up the phone and called Steve. "Hey, Steve, this is Tim."

"What's up, Tim?"

"I guess you guys are good friends with Scott Smith, the driver in Dayton?"

"Yeah, we are."

"Well, Dagger just fired him. He's headed to you to do deliveries. He says he'll be there in less than an hour."

"That's fantastic timing. The way Dagger is going, he'll fill up our office for us." Steve laughed.

"I know, it's funny. At least now I've got a safe haven for Dagger's victims. Call me tonight and let me know if you made any sales. I'll talk to you later." I hung up the phone.

The phone rang. I answered. "New Day Marketing."

"Timmy, where's Johnny? He's not on your close out sheets." Dagger demanded.

"He's been missing for two weeks. Two weeks ago, he earned as much as he wanted. Per your orders. He went on a bender and disappeared. Just as I said he would. So, we have lost two weeks of income from him. Plus, he may be dead. Who knows?" The phone was silent for a minute.

"Get him back to work," Dagger said. I didn't expect him to admit he was wrong. He was never wrong.

"I have no idea where he is. How should I do that?" Again, the phone was silent for a minute.

"Alert me on any updates," Dagger said. He hung up.

I finished the night out and closed the office at 9:30. I hadn't heard from Steve yet. I was worried something was wrong, so I drove to Bexley. I parked and walked up to the building. Night looked much different in Bexley. Spotlights in the grass lit the yard sign and bricks on the building. The neighboring buildings also had lights. It made the nighttime feel safe, unlike outside the Whitehall office. The light from our office shone through the window. I walked inside and up the stairs. Steve and Crystal were sitting in their chairs.

"Guys, how'd it go tonight?" I asked. Steve, with a deadpan face, slowly shifted his head and looked at Crystal. Crystal got a big smile on her face.

"Come on, how'd it go?" I asked.

Chapter 39

"WE GOT $500 IN sales. Scott's out picking them up. He should be back any minute now," Crystal squealed. She jumped from her chair and twirled like a cheerleader into Steve's lap, one leg in the air. Then, she bounced to me and gave me a hug.

"Oh, my God, that's great news," I said. We heard rapid steps coming up the stairs. Scott came in with a big smile. He had a mostly empty shoebox with inventory. He sat it on the table and pulled out a stack of tickets, checks and cash.

"Hi, Scott, how'd your night go?" I asked. I already knew from that pile of tickets.

"Not bad. I made fifty bucks in two hours. I'm going to love this office."

"We got our delivery guy," Steve said. Scott walked over to high five Steve.

"Tim, can I make sales and deliver?" Scott asked. "I was selling in the Dayton office, that's why I saw Dagger." He put his hands in his pockets. His legs shivered. Scott was a bundle of energy. Just one good reason he was a skilled driver.

"Wow, a salesman and a driver. Man, we got ourselves a crew, don't we?" I asked.

"Yeah, we do," Crystal said. Steve and Scott let out a whoop. Crystal took the tickets and money from Scott. She pulled out an inventory sheet, sat, and logged the sales.

"Y'all feel like coming by my house to celebrate?" I asked.

"Yes," Crystal said. She raised her hand like she was in class.

"Sure, we'll see you there shortly," Steve said.

"Scott, you can follow Steve, or you can follow me if you like, or I can give you the address," I said.

"I'll just follow Steve," Scott said. He sat and put his feet up on the table. "I love this place and I want my pay."

I walked out to my car and drove home. When I entered, Candy was reading a book to Colin. Colin was hanging on her shoulder, watching the book as she read.

"Honey, guess what?" I asked. I walked over to sit by Colin.

"Daddy!" Colin jumped on me, knocking my glasses off. I gave him a hug and sat him on my lap.

"What?" Candy asked.

"Our new Bexley office made $500 in sales tonight."

"Is that good?" Candy set the book on her lap. Colin grabbed it.

"Yeah, it is. I asked Steve and Crystal and our new guy, Scott, to come over. I hope that's okay. We want to celebrate."

"Oh, that'll be great. I can fix some snacks." Candy stood, letting Colin have the book, and sat Sapphire in the child carrier. Colin flipped through the pages and started telling a story. He couldn't read yet, but that wouldn't stop him. I picked up Sapphire and cuddled her. She looked at me and cooed with her lips forming an O shape.

"Are you sure you feel like preparing snacks?" I asked. I remembered when Candy would get so giddy preparing snacks for the AmericPlan zombies in Denver. It brought her to life.

Candy was already in the kitchen when she answered. "Yes, I do." She pulled serving plates out of the cupboard and slid the silverware drawer open. It made a shh sound from the wood and then jingled as she grabbed forks and spoons.

"What a good day. What a good day." I reached to tickle Colin.

The crew arrived and visited with us until eleven. We were in a celebratory mood.

Over the next week, Steve, Crystal and Scott did $4000 in sales. They had a sanctuary to work without unjust termination. They were making more than they were in Dagger's office. I was putting the profit from that office toward my $50,000 fund to start my disaster restoration and carpet cleaning company.

On Monday night, Dagger came into my office. He stopped at the door. The salespeople straightened up in their chairs as he watched them. He sat in an empty chair and listened to their presentations. He folded his arms and looked from person to person. The salespeople spied him from the side of their eye, but never directly.

After he sat for thirty minutes, he stood and walked over to me. "I need you to fire Michael," he said.

"What? Why? He's doing good?" I asked.

"He insulted Sammie."

"Michael? Hard to believe. He's pretty mild mannered."

"Are you calling me a liar?" Dagger put his hands on his hips and glared at me.

"I'm not calling you a liar. I'm just surprised. And, I don't see why I have to fire him because he insulted Sammie, that's between him and Sammie, right?"

"This is my company. You do what I say." Dagger crossed his arms and squinted at me. "Bring him back here and fire him. I want to listen."

"Let me do it after the shift so we don't interrupt our sales. Is that alright with you?"

"No, it's not. I want it done now." Dagger squinted and set his jaw.

I walked over to Michael and tapped him on the shoulder. "Michael, come back here please," I said. Michael got off the phone and followed me to my desk. He looked at Dagger and squinted.

"Michael, Dagger says you insulted Sammie."

"No, I didn't. I mean, I called her a bitch, but we were joking around," Michael said.

"Where did this happen?"

"Last night, at the Brass Rail. But I was just kidding."

"Nobody calls my mother-in-law a bitch even if they're kidding," Dagger said. "You're fired. Get the hell out of this office."

Michael's mouth hung open. He looked at me.

"Michael, come back and get your pay tomorrow, okay?"

Michael picked up his notebook. He went to the bus stop, walking with his shoulders slumped like a defeated man and sat on the bench. The next bus was due in thirty minutes.

Dagger smiled, put his hands on his hips, surveyed the room, then left.

"What happened?" Larry asked.

"Michael called Sammie a bitch, so Dagger fired him," I said.

"That bitch," Don said.

Everybody laughed. I told my trainee to watch the phone. I walked out to the bus stop and sat by Michael. He had tears in his eyes.

"I don't want to live under a bridge. This job saved me. I love working here." Michael wiped his eyes with his sleeve.

"I know, Michael. Dagger will probably change his mind later. But in the meantime, I've got a job for you."

"Yeah? What is that?" Michael's eyes widened.

"I started an Anti-Dagger room. Get off the bus in Bexley. Go to this address. Here, give me your notebook, I'll write it down. We're selling Kodak film. Anytime Dagger fires somebody, I put them to work there."

"Really?" Michael's face became alive with a smile and bright eyes.

"Yes. You'll probably be back here. But this is your safe haven where you can make money. Okay?"

"Yes, thanks, Tim."

"It's best to not tell anyone about it. The longer we can keep it a secret from Dagger, the better."

"I understand. Who's in that office?"

"Right now, there's Steve, Crystal, and Scott. You don't know them, but they are good people. You'll love working with them. They are kind."

"Thanks, I'll get off the bus in Bexley."

"I'll let Steve know you're on the way." I walked back into the office to call Steve. "Hey, Steve, a guy by the name of Michael's coming there. He's one of my best salespeople. He's going to work for you."

"Sure, keep sending them. Is this a Dagger firing?" Steve asked.

"Yes."

"Why?"

"He called Sammie a bitch. Sammie is Dagger's mother-in-law."

"Well, is she a bitch?"

"Yes, actually. Michael's a good man, take care of him."

"We will, Tim."

I hung up the phone and smiled. Things were going my way. I hadn't heard from Kenny; I hadn't heard from Vernon's lawyer. I could take care of people that Dagger fired and I had extra money coming in to build my cleaning company fund. Dale must've been so busy taking care of Northern Ohio that he wasn't thinking about me anymore. I hadn't felt his evil energy in over a week now. As far as Jeff's sexual harassment, if it shuts down the company, I own a business. Things were looking good.

The next afternoon, the phone rang. "New Day Marketing, this is Tim.

"This is Attorney Isaiah Sheldon, is this Tim Drobnick?

"Yes, it is. You're the one that was representing Vernon, right?"

"Correction: Is representing."

My heart smacked my chest. It had hoped we were done with this lawsuit.

Chapter 40

"I THOUGHT YOU'RE GOING to come in and talk to me about this. I never saw you, so I figured you weren't pursuing the case."

"Oh, we're pursuing it. We have enough evidence to go to court."

I searched my mind for any memory of wrongdoing I did to Vernon. I knew he was pissed that I wouldn't hold a phone for him past five o'clock. I never treated him unkind. He got the same share of taps as everyone else. He got more, since his sales were higher than most.

"What evidence?"

"We'll bring that out in discovery."

"You can't possibly have evidence because I'm doing nothing wrong. Even if you had a hidden camera, there's nothing to find."

"Mr. Drobnick, I'm calling to see if you want to make a settlement. As it is now, we plan to sue you and your company."

"What is Vernon's complaint about me?"

"Many times, you've sent him home from work because he's a black man."

"That's just bullshit. He's always welcome to work here if he shows up on time."

"Mr. Drobnick, Mr. Jefferson claims he's the only one you made that rule for." I could hear the attorney shuffling papers.

"He claims wrong and I won't settle."

"Then we'll see you in court." He hung up the phone. I sat down with my mouth hanging open. I was stumped. But I knew that people could win lawsuits if they got a sympathetic jury, right or wrong. I could lose everything.

The phone rang. I answered, "New Day Marketing."

"This is the operator. Will you accept charges for a long-distance call from Johnny Bardo?"

"Yes, operator, I will."

"Thank you, please hold while I connect you." I waited for ten seconds and then I heard Johnny's voice. It sounded like a casino in the background, bells and dings and coins pouring out of slot machines.

"Tim, this is Johnny."

"Johnny, I'm glad you're okay. I've been worried about you."

"I know man, I'm really sorry."

"Where are you?"

"I'm in Vegas." I could hear a big jackpot.

"Vegas? How did you get out there?"

"I have no idea. I just sobered up today. Last I remember, I was at the Brass Rail, drinking."

"Johnny, I thought you wouldn't have enough money to go on a binge."

"I didn't. But then I started drinking. And I wanted more. So, I pawned my VCR."

"Your brand-new VCR?" I asked.

"Yes. You were right, Tim. I should have stopped at $400, but I can't. It's best if you force that on me."

"Okay, Johnny. Are you going to come back? Do you need me to wire bus money to you?"

"Yes, if I'm not fired, I'll come back."

"You're not fired, Johnny. I want you back. Do you need money?"

"Okay, thanks, Tim. I don't want more money. I'm going to hop on a freight train. I'll get back as soon as I can."

"Okay, Johnny. Please be safe."

"I will, Tim. Thank you."

I hung up the phone. Dagger wanted updates. I called him.

"Dagger, this is Tim, I have an update on Johnny."

"Hi Timmy, what is it?"

"Dagger, every time you call me Timmy, I tell you my name is Tim. I don't want to be called Timmy." He didn't respond. "Anyway, Johnny is in Vegas. He said he earned too much money and went on a bender. He just sobered up today. He doesn't know how he got to Vegas."

"Well, get him back here."

"Why? You'll let him earn as much as he wants, he'll go on another bender, and then he may die next time." Dagger was silent for a full minute. I waited.

"Get him back here, Timmy."

"My name is Tim. I will get him back here, but I won't let him earn more than $400 per week." I hung up. I waited for Dagger to call back, screaming, but he never did.

At closing time, I stepped outside and locked the door. The shadows were darker here than at my Bexley office. I watched for any movement from Dale or his blob of whatever matter that is that he attacks me with. I didn't see any. I rushed to my car and drove home.

"What's wrong, Tim? Did somebody die?" Candy asked as I came in the door. I must have had a billboard on my head displaying my despair. Colin ran to me and I picked him up. Sapphire was in Candy's arms. I kissed Candy and then brushed Sapphire's cheek. She cooed and kicked her legs and flung her arms.

"I found out Vernon is still suing me. If they win a million-dollar lawsuit, I'll never save enough money to start a cleaning company. I'll lose my job and I'll lose my Bexley telemarketing office."

"Well, how can they win if you're not doing anything wrong?"

"I don't know. This attorney seems to think they can win."

"Why don't you go sit out back and watch the glass people. That helps you relax. I'll bring dinner out," Candy said.

"Thank you, Candy. Come on, Colin, let's go outside." I sat Colin down who ran out the door. I took Sapphire from Candy and cradled her in my arms. I went to the patio to watch Colin run.

"Look at that brother of yours, Sapphire. He's got more energy than the sun." Sapphire watched my eyes as I talked to her.

"Let's watch the glass people, Sapphire. Can you see them?" I propped her up. She wiggled her arms. I relaxed for twenty minutes watching the glass people. Colin ran through the grass as if he was chasing them, although, I'm pretty sure he couldn't see them. Then I saw the two figures in yellow raincoats. I recalled one night in my other reality flying over two men in yellow raincoats and wondered if somehow the glass people were related to my other reality?

The people looked like they were going and coming from buildings in downtown Columbus, like the people I see when I'm flying.

"Here you go, honey," Candy said. She had my dinner.

"Thank you, dear." She sat the carrier next to me and I put Sapphire in it. Candy handed me the plate and sat next to me.

"Look at that boy running," I said. Candy nodded.

"Can you see the glass people tonight?" She asked.

"Yes. It's funny, it looks like Colin is chasing them."

"Do you think he can see them too?"

"I don't think so. He doesn't react on the mark."

At night, we lay in bed. I closed my eyes but opened them. I felt Dale. His sinister anger overwhelmed me and I froze. I hyperventilated. As I looked at the ceiling, I saw Dale's blackness floating over me. I did my best to hold on to consciousness. After thirty minutes he left. I couldn't imagine this would keep going on for the rest of my life. Somehow this had to stop. But how do you stop an evil emanation? I could choose to not be afraid of Dagger, but I could not choose to not be harassed by Dale.

The next afternoon, I was in the Whitehall office. I was pinning tickets on the map. Kermit was loading up his car with light bulbs. He snapped his gum and walked with a half sprint as if he were the happiest man in the world. Kermit filled out his driver's inventory sheet and handed it to me.

"Here you go, boss. Want to check my count?"

"No, I trust you, Kermit." And I did. Kermit had never given me any reason to not trust him. He was efficient, honest, and had a good attitude.

"Thanks, boss."

"You're welcome. Grab your route off the map," I said. Kermit picked them off and even took two out of the way. "Do those two last, I'll try to get another one or two near it for you."

"Okay, boss, see you later." Kermit bounced out the door doing his stiff wave to the salespeople.

The phone rang, I answered, "New Day Marketing."

"Hey Tim, this is Kwame. Jeff was down here again last night. Hitting on all the ladies. He took two of them to a bar."

"How many ladies you got down there?"

"Four."

"Jesus, that's more than most offices."

"I think that's why he spends so much time down here," Kwame said. "He's disturbing my sales."

"Alright, I'll give Harley a call. Thanks for letting me know."

I called Harley. "Harley, this is Tim."

"Yes, Tim."

"Jeff's up to his tricks. He's in Cincinnati, hitting on all the ladies. He took two of them to a bar after work last night. We're going to get sued for sexual-harassment and then we won't have a company."

"I already chewed his ass about this once. I'll get on him again."

"Thanks, Harley." I hung up. Two hours later, Jeff drove over the curb into the parking lot and squealed his tires to a stop. He parked sloppily, taking up two spaces. He exited the car and slammed the door. He clacked his boots up to me and put his finger in my face

"You son of a bitch. I warned you," Jeff said.

Chapter 41

"I TAKE IT HARLEY talked to you." I smiled. I thought about this. I had always been bold with Jeff. I was so afraid of Dagger that I couldn't see I had boldness in me. Sheena was right.

"I warned you about going behind my back." His face was flushed.

"Well, I warned you about sexual-harassment." I crossed my arms.

"I've had it with you, you are fired."

"You're kidding me right?"

"No, I'm not. Get out, you're fired."

"No thank you," I said.

"What do you mean, no thank you?" Jeff asked. His face got redder by the minute.

"I mean, I'm not letting you fire me tonight."

"You don't have a choice in the matter."

"Well, I guess you better call Harley, then. Tell him I'm not obeying you," I said.

"You can bet your ass that I will," he turned around and stomped across the room, kicked the door open and left. He started his car and squealed his tires as he backed out of the parking lot.

The phone rang again, "Hello, New Day Marketing."

"I need to speak to Sammie."

"I'll have her call you back," I hung up. "Sammie, call your kids."

The phone rang again, I answered, "Hello, New Day Marketing."

"I told you, I want to talk to Sammie. Don't you hang up on me," the child's voice said.

"Which of her kids is this?" I asked.

"It's none of your business, put her on the line."

"She's probably trying to call you back right now. I told her to call you." I Hung up. The phone rang again, this time, it was Dagger. He was screaming, I held the phone away from my ear, listened for twenty seconds then hung up.

The phone rang again, "Hey, Sammie, I think this is for you, come pick it up," I said.

Sammie came over and picked up the phone. "Hello? (Pause) Yes, he's standing right here. (Pause) I'll tell him." Sammie hung the phone up. "Dagger is really pissed. He's on the way to see you."

"Great, there goes our sales goals for tonight," I said. I felt shivers come over me, my knees shook. But then, I reminded myself that the worst-case scenario is he would fire me. Or kill me. If he fired me, I had a place to go, unless of course, Vernon sued me, or Kenny killed me. If Dagger killed me... I had no control over that. I couldn't worry about it.

"Thirty minutes later, Dagger showed up. He slammed his car door and marched in the front door. He picked up my coffee mug and threw it against the wall. Pieces of mug and coffee flew everywhere. That seemed to be his modem operandi.

"You motherfucker, don't you ever hang the phone up on me." His breath smelt of whiskey.

"Well, I'm tired of you screaming at me. All I'm trying to do is make you money. Your screaming doesn't help me do that," I said.

"This is my company." He put his finger in my face, his palm up.

"Sure, it's your company, but if I don't get enough sales, you get pissed. When you scream over the phone or come into the office like this, sales go down." Dagger stopped and looked at me for a minute. He pulled out a cigarette pack, tapped it, put one in his mouth and lit it. He had a big smile on his face.

"After you close the office tonight, you're fired. I'll stand here to make sure you don't steal from me."

"That's the second time I've been fired today," I said.

"Who else fired you?"

"Jeff."

"That pissant can't fire anybody without my permission."

He stepped away ten feet and sat down on a chair. I went about my business. I roamed the room, trying to motivate everyone again. I remembered how Harley had patted the crew on their shoulders and said, doing a good job, doing a good job. The crew didn't recover, however. Kermit and Ralph came in and I checked them out and paid them. I walked over to Dagger with the inventory sheet.

"Ready to inventory me?" I asked.

"I think I'll wait till tomorrow night to fire you." He stood and left.

I guessed Dagger got more pleasure out of watching people squirm than firing them. But I wasn't going to squirm. I was going to fight back. I was also going to fight back against Vernon, Kenny, and Sammie's kids. Screw them all.

The next morning, Harley called me.

"Hi Harley, what's up?" I could hear music and laughing. Party at Harley's.

"Jeff said he fired you and you refused to leave." Someone squealed, Harley laughed.

"That's right," I said. I wasn't sure Harley heard me. "Harley?"

"I'm here, Tim. I promised Jeff I'd talk to you about refusing to leave."

"Ok, go ahead." I listened to the party for twenty seconds. "Harley? Are you going to talk to me?"

"I just did. Keep up the good work. Bye," Harley said. More females squealed as he hung up. I hung up the phone and laughed.

The phone rang. I answered. "New Day Marketing."

"May I speak with Tim Drobnick?"

"This is he."

"This is Attorney Isaiah Sheldon. I want to give you one more chance to settle. If not, I have the papers ready to file in court." I heard papers shuffling and what sounded to be a paper shredder.

"I already gave my offer. Come here and talk with me about it in person," I said. I listened for clues. Maybe Vernon was there listening. What would they be shredding?

"Is that a threat? I sure hope it is."

"It's not a threat. I just don't think we can communicate well over the telephone. Come in, I'll be reasonable. Maybe we can work out a deal." More shredding. Then I heard another voice. Muffled. Male. Deep. Maybe Vernon. Attorney Sheldon said nothing for twenty seconds.

"When should I come in?" He finally asked.

"Anytime between five and nine PM Monday through Friday is fine. You could also come in on Saturday morning from nine to noon."

"So, you don't care which day I come in?"

"No, surprise me." Again, I heard the muffled mystery male voice. He remained silent for twenty seconds.

"I'll come in and talk. I'd rather make a deal than go to court. Give me your address again," Attorney Sheldon said.

"3872 East Main Street in Whitehall." Three salespeople handed me tickets. I lay them on the desk.

"Okay, I have it. Thank you. I'll see you soon."

"I look forward to meeting you," I said and hung up the phone. I picked up the tickets to pin on the map. The morning shift only had seven salespeople, but they were kicking butt. Kermit and Ralph would be busy.

I ripped open a coffee packet and put it in the Mr. Coffee. For the non-gourmet drinkers, I emptied the ten-gallon pot in the bathroom sink and rinsed it out. I sprayed 409 onto the inside, then scrubbed with a Brillo Pad. Then, I rinsed again and cleaned the outside. As I was carrying it back to my desk, the phone rang.

"Hello, New Day Marketing," I answered. I sat the shining coffee maker on the snack table. I cradled the phone on my shoulder with my ear and opened a three pound can of Folgers Coffee.

"Tim, this is Kwame. Hey, guess who's in my office?"

"Jeff?"

"No, Kenny and Cheryl." Kwame spoke in a hushed voice.

"No shit."

"Yes shit. They came in and used fake names. I've got them on the phone, working. Man, they look rough like they've been living underground."

"Alright, try to keep them there. I'll call the police."

"Okay. Get the cops here soon, they make me nervous."

"I understand, Kwame, I'll call the detective now." I hung up. I picked up the card that Detective Tallridge had given me and called him. He was in the field, so dispatch patched me though to his car radio.

"Detective Tallridge, this is Tim Drobnick. I manage the office in Whitehall by the Brass Rail. You were looking for Kenny and Cheryl Artiside."

"Yes, do you have news?"

"Kenny and Cheryl are in our Cincinnati office right now. Can you get someone there quickly?"

"Yes, I can dispatch a black and white. What is the address to that office?"

"It's 6200 Daly Road, in Cincinnati."

"Thank you, try to keep them there as long as you can."

"I already instructed the manager to do that. They came in under a fake name, so we're pretending we don't know who they are. They don't know Kwame, but Kwame knows them. That's the manager."

"Thank you, sir. Please call me back if they leave."

"Yes, I will."

The detective hung up. I called Kwame. "Kwame, I called the detective on the case. They're going to get local cops in there ASAP. Just play it natural like you're already doing. Good job, man."

"Thanks, Tim. Man, I'm nervous."

"I know. I really appreciate this. I've been nervous about them being on the loose. Worried they were coming for me," I said.

"I get that. I'm glad I can help."

I hung up and scooped out two cups of coffee grounds and spread it over the coffee sifter. I put the lid on and plugged it in. Fresh coffee was coming. I went about my business, but I couldn't stop thinking about Kenny and Cheryl. After thirty minutes, I called Kwame to see if the police had arrived.

"No, not yet," Kwame said.

"Call me when they do, okay?" I asked.

An hour later, the phone rang. I answered, "New Day Marketing."

"Hey, Tim, this is Kwame, they got them."

Chapter 42

"THEY DID?"

"Yeah, scary as shit, man. They came in with their guns pulled and arrested them. They handcuffed them and took them away."

"Wow. Did they say anything to you?"

"Not a word."

"They didn't even ask which ones were Kenny and Cheryl?"

"No. They knew exactly who they were."

"Geez, I'm glad they got them. That's a gigantic relief for me."

"Yeah, me too. I was a little nervous about having murderers in here," Kwame said.

"Well, we don't know that they're the murderers."

"The police think they did something wrong."

"I'm glad you're safe, Kwame. Thanks for helping me out."

"Anything for you, Tim."

"Thanks, talk to you later, Kwame." I hung up.

That night at home, I watched Colin playing on his new swing set I built. Candy came out with a plate for me and sat next to me.

"Guess what? The police caught Kenny and Cheryl," I said.

"Who's Kenny and Cheryl?"

"Kenny robbed me of twenty dollars a while back. He worked in my office. Cheryl is his wife. Some of my people think they killed that person at the Brass Rail. They arrested them in my Cincinnati office."

"Well, that's scary. You had murderers working in your office. And why didn't you tell me he robbed you before?" Candy asked.

"I didn't want you to worry. And we don't know that they're murderers. I don't know why the police wanted them."

"Well, I'm glad they caught them."

"Yeah, me too."

That night in bed, I lay awake thinking about the day's events. And the week's events. Candy breathed rhythmically beside me. Sapphire was making baby noises while she slept in the bassinet.

A darkness formed and pressed on my chest. I didn't recognize the shape, but I sensed it to be Dale. I panicked when that happened, as that darkness would seize my throat and halt my breathing. I could feel it tugging at my soul as if it may rip it from my body. I lay still in my fear and became dizzy. I realized I was hyperventilating and closed my eyes. I imagined my ghosts were standing by my bed. I hoped it was true. I concentrated on Sheena. In my mind, I asked for help. After what I imagined being thirty minutes, the darkness and oppression left. From my exhaustion, I fell asleep.

I'm flying over Columbus. Crowds of people are near the skyscrapers. Among them are two men in yellow raincoats. These crowds look like my glass people crowds. Except, they don't look like glass.

I leave the city to fly to the country. I see Sheena on top of the old country church. I land next to her.

"Sheena, I'm happy to see you."

"I'm happy to see you too, Timothy Tibb." She hugs me.

"Sheena, I don't know what to do about Dale. I thought he had quit harassing me, but he's back. His emanation is attacking me every night. How can he have that power?"

"It's the power of hate." Sheena looks at the cornfield. She closes her eyes and lifts her arms. Her flowing robe waves in the gentle breeze. "When Dale is deep in loathing and seething, his energy attacks. He does not know his energy is attacking or that it has traveled from his body. He only knows that he hates."

"How long must I tolerate it?" I ask. She looks at peace.

"I will help you. I want you to imagine a violet egg surrounding you and your family. And then, I want you to imagine the egg evicting Dale's evil from your home, bouncing into space where it can't hurt anybody." She says this without opening her eyes or lowering her arms.

"Will that work?"

"Yes, Timothy, it's powerful."

"Why didn't you show this to me before?"

"You weren't ready for it. You could not summon the violet egg until now." Sheena lowers her arms and looks at me.

"Why? Why not until now?"

"You are banishing your fears. Little by little. Piece by piece. You have chipped away enough to gain this ability." Sheena puts her hands on my shoulders and looks me in the eye. "Fear cannot fight evil. Love, hope, and faith can. Your hope has grown. You have expanded your love to many people. The more people you love, the more hope and faith you have, the more powerful the violet egg can be."

"I guess these were some of my lessons to learn?"

"Yes. Some."

"Thank you, Sheena."

"You're welcome, Timothy Tibb."

"Sheena, I see what I call glass people in the backyard. It is very calming. But now I'm suspecting what I'm seeing is in this reality while I'm in the other one. Is that what it is?"

"I can't tell you that right now, Timothy," she says. "Go fly some more. Keep flying every night."

"Thank you, Sheena I will."

The next Tuesday night at seven, a man hauling a briefcase and wearing a suit strode into the Whitehall office. He paused and studied my salespeople.

"Hello, welcome, I'm Tim. What can I do for you?"

He walked to my desk. "Are you Tim Drobnick?"

"Yes, I am."

"I'm Attorney Sheldon." He laid his briefcase on my desk. He scratched his head and looked at the salespeople near the coffee machine.

"So, you're here to discuss a deal with me?" I asked.

"Yeah." He looked around the room again. He shook his head and mumbled something to himself.

"What kind of deal?" I asked.

"Well, it seems we may have trouble pursuing this case. I see that half of your salespeople are black."

"Yeah, that's about right," I said.

"You didn't mention that to me." He glared at me.

"I didn't think it was important." I leaned against the wall and crossed my arms.

"Vernon asked others to join him in the lawsuit, but he couldn't snag anyone. And he didn't mention that half of his coworkers were black."

"You're welcome to solicit for your case, if you like," I said.

"Well, I tell you what, we're dropping this case." He shook his head again and snatched his briefcase, which knocked a pile of tickets and pens onto the floor. He stormed out the door. Watching him leave made me feel thirty pounds lighter. I floated up three inches.

"Who is that?" Ron asked. He dropped a ticket on my desk. I stooped over to pick up the spilled pens and tickets on the floor.

"That was Vernon's lawyer, here to make a deal."

"Where'd he go?"

"He said he's dropping the case. He said he couldn't pursue it since half the room was black," I said. Ron laughed and went back to his phone.

The phone rang. It was Steve. "Hey Steve, how's it going in Bexley?"

"We're kicking butt, it's going to be a stellar week. Michael's doing a good job."

"Yeah, I knew he would. I appreciate you taking care of him."

"Hey, that's what we're about. The refuge from the Dagger storm. Hey, I got a call from Kathy in Zanesville. Jeff's been out there hitting on her again." Steve sighed. I could hear Crystal talking with a customer. Then I heard Scott.

"That idiot is out of control. Harley chewed him out yesterday. I doubt it will matter because Jeff cussed me out for reporting him to Harley."

"Well, Kathy will quit if it doesn't get taken care of."

"Alright, I'm going to give Jeff a call now."

"Shouldn't Harley be taking care of this?"

"Why? The more I do for Harley, the more he depends on me. He certainly doesn't complain about my help." I hung up and called each of the offices in southern Ohio. I told them if Jeff shows up, tell him to call me. An hour later, Jeff called.

"Tim, this is Jeff. What do you need?" He snorted and sounded tense. His words were short.

"Jeff, we're about to lose our manager in Zanesville, Kathy," I said.

"Why's that?"

"Because she's tired of your harassment. She doesn't want to date you. She doesn't want you flirting with her. She wants you to keep your hands off her." I heard the phone hit something. Jeff probably hit the wall or desk. I waited ten seconds for him to reply.

"You just can't get it, can you, Tim? You can't tell me what to do," Jeff said. He pitched his voice. I imagined his face turning red and sweat coming from underneath his cowboy hat.

"So, I guess you don't care if you lose a manager?"

"I can always get another one."

"Only if I send one to you. And I won't. You have the wrong attitude. You need to nurture your managers and give them what they need to be successful. You don't want to slow them down like Dagger does."

"Well, there's a reason Dagger is the owner and you're not. There's also a reason I'm the district manager and you're not." Jeff slammed the phone. I guessed he finished talking.

Jesus, I didn't know what to do about him. I could call Harley again, but I didn't think it'd make a difference. I called Kathy in Zanesville.

"Hi Kathy, this is Tim in Whitehall."

"Hi Tim, how are you doing?" Her voice was stressed and high pitched. I could hear her salespeople talking in the background.

"I'm doing good. I'm sorry Jeff is harassing you. I'm trying to get it taken care of. I told him to keep his hands off you, but he ignores me."

"If he doesn't stop, I'm going to quit." Her voice raised.

"I totally understand that I just want you to know I'm working on it. Next time he comes to your office, would you call me as soon as he's there?" I listened to her room for five seconds.

"I'd be happy to," she finally said. Her stressed voice relaxed.

"Alright, thanks, Kathy. I promise I will fix this. You're doing a good job out there. Keep it up."

"We have a right to not have Jeff's harassment."

"Yes, I agree, Kathy. I'll make it stop."

I hung up the phone.

Chapter 43

A FTER WORK, I LOCKED the door. Per my routine, I
stood to watch the dark parking lot. After five minutes, I
felt safe to get into my car.

"Candy, I'm home." I threw my keys in the bowl by the door.
Colin ran up to me and I swung him up over my shoulder. We
had dinner and then sat outside on the patio. The spotlights on
the house let Colin play on the fort. Sapphire was already
sleeping in her carrier.

I felt Dale's energy attacking me. I remembered Sheena's
instructions about the violet egg. I closed my eyes and imagined
one forming around my family and house. I concentrated until I
could see it clearly in my mind.

Next, I imagined Dale's evil energy bouncing off the egg and
into space. After ten minutes, it felt like it was working. I could
feel the attacks, but only slightly. Like a bird tapping on a
window. But, I no longer felt overwhelmed. It was going to take
energy on my part to keep the violet egg protecting us, but so
much less than the energy I lost in fear of Dale.

After the family and I were in bed, I felt at peace. All I could
feel was the tap, tap, tap of Dale's evil energy bouncing off the
egg. I fell asleep. For the first time that year, I slept peacefully.

The next morning, I went to the Whitehall office. Dagger
never finished firing me, but I was able to not worry about it. I

refused to let him scare me. The phone rang and it was Kathy in Zanesville.

"Tim, you wanted me to alert you when Jeff got here. He just arrived." Her voice was worried.

"Thank you, Kathy, would you hand the phone to him, please?" Jeff took the phone.

"What?" Jeff said. I heard anger.

"Jeff, there's no reason for you to be in that office. I want you to get out now." I said this with a stern, strong, matter-of-fact voice.

"Listen, you peon, you can't tell me what to do." Jeff spoke loud enough to disturb the salespeople.

"If you don't leave now, I'm going to have Kathy call the police."

"You can't do that. You're not my boss." He hung up the phone. I called back and Kathy answered.

"Kathy, if he's still there, call the police and tell them he refuses to leave."

"Actually, he just squealed out of here. He said he was coming to chew you a new one." Kathy's voice had relief.

"Alright, great. I'm glad he's out of your way. You'll never see him again. I have a plan."

"Thank you," Kathy said. Her voice softened.

"I'm so sorry he has put you through this." I tried to relay sympathy.

"No one should tolerate that harassment. I appreciate you taking this seriously." Julie sniffed.

"I do. Harley does too. Relax now, it's over." I listened to Julie for thirty seconds. I could hear her crying.

In a strong voice, she said, "Thank you, Tim. My salespeople need me." She hung up the phone.

"Hey, everybody," I said. The seven sales people looked at me. "Jeff is on the way here. Hang up the phone when you see him, as I expect he's going to be loud. He's pissed."

"Sure, Tim," they said. A few just nodded.

The phone rang. I answered. "New Day Marketing."

"Let me talk to mom," a child's voice said.

"I'll have her call you." I hung up. "Sammie, call home," I said. She picked up her phone.

My phone rang again. I answered. I heard the same child's voice. "Look, you tiny pissant, don't hang up on me. Give me my mom."

"She's trying to call you now." Sammie looked back at me as she hung up the phone. I hung up and did a swirl with my finger, signaling for her to try again. I wouldn't allow Sammie's kids to control me.

At noon, Jeff's car swooped into the parking lot, bouncing off the edge of the curb. His tires squealed as he came to a stop in front of the office. The salespeople saw him and hung up their phones. Jeff kicked his door open and crawled out. He stared in the window for thirty seconds. If his face froze in place, it would make his mother sad. He reached in and grabbed his cowboy hat and positioned it slightly forward to hide his eyebrows. He kicked his car door shut with the side of his boot.

"Tim, do you need backup?" Larry asked me.

"If he takes a swing at me, sure," I said. Larry and Don both stood. Don scooted his ash tray and coffee cup toward the back of the table so he could sit on the edge. Don was a brave man. Missing a leg but ready to take on an angry cowboy. Don took shit from no one. His sinewy muscles looked strong, although thin. I imagined he could put a vice grip on someone's throat or give a powerful blow with his crutch. Larry, brave also, was big enough to bear hug any threat.

Jeff stepped forward and kicked the door with the bottom of his boot. I assumed to open it, but the door opened outward. The door stood still.

"The door pulls out, you idiot," Don said. Not that Jeff could hear him. Everyone laughed, however.

Jeff stood and recomposed, then pulled the door open. He could see salespeople smirking as if he was the butt of a joke. Which he was. He clenched his hands into fists and stomped toward me. I stepped away from my desk, toward the bubbling ten-gallon coffee maker, in case I needed space to dodge a punch. The other four salesmen rose from their chairs. This was a good crew. They had my back. Sammie turned to watch, still seated, cigarette between her fingers.

Jeff stopped three feet from me. "Why are you still here? I told Harley that I fired you. He said he talked to you."

"Yes, he talked to me about that." I folded my arms and took half a step back, keeping my right foot back to brace myself.

"Then why are you here?"

"Maybe, you should talk to Harley about that," I said.

"Who the hell do you think you are, threatening to call the police to evict me from my Zanesville office?" Jeff stepped toward me again and lifted his index finger six inches from my nose. He was so angry he was frothing spit from his mouth.

"Who the hell, Jeff, do you think you are, harassing our female employees?" I squinted and stared him in the eye.

"That is none of your business. You are my minion, Timmy." He said my name slowly and distinctly.

"Jeff, you apologize to me right now. I have told you I don't want to be called Timmy."

"What are you going to do about it, Timmy?" Jeff stepped toward me again and tapped my chest with his finger. The salesman stepped forward. I put my hand up, signaling them to wait.

"I'm waiting," I said.

"I don't apologize to my underlings. You think you can call the police on me? I'm going to call them now and tell them you're trespassing. I have fired you and you're not supposed to be on company property." Jeff walked to my desk and picked up the phone.

"Jeff, if the police arrive, you're the one that will be arrested for your threatening behavior. Is that what you want?"

"I'm not threatening you." Jeff slammed the phone down and turned to me.

"Guys, is Jeff threatening me?" I asked the room.

"Hell yes," Don said.

"Yes," Larry said. The others nodded.

"This is bullshit," Jeff said. "I'll fire the lot of you. You're just sheep shit on my boot to scrape off."

"Jeff, you're a danger to this company. You're running off good salespeople. You're sexually harassing our female employees. Take this as your official notice." I put one hand on my hip and lifted the other as I stepped toward Jeff. I tapped his chest with my finger as I said each word.

"You are fired."

Everyone in the room clapped. Even Sammie.

"Yes!" Three of them exclaimed in unison.

Jeff stuttered and puffed his chest. His face became red. "You can't fire me," he yelled.

"And yet, I just did. You can work as a salesman. You must work here so I can monitor you. But you're not working in Zanesville, and you'll stay away from Kathy."

Jeff's froth spit out of his mouth and he stomped his foot and yelled again, "You can't fire me!"

"Hold that thought, Jeff." I lifted my finger for him to pause. I picked up the phone and called Harley. "Harley, this is Tim. I'm handing the phone to Jeff. Please tell him he's fired." I handed the phone to Jeff.

"Hello?" Jeff said. (Pause) "What? Why?" Jeff sputtered. (Pause) "Because Tim says so?" Jeff's puffed chest collapsed. His arms dropped beside him. Then, he handed the phone back to me. All the salespeople chuckled.

"I didn't know that you could fire me," Jeff said. The salespeople burst out laughing.

"Jeff, you could've continued being district manager, but you're an asshole. You are a sexual horror. And you're putting our company at risk. You can work here. Nowhere else."

"I won't work with you jerks." Jeff grabbed his hat and waved it. "You guys can all go to hell." Then Jeff stomped out.

The salespeople laughed and clapped as Jeff stormed to his car. I waited for them to calm down, then I called Harley. "Harley, this is Tim. Give me three percent and I'll be your district manager."

Chapter 44

"**D**ONE," HARLEY SAID. NO hesitation. I hung up the phone.

I called Zanesville. "Kathy, I fired Jeff. Do not let him in your office. If he shows up, tell him to leave or you're going to call the police. I'm going to be your district manager now," I said.

"Oh, that is such an enormous relief," Kathy said. The words flowed easily from her mouth. "Thank you, Tim. Thank you."

"You're welcome, Kathy. I got your back."

"Yes, you do. Thank you."

I hung up and called each of the other office managers. It thrilled them to be done with Jeff and they were even more thrilled that I'd be their district manager.

Now I needed a manager for Whitehall to replace me. Kermit was my first choice. Dagger believed a driver couldn't be a manager, but I had proved him wrong. I'd talk to Kermit when he came in for the evening shift. After that, I'd tell my crew I won't be their manager. I knew everyone loved Kermit and I knew Kermit had the discipline to follow my system.

"Here comes that religious nut," Don said. I looked up to see Vernon. He walked into the door rather sheepishly. He wasn't holding his bible. He was missing his self-righteous look where he held his chin up and squinted.

"Hello, Vernon. What can I do for you?" I asked.

"I'd like my job back," Vernon said. I looked at him for twenty seconds. I wanted him to think I was mulling over the decision. The fact was, he was an excellent salesman and never gave me trouble except for the attempted lawsuit. I knew in advance I'd hire him back, but I didn't want it to appear too easy for him. I wanted him to consider himself fortunate to be hired back.

"Do you understand I've been enforcing the same rules for you as for every salesperson?"

"Yes, yes I do. Now anyway. I got blinded with rage when I thought you were treating me differently because I was black. Ron talked to me. He said you were the fairest white man he'd ever met. He said he had to arrive by five for a guaranteed phone. All the white guys did too. He made sense."

"Vernon, I get it. I'm sure you face prejudice every day of your life. If ever you think I'm being prejudiced, just flat out tell me. Okay?"

"Yes, I will," he said. He put his shoulders back and looked me in the eye.

"Great, then you're welcome to work here," I said. I stuck out my hand and Vernon shook it heartily.

"Get to work, Vernon." I smiled. Vernon smiled back.

Kermit showed up for work with his deliberate steps, snapping his gum, and his usual gigantic smile.

"Hey everybody," Kermit said. He waved his hand.

"Hey, Kermit," most of the room replied. Everyone loved Kermit.

"Kermit, come to the back with me. I want to talk to you." I walked to the back alley; Kermit followed me.

"Yeah, buddy, what's up?" Kermit asked. He had a puzzled look.

"How would you like to manage Whitehall?" I folded my arms, cocked my head, and looked at him.

"Really? I'm not a salesman. Dagger says drivers can't be managers. That's why he fired Steve."

"First of all, fuck Dagger. Second of all, Steve was an amazing manager. He still is. Drivers can be brilliant managers. If I give you a system to follow, will you?"

"Of course, buddy, you know I will." Kermit bowed forward and twirled both hands at me.

"Yes, I know. That's why I'm asking you to be a manager. But this office needs a lot more than a manager. I don't think most of my managers could handle it, but I believe you can, Kermit."

"Like what?"

"Well, I need to keep recruiting and training managers here. I'll show you how to do that. You won't be alone because I will be here often helping you. Not always. I need to visit the other offices."

"So, you're going to be district manager?"

"Yes."

"What happened to Jeff?"

"Oh man, you should have been here. I fired him. It was hilarious. Everyone in the entire room laughed and clapped."

"You fired him? Not Harley or Dagger?"

"Yes."

"Man, you're like the wizard behind the curtain," Kermit laughed.

"Hey, that's what I always say." We both laughed.

"What, do you mean Steve is still a manager?" Kermit asked.

"I'll explain to you later."

"Ok, but how do I train salespeople? I can't sell."

"I'll train you how to train them. I have a system. I have a script for calls from the advertisement. For when they walk in the door. I have a system to train them to sell. I have a system to train managers. It's in a system. You are intelligent, everyone loves you, you're honest, you're reliable, you've never been a problem, you can do this. You'll be the best office manager in the entire organization."

"That'd be great!" Kermit's eyes widened and that smile of his almost exploded off his face. "We'll have to get a driver to replace me, right?" Kermit asked.

"That's right. Hire three part-timers to replace you. I don't think you need my help to hire drivers, so I'll put an ad in the paper for that, okay?" I asked.

"Fan-fuckin-tastic! thanks, boss!"

"You're welcome, Kermit, you deserve this. Let's go make the announcement." Kermit followed me, almost dancing. I walked to the front. No one was on the phone yet. They were getting their coffee, talking with each other, having a smoke, and milling around. Preparing for five PM.

"Everyone, please, I need your attention. I have important announcements." Everyone stopped talking and looked at me. Several sat in their chairs.

"First announcement. For those not here this morning, I fired Jeff. He is no longer our district manager." Those holding coffee sat it down and everyone started clapping and whooping. The ones from the morning crew were laughing their ass off.

"Second announcement. I'm leaving to be your district manager." Everyone cheered and clapped for me.

"Who's going to be the manager?" Sammie asked. Oddly, she looked worried. Could it be that she'd miss me?

"My choice is Kermit." I stood aside and motioned my arms toward Kermit. I didn't get an immediate reaction from the crew.

"Who's going to get our tickets delivered?" Don asked.

"Guys, we'll hire three drivers to replace him, because he's as good as three drivers combined, right?"

"Right," most answered.

"And who else knows more about drivers than Kermit? And who else can anticipate delivery problems better than Kermit? Right?"

"Right," everyone answered, more strongly.

"I know you all love Kermit. Don't you think he'd be a good boss?"

"Yes," most responded. Everyone nodded their heads and looked at the other salespeople for confirmation.

"So, who wants Kermit to be manager?" I asked.

"We do!" Larry yelled. Everyone clapped and started coming to shake Kermit's hand and pat him on the back. I stood back to let the bonding begin. Kermit was thanking everyone one by one, grabbing their hand, looking them in the eye, and smiling a smile that could've been seen from space. I stepped outside to get fresh air.

Kermit would deliver until we got new drivers. When not driving, he would be a manager trainee. After he finished delivering that night, I had him sit with me to learn management paperwork. We paid everyone and then only he and I were left in the office.

"Kermit, I'm having a barbecue at my house this Sunday. I'd like you to be there. Steve, Crystal, Scott, Michael, and Harley will come too. Can you be there?"

"Sure thing, buddy. I thought those guys were fired?"

"From Dagger's business, yes. But I built a refuge for Dagger's victims. I'll explain it all on Sunday, okay?"

"Sure." Kermit looked curious.

"Let's get home, Kermit, it's been a long day."

"It sure has."

The next day, my morning crew had just got their coffee and prepared to make calls.

"Holy cow, look at that," Gary said. We all looked out the window. A man with tattered clothes covered head to toe with filth was tromping toward us. He had a three-inch beard covered in soot or something black. His face was haggard. His hair was a dirty mop. It was Johnny. He came into the office. I sprinted over to greet him.

"Johnny, I'm so glad you're safe."

"I need food, please."

"Go get it, Johnny." He ran to the fridge and grabbed a sandwich in each hand.

Chapter 45

THREE DAYS LATER, ON Sunday, Candy and I were
hosting the barbecue at our house. Scott, Crystal, Steve,
Michael, and Kermit showed up at noon. I had invited them to
arrive before Harley.

"Kermit, you old dog, how are you?" Steve swung his hand
sideways to grab Kermit's with a slap. He shook his hand and
pulled him in for a hug. Steve and Kermit had bonded as drivers
during the Christmas period when I ran the Newark crew in the
back of Whitehall.

"It's great to see you, buddy," Kermit said. "Where have you
been? I thought Dagger fired you?"

"He did fire me. Since then, Crystal and I have overseen a
secret operation." Steve flashed a smile at me.

"Dagger said he fired you because drivers can't be managers,"
Kermit said.

"That's bullshit. Crystal and Steve were turning in the best
numbers per phone in the entire business. Dagger fired him
because Steve chewed Dagger out for abusing Crystal." I carried
a plate of red hamburger patties out the back door to the grill.
Everyone followed me.

Candy set up folding chairs on the patio. Crystal helped. They
were giggling about something.

"I hear the best Whitehall driver is going to be the Whitehall manager now," Steve said. He gave his devious look to Kermit.

"Yeah and I'm going to be the best manager." Kermit nodded as he responded.

"Well, best, next to me and Crystal." Steve laughed.

I opened the grill, which released a cloud of steam. I lay the hamburgers one at a time which immediately sizzled aroma to our hungry crowd. The guys gathered around the grill.

"Hey guys, beers are in the cooler." I pointed. Steve leaned over and plucked them out, handing them to the other guys and one to me.

"Michael, where have you been?" Kermit asked. He lifted his beer to his lips.

"Working for Crystal and Steve," Michael said. He took a long drink of the cold beer and smacked his lips in approval.

"I don't get it. What are you guys doing?" Kermit asked.

"I set up another telemarketing room in Bexley," I answered. I lifted the grill to poke at the hamburgers. Not ready to turn yet. "We're selling Kodak film coupon books. Whenever Dagger fires someone, I send them there. It's our refuge for Dagger victims.

"And, we're making good money," Scott said. "I'm Scott, by the way." He nodded toward Kermit.

"I think I remember you," Kermit said.

"Yes, I was a driver for a week in Whitehall, and then Tim sent me to Dayton to be their main delivery guy."

"And Dagger fired you too? I remember him firing Michael."

"Yes, Dagger didn't enjoy my humor." Scott laughed.

"Wow. I had no idea. Tim, you are one sneaky dude!" Kermit said.

"Yep, the wizard behind the curtain," I said. Everyone laughed.

"I thought you said Harley was coming?" Kermit asked.

"Yes, I told him we were starting at one. I wanted a chance to brief you before he got here. He doesn't know about our side business." I flipped a hamburger. It looked right. I flipped through the others.

"Is he going to be pissed?" Steve asked.

"No. Not Harley. He's happy to let me take care of all the problems. He's busy with parties at Harley's." I laughed. The doorbell rang. "That's probably him now."

"I'll get it," Candy said. She and Crystal walked inside. I could hear Harley's boisterous voice greeting the ladies. He always had a joyous laugh. He walked through the kitchen to the patio.

"Hey, it's the missing crew!" Harley laughed. He shook hands with everyone. "I thought the Devil's Triangle got you."

"Almost. Dagger's Triangle. Harley, you're just in time. The burgers are ready," I said. I started sliding them onto a plate and sat them on the patio table. "Steve, grab Harley a Bud."

"I'll get it," Harley said. He opened the cooler and reached into the ice to find a Bud. Crystal and Candy brought out condiments, plates, napkins, and silverware and sat them on the table.

"Did any of you see today's newspaper?" I asked.

"Oh yeah, they caught the guy that killed the bartender at the Brass Rail," Kermit said. "I didn't see it, but I heard it on the radio."

"Was it Kenny and Cheryl?" Crystal asked. Candy stopped and looked at me.

"No, some other guy," I said. "I don't know why they arrested Kenny and Cheryl, but I'm happy they weren't the murderers."

"Me, too," Candy said. She walked back into the kitchen and brought out a bowl of potato salad. "Dig in, guys."

Michael and Kermit grabbed a bun and assembled their sandwiches.

"If you want your buns toasted, bring them to me," I said. "So, Harley, I have a story for you."

"I like your stories," Harley said. Everyone laughed.

"Remember when Dagger fired Steve and Crystal?"

"Yes." Harley sat down with his plate and raised an eyebrow.

"Remember that I asked what we should do with them?"

"Yes." Harley balanced his plate on his knee and took a big swig of Bud.

"And you said to tell you if I had an idea?"

"Does this story end?" Harley laughed.

"Yes. Well, I got an idea, but I never told you. I opened another phone room in Bexley. We're selling Kodak film coupon books. We're not competing with your business. But now, when Dagger fires someone, I have a place for them."

"Does Dagger know about this?" Harley asked.

"Hell no," Steve and I said in unison. The others laughed.

Harley looked at each of us, then he burst out laughing. He slapped his knee and I grabbed his plate so he wouldn't spill it. He laughed until tears came to his eyes.

"That is hilarious." Harley wiped his eyes with his napkin. We all laughed. "Tim, that's the best story I've heard all year. Cheers." Harley lifted his beer to us. We all lifted our drinks to him.

We sat on the patio for the afternoon, swapping stories and enjoying each other's company. At five PM, I saw the glass people. I recognized the crowd, buildings, and figures in yellow raincoats. I was right, it was my other reality. Maybe that's why I relaxed when I watched it.

"Tim, what'll you do when Dagger fires salespeople too far from Bexley?" Crystal asked.

"Then we'll open new offices. We can expand as fast as Dagger can fire." Everyone laughed. Harley laughed the loudest.

It was a brilliant group of talented people. They had positive energy and attitudes. All enjoyed their time visiting until dusk shrouded the patio. Steve and Crystal left for their drive back to Newark. Then, Scott and Michael left, since Scott was Michael's ride. Then Kermit followed Harley out, saying their goodbyes. They left Candy and me alone with our family. We bathed the kids and put them to sleep.

I went to the kitchen with Candy to finish cleaning what they left of the party food and dishes, then we sat at the breakfast table to relax.

"Candy, there's something I want to know," I said.

"What?" Candy pulled the French braid in her hair loose, letting her hair fall into her face.

"How did you get money out of my locked briefcase? And how did you find it behind the light switch?"

"I told you I didn't steal your money." Candy frowned.

"Oh, come on. I know it was you. One of those weeks, you bought extra clothing and toys for you and Colin. More than you could have with the $300 per week I was giving you."

"I didn't do it." Candy's voice became shrill. We both sat silently for five minutes.

"Well," I said. I looked at her and cocked my head. "You impressed me. Amazed me. However, you did it, you showed master skills."

At this, Candy's lips turned into a slight smile. So slight, it was hidden to most people. But not to me.

"Ah, ha!" I said.

"What?" Candy asked.

"You smiled. You are proud that you fooled me. I know you did it. Just admit it. I want to know how. It's driving me crazy not knowing."

Candy smiled and squinted. She looked at me for thirty seconds. Finally, she blurted, "Okay, yes, I did it, but it was my money too. We are married. I wasn't stealing."

I wanted to argue this point with her. I wanted to explain it wasn't my money. It belonged to Harley and Dagger. I was just managing it. But if I did that, she'd get pissed and not answer me.

"Okay, Candy. You make an excellent point. I won't argue. So, please tell me how'd you get the money out of my briefcase?"

"Well--" Candy smiled again. She was going to make me sweat it out. She was enjoying this.

"Come on, Candy. Please."

"Okay. Remember, in Denver, you had forgotten your combination to your briefcase?"

"I think so."

"Phil was at the house and he showed you how to open it. He said cheap briefcases had cheap locks. He turned each dial slowly until he felt a click and got your case open." Candy leaned back, very pleased with herself. "That's how I opened your cheap briefcase."

"I vaguely remember that. I don't remember you being near us. But the dial was at 427, so I'd know if you attempted to open it. And, I had the envelope facing away inside the pocket of the briefcase."

"Yes, I was careful to leave it exactly as I found it."

Now, Candy impressed the socks off me and left me a bit fearful. Candy's skill for deception was greater than I knew.

"Okay, so that explains the briefcase. But what about the light switch? That had to be impossible, but you did it anyway."

"Give me $50 and I'll tell you." Candy held out her hand. I wanted to refuse, but then I'd never know the truth. I handed her $50.

"Now, tell me. Please," I said.

Candy pushed the money into her brazier. "You locked the door. You never lock the door. I figured something was up."

"How'd you know I locked the door?"

"I wanted to grab my lotion. The door was locked."

"Oh." Suddenly I wasn't feeling like a genius.

"I lay on the floor and looked under the door. Your feet were by the light switch. I stood and put my ear against the door. I could hear you using a tool on the wall."

"That's it? That's how you knew?"

"Yes. It took me a while to figure it out. What you were working on. Nothing was on that wall except the light switch. I removed it and saw the money."

"Oh, my God. But I put the screws in positions. I'd know if you turned them."

"Well, I made sure it was exactly as I left it."

"Incredible. Just Incredible." I shook my head and leaned back in my chair. I marveled at her sneakiness. "Candy, the next day, I put it behind the light switch."

"I know. I figured that out."

"Well. That was worth $50 to find out. Thank you for telling me." After that, I could have explained why it wasn't her money. But then, she'd get mad and want to argue. I decided against the argument. She no longer had access to the company money, so there was no point.

We went to bed and turned out the lights. I lay for five minutes in the dark with my eyes open. Then, I closed them and imagined the violet egg around my family for another five minutes. I got out of bed and walked quietly to Colin's room. He was sleeping, spread eagle. I pulled the blanket over him. I walked back to our room and peeked in the bassinet. Sapphire was sleeping, breathing evenly. Candy was facing the bassinet, but asleep. I could hear the taping on the violet egg, but it was slight. We were in an oasis of positive energy, like sheltering in a shack during a thunderstorm, the rain tapping at the windows. I crawled into bed and lay on my back. I stared at the ceiling until my eyes drooped slowly shut.

My family slept peacefully inside the violet egg, but as I fell asleep, I had a fleeting thought. Was there evil the egg wouldn't evict? Was there evil within the egg?

Disclosure

I have tried to recreate events, locales, and conversations from my memories of them. In order to maintain their anonymity, in some instances, I have changed the names of individuals and places. I may have changed some dates, identifying characteristics, and details such as physical properties, occupations, and places of residence.

About the Author

Timothy L Drobnick Sr

I have had a rich life.

I have a good history in business. As an entrepreneur, I started several successful businesses.

I have enjoyed being an artist, potter, teacher, inventor and much more. I have been a small plane pilot experiencing flight which had been a dream of mine since a child.

I have spent much of my life seeking truth and my spirituality.

From 1994 to 2015, I was a stay-at-home dad and raised seven children. I supported my family by providing services for the Internet, preparing taxes, and writing stories.

In 2015, after last child graduated, I moved my business out of the house.

My patio is where I love to write. This is where my writing partner, (Maddie a Chihuahua but insists she is human), loves to take naps as long as it's next to me.

I am writing seven books, or more, for "My Ghosts" series. After that I will write paranormal thriller fiction.

Free Audiobook

For a limited time you can get my eleven hour audiobook of book one, "Rescued by Ghosts," on my website.

You may also join my author's group on Facebook to talk with me and get on my updates to be notified when I have new books published.

My website is https://RescuedbyGhosts.com

Please Leave Review

Please leave a review of this book on Good Reads or Amazon. This helps me to continue to write for you. Believe it or not, less than one out of every 100 readers leave a review.

I appreciate you. Thank you.

Other Books

THIS IS BOOK THREE of a seven part series.
Book One: Rescued by Ghosts
Book Two: Deceit in Denver
Book Three: Evict Evil
Books Four through seven coming soon.
Find them on Amazon.
Join my author's group at https://RescuedbyGhosts.com

Made in the USA
Monee, IL
08 September 2022